THE EUROPEAN SINGLE MARKET

The European Single Market Monetary and Fiscal Policy Harmonization

Edited by

H.M. Scobie
Executive Director,
European Economics and Financial Centre,
London, UK

SPRINGER-SCIENCE+BUSINESS MEDIA, B.V.

First edition 1994

Originally published by Chapman & Hall in 1994
Softcover reprint of the hardcover 1st edition 1994
Typeset in 10/12 Times by Interprint, Malta.

ISBN 978-94-010-4569-8 ISBN 978-94-011-1304-5 (eBook)
DOI 10.1007/978-94-011-1304-5

A catalogue record for this book is available from the British Library

Library of Congress Catalog Card Number: 93-74443

∞ Printed on permanent acid-free text paper, manufactured in accordance with ANSI/NISO Z39.48–1992 and ANSI/NISO Z39.48–1984 (Permanence of Paper).

Contents

Contributors

C.A. Bollino	Director General, ISPE, Rome
P.C. Padoan	Professor of Economics, Università La Sapienza, Rome, Italy
C. Dunis	Chemical Bank, Capital Markets Group, 125 London Wall, London EC27 5AJ, UK
F. Ettlin and M. Bernegger	Swiss National Bank, Postfach, CH-8022 Zurich, Switzerland
R. de Groof and M. van Tuijl	Tilburg University, PO Box 90153, NL-5000 LE Tilburg, The Netherlands
A. Gubitz	Commerzbank AG, Economic Research (ZKV), 60261 Frankfurt am Main, Germany
M. Gudmundsson	Central Bank of Iceland, Kalkofnsveg 1, Reykjavik 150, Iceland
D.P. Hanson, C. Lackman, T. Petinaux	Associate Professor of International Business Associate Professor of Marketing Graduate Student Graduate School of Business Administration, Duquesne University, Pittsburgh, Pennsylvania 15282-0107, USA
J. Michielsen	National Bank of Belgium, Boulevard de Belaimont 14, B-1000 Brussels, Belgium
H.M. Scobie	European Economics and Financial Centre, PO Box 2498, London W2 4LE, UK
P. Moutot	Banque de France, 31–39 rue Croix des Petits Champs, 75001 Paris, France
P. Pollard	The Federal Reserve Bank of St Louis, PO Box 442, St Louis, Missouri 63166, USA
H. Skånland	Bank of Norway, Postboks 1179, Sentrum 0107, Oslo, Norway

Glossary

BIS	Banking Information Service
CMEA	Council for Middle Eastern Affairs
COMECON	Council for Mutual Economic Assistance
EC	European Community
ECB	European Central Bank
EEA	European Economic Area
EFTA	European Free Trade Association
EMS	European Monetary System
EMU	European Monetary Union
ERM	Exchange Rate Mechanism
ESCB	European System of Central Banks
GNP	Gross National Product
IMF	International Monetary Fund
OECD	Organization for Economic Cooperation and Development
UNCTAD	United Nations Conference on Trade and Development

Introduction

THE EUROPEAN SINGLE MARKET

This volume comprises a collection of papers, some of which were presented at different workshops organized by the European Economics and Financial Centre (London), in conjunction with various European central banks.

In addition the book contains, in Chapter 2, the text of a memorial lecture on Trade and Financial Relationships of the US and Europe given by this author in New York. The lecture, known as the Henry George Lecture, was given at St John's University in New York in April 1993.

The workshops were part of a series of workshops, the first of which was hosted by the Central Bank of Finland. At these workshops usually some 20 central banks from Europe, the Federal Reserve Board and various other central banks were present. Furthermore the workshops contain papers from international organizations such as the OECD, European Commission, Bank for International Settlement, government ministries, commercial banks, research institutes and academics from Europe and elsewhere.

The two workshops from which some of these papers were drawn were those held at the Central Bank of the Netherlands and the Central Bank of Austria. The workshop held at the Central Bank of the Netherlands (De Nederlandsche Bank), was on Policy Coordination, and took place during 2–4 November, 1992. The one held at the Central Bank of Austria (Östereichische Bank), was on Policy Formulation in Interdependent Market, and took place during 24–26 March 1993.

The European Economics and Financial Centre acknowledges the help of these central banks in hosting these workshops.

The workshop topics were chosen for two prime reasons.

1. It is often the incorrect assessment of the present conditions that can lead to incorrect predictions.
2. Incorrect predictions can result in inappropriate policy prescriptions.

Thus, there is a powerful argument and emphasis for an accurate grasp and assessment of the economic and financial conditions.

Policy formulation embodies three main stages:

1. Accurate assessment of a given econonic state,
2. Enlightened prediction of the future, in order to come to the third stage which is
3. Prescription of relevant policies.

In today's climate of European Community both the members and the satellite countries have to introduce checks and balances on all the diverging pressures across the participating countries. While effective coordination can prevent such tensions, the risk remains that these tensions could resurface. We are privileged here to have attracted many papers in this area.

It is an honour that Mr Skånland, the Governor of the Bank of Norway, accepted our invitation to contribute his paper to this volume which was given as the keynote address at the meeting held at the Central Bank of Austria.

The principal criterion behind the selection of the papers has been to give an overview of some of the thinking and new developments in the current climate of the European economy.

Copies of the papers that were presented and were not included in this volume together with information about the workshops and forthcoming ones can be obtained from the European Economics and Financial Centre, PO Box 2498, London W2 4LE, UK.

Given the present transformation of European economies, the formulation and harmonization of economic policies, both on the monetary side and the fiscal side, across this continent will remain a key issue in the years to come.

These workshops (and, hence, this volume emerging from them), were set up with several objectives. First, they attempted to bringing into light the new thinking, new findings, developments and advances within the public and private sector and to capture the responses from both sides. It was intended to portray their outlook, focus and direction towards policy making and interaction with each other, both within the government sector and in relation to the private sector.

Second, they were called with a view to portraying different monetary and fiscal policies formulated within the public sector among the different countries. Clearly domestic policies are formulated in the light of economic developments externally and account is taken of such events. These workshops were designed to highlight such influences.

Third, and finally, they were designed both to highlight and capture attempts at policy formulation and bring into focus the constraints, choices and instruments in an interdependent economic environment. In this respect the workshops and this book contain papers that are focused on a specific domestic issue within a given country as well as papers providing an overview of policy formulation and harmonization.

Finally, I would like to thank Mr Anthony Watkinson of Chapman and Hall for his help and valuable support in putting this collection together.

It is hoped that this volume brings to light some of the key issues in the fast changing era of the new Europe and trigger new ideas and stimulate further research in this area.

H.M. Scobie
Director
European Economics and Financial Centre
London, August 1993

1

Concerns and uncertainties for macroeconomic policy

H. Skånland

1.1 INTRODUCTION

Developments in Europe since last summer have been quite dramatic for those assigned with the responsibility of defending exchange rates. Not everyone has been equally successful and this has been perceived as a setback to the fixed exchange rate policy of the Exchange Rate Mechanism (ERM) and in Nordic countries.

This chapter will look at the most important concerns and uncertainties facing the authorities in European countries. In addition to the turmoil in foreign exchange markets over the last months, the basic concern of macroeconomic policymakers is the prolonged stagnation in industrialized countries. The recession and the currency turbulence may have jeopardized the long-term efforts to achieve price stabilization and lower unemployment in Europe because budget deficits have shown an appreciable increase, progress towards European monetary union has been dealt a blow, and there is some risk in a number of countries that inflation which had been brought under control will rise again.

1.2 INTERLINKAGES BETWEEN FOREIGN EXCHANGE MARKETS AND THE BUSINESS CLIMATE

Let us start with the currency turbulence and the cyclical downturn and their interlinkages. Was the crisis within the ERM system triggered by the recession, since the downturn in Europe – with the exception of Germany – was so deep that the countries were entering a period of deflation? Taking this a step

The European Single Market – Monetary and Fiscal Policy Harmonization.
Edited by H.M. Scobie. Published in 1994 by Chapman & Hall,
London. ISBN 0 412 57520 5

further, does the breakdown within the ERM permit greater leeway for expansion in Europe, or is it a zero-sum game with greater expansion in the UK, Italy and other countries being offset by continued stagnation in Germany?

The exchange rate changes are in themselves probably a zero-sum game, but the recent appreciation of the Deutschmark should bring down German interest rates more rapidly than would otherwise have been possible. A reduction in German rates will be a source of growth impetus to European economies.

On the other hand, it may be natural to ask if the appreciation of the Deutschmark could not have occurred at an earlier point in time and in a less disruptive manner. This could have contributed to bringing down interest rates in Germany and elsewhere in Europe, which would have reduced tensions in the ERM. A different approach could perhaps have contributed to curbing the recession in European countries in addition to Germany.

A paradox in this connection is that short rates in Germany may have more of an impact on the level of activity in other countries such as the UK or Norway than in Germany itself. In Germany, borrowing at long rates is most common, but the situation is the opposite in the UK and Norway where loans to households and the business sector usually depend on short-term rates in the money market. Whereas the Germans are concerned with interest rates in the capital market, the British and Norwegians focus on short-term rates. The interest rate is therefore much more politicized in these countries than in Germany, where they are more preoccupied with the factors contributing to high rates in the capital market. Here monetary policy is only one element. Equally important, and perhaps even more crucial, are inflationary expectations and the government budget deficit.

This observation begs the question of why the long-term capital market is much less developed in countries like the UK and Norway than in Germany. I do not know the full answer but one important factor may be that in the UK and Norway there seems to be a lack of confidence in the authorities' commitment to keeping inflation at a low level. The historical inflation figures indicate that there are good reasons for this lack of confidence.

Is the depreciation of pound sterling, the Italian lira, the Swedish krona and the Finnish markka excessive or is it just what is required to bring real exchange rates into sustainable balance once the price effect has worked its way through the system? So far the exchange rate changes are in the order of 15–25%, which deviates considerably from previous very moderate realignments within the ERM. Why have exchange rates moved with such force?

The only parallel to these major fluctuations is the strong swing in the dollar exchange rate. However, the US economy is of a completely different size than European economies and imports account for a much smaller share of domestic demand. As a result, US monetary policy will primarily influence the economy directly through the interest rate level and its impact on investment and consumption. In small open European economies imports represent a much larger share of domestic demand, and the price impulses associated with the interest rate's impact on currency rates therefore have a much more rapid and direct impact on the economy.

So far the inflationary impact in the countries that have depreciated has been quite small, probably because trade margins have absorbed some of the pressure. A 20% depreciation in countries like Sweden and Finland should directly raise the price level by about 6% as a result of higher import prices, while the effect will be somewhat smaller in the UK and Italy. Second-round effects stemming from higher wage demands come in as well. These effects may become stronger as economic activity gradually picks up.

The next question then is what measures should be taken to counteract the increase in inflation that will eventually occur. If an active monetary policy is indeed being pursued, an adjustment of interest rates will be required for price stabilization. This raises several interesting questions.

1. How much will interest rates have to be increased to halt a depreciation or achieve an appreciation which can contribute to renewed price stability?
2. Will it be politically acceptable to raise interest rates sufficiently if economic activity is still unsatisfactory?

Or to put the question in a different manner:

> Are the authorities in the countries that have recently floated their currencies prepared to let the central bank take the steps necessary to keep inflation at a low level, even at the cost of continued high unemployment?

A common feature of the countries with floating currencies is their severe fiscal problems. Sweden has the largest government budget deficit among the OECD countries, possibly with the exception of Greece. Italy is close behind followed by Finland and the UK. The large budget deficits have been cited as one reason why these countries were forced to float their currencies. It has been maintained that an appreciable improvement in the budget balance would suffice to reduce the danger of inflation. Can this be achieved quickly enough and to a sufficient degree to produce such an effect?

The downturn in Europe seems to be more protracted this time around than normally. In the US the recession spanned three years and in Europe it may last even longer.

In the 1980s only Japan accumulated such fiscal room for manoeuvre which today allows the country to use fiscal policy measures to stimulate the economy in order to shorten the recession. In many European countries fiscal balances are so weak that the debate is more concerned about whether automatic stabilizers should be allowed to work or not.

It may be worth recalling that in the Nordic countries the strains on financial markets emerged only after several years of losses in the business sector. Europe and Japan may still be heading for harder times in this area.

One reason why the current downturn may last longer than previous recessions is that it presents somewhat different characteristics than those that we have seen. One distinctive feature is the efforts by households and businesses to reduce their debt burdens. Financial consolidation on this scale can only be found in the inter-war period. This does not mean that the current downturn will be as serious as it was then, as some seem to fear. Most countries are now experiencing slower growth, not a decline. In several areas there are important differences with respect to how the economy functions now as compared with the 1930s.

1. The social safety net is better developed and dual-income families are far more common.
2. A relatively stable public sector plays a far greater role today than it did then.
3. Today, the authorities will not permit a crisis to spread through a collapse of the financial sector as then was the case.

The efforts to reduce debt are an effect of both the rapid growth in indebtedness and the rise in real interest rates to the current high level. High real-interest rates directly affect debt-servicing costs and have an indirect effect through the fall in the value of the fixed assets the loans have financed.

The US has shown that even by a very determined and long-lasting easing of monetary conditions it is difficult to make demand respond. Admittedly, short rates do not play a very significant role in the US economy. Investment is chiefly financed by long-term loans as in Germany, and long rates have fallen much less than short rates. The slow response of the private sector to the expansionary monetary policy is, however, also an indication that debt imbalances and the boom in the housing and property markets were allowed to go too far before the turnaround. Restoring balance-sheet equilibrium takes a long time and may require substantial adjustments in the flow of saving and consumption.

One lesson that can be derived from this experience is that business confidence is not easily restored when these sectors are caught in a debt trap. It may be useful to recall that the sheltered sectors of the economy have been the hardest hit, i.e. households and the non-export industry. This raises the question of the extent to which exchange rate changes can be expected to affect demand in light of the nature of the current downturn in many European countries. Households and sheltered industries are experiencing a reduction in their purchasing power as inflation increases, and cannot easily shift their resources into new activities.

1.3 PROSPECTS FOR A RECOVERY

Efforts to reduce the high level of structural unemployment in Europe have been thwarted by the recession. Before the downturn started, some headway had been made in terms of drawing up a long-term policy to boost employment. The question now is whether those in this field will emerge from the downturn as strong as when they entered it.

In the short term the rise in unemployment almost always appears to be cyclical in nature, as is true this time. Only in retrospect can the difference be perceived between cyclical and structural unemployment.

After a steep rise in structural unemployment up to the mid-1980s, it appears to have levelled off. Actual unemployment decreased somewhat at the end of the 1980s, but it is still uncertain to what extent this is due to the prolonged and – in many countries – strong upturn or whether structural policies have gradually had an impact.

In the 1980s there was growing recognition that the unemployment problems could not be solved by traditional macroeconomic measures.

After a rather pronounced weakening of government budget balances following the oil crisis in 1974 and up to 1979, European countries spent the 1980s attempting to reduce these deficits. Despite their efforts, the deficits were not brought down to below 2% of GDP, which was the approximate level in 1974, until the end of the boom in 1989. Persistently high budget deficits have resulted in a steep increase in public debt in European countries, from 18% of GDP in 1974 to 43% at the end of 1992.

The recession which took hold in 1989 has resulted in a severe deterioration of budget balances, and in 1992 the deficits in the European countries were more than 5% of GDP on average. Countries which were forced to float their currencies experienced the greatest deterioration. The exception is Italy, but the deficit in that country was record high at the outset. Fixed exchange rates thus seem to be incompatible with a substantial worsening of government finances.

This would be a good reason to apply the Maastricht criteria to public finances before EMU enters into force. The criterion stipulating that the government deficit should be limited to 3% of GDP is, however, not sufficient to prevent debt from growing to unacceptable levels. It is a criterion for participation, not one of good behaviour.

The freedom of manoeuvre used to accumulate high public debt in the past decade should rather have been used to reduce the deficits and even to eliminate them, and ideally record a surplus for a period. As things have developed, real interest rates are likely to remain high, and higher than the growth in GDP. An increasing share of the government's resources will therefore be used to service debt. In several of the most heavily indebted OECD countries net interest expenditure already comes to about 20% of total public spending.

The lack of fiscal room for manoeuvre could be one reason why the European countries whose currencies are now floating appear to be using monetary policy rather actively in order to stimulate economic growth. In this context fixed exchange rates represent a less active monetary policy approach, but as long as the intermediate targets for inflation remain unchanged the difference over some time will not necessarily be that great. Like fiscal policy, monetary policy cannot contribute to a sustainable reduction in unemployment. An active monetary policy can, barring ill-luck, help to stabilize economic developments, but structural unemployment cannot be solved through an expansionary monetary policy. On the other hand, if a firm medium-term monetary policy is not conducted, structural problems may be amplified by higher inflation. Monetary and fiscal policy are similar in this respect – in the short term they can reduce unemployment, but in the medium term their impact is extremely limited. However, an excessive relaxation of fiscal and monetary policies in the medium term will probably have a negative effect, resulting in higher real interest rates and inflation.

So, where shall we turn? Is there anything we can do to increase employment? Let us first look at the areas in which employment can be expected to rise in the years ahead.

The distribution of employment by industry has shown a very similar trend in most countries. There has been a steep decline in employment in primary industries, whereas the goods-producing industries such as manufacturing have either accounted for a constant or falling share of employment. The service sector has shown the strongest employment growth, both in the public and private sector. In the private sector the composition of services has shifted away from consumer services to business sector services.

In what sectors, then, will employment exhibit the strongest growth in the years ahead? In the goods-producing industries production growth will probably be stimulated by productivity gains and not be the result of higher employment. Improved competitiveness will boost exports and value added but will not create new jobs. Employment growth will therefore have to be generated in the service sectors.

The next question is whether employment will increase in the public or the private sector. The growth potential in the public sector is limited if governments are to refrain from increasing the budget deficits or raising taxes. One sector which could expand – and probably at a rather fast pace – is paid public services.

In the private sector, growth in business sector services will to a large extent be determined by output growth in industry and commerce. Consumer services should, however, have a large growth potential.

Which policy measures must be implemented in order to boost employment? As long as we adhere to the principle that neither budget deficits nor taxes should be increased, we are left with the following possibilities:

1. Transfer payments can be cut and more public resources can be devoted to job creation measures. Attempts are being made to do this in Norway, but it is hardly realistic to assume that this will have any substantial effect. In most countries government finances are in such a poor state that a

reduction in transfer payments should rather be used to strengthen the budgetary position. The growth in transfer payments will inevitably have to be limited in order to avoid a continued weakening of public budget balances.
2. An increased use of payments for public services has already been mentioned, but it is important that competition with the private sector is permitted to ensure efficient services.
3. There must be a change in the price of hiring the unemployed, partly through greater wage differentiation and perhaps also through lower taxation of labour provided by youths and unskilled workers. In addition, the alternative income of the unemployed must be modified.

As mentioned earlier, private services appear to be the primary source of employment growth in the longer term. In the US job creation has been considerably higher than in Europe in the past 10 years, and the largest number of jobs has been created in the service sector.

In other words, the solution to unemployment problems in Europe cannot be found in fiscal and monetary policy, but in a long-term approach involving structural policy measures. The elimination of arrangements which prevent job-seekers from trying their hand in the labour market is of particular importance.

Even though many European countries which introduced structural policy measures in the 1980s have had only limited success in reducing rigidities in the labour market, there appears to be no other solution to the unemployment problem.

1.4 EUROPE BACK ON TRACK TO EMU?

The EC single market and the Maastricht Treaty were meant to be a continuation of the structural policy pursued in European countries. A key element was the removal of barriers and, eventually, the establishment of a single currency.

Following the collapse within the Exchange Rate Mechanism (ERM), many have raised the question if and when Europe will be back on track to EMU.

The first test will be whether the ERM will survive in its existing form. Many have expressed an opinion. In addition to the hope that the system will not again be exposed to such strong asymmetrical shocks which the unification of Germany entailed, it has been stressed that changes must be made by the following.

1. Improving the system for reciprocal intervention obligations so that a country whose currency comes under pressure can rely on assistance from the countries to which its currency flows.

2. Sharpening the recognition that even though exchange rates are fixed, they are *adjustable.*
3. Improved harmonization of economic policies.

The first point is essential to the success of a fixed exchange rate regime in Europe. The magnitude of currency flows this past autumn demonstrates the structural shift we are facing. When a single maket participant can move foreign exchange equivalent to $10–15 billion, there is little that can be done about it. This amount is about the same as Norway's total foreign exchange reserves. Moreover, these operators learned last autumn that they can succeed. It seems quite obvious that it is now both more difficult and dangerous to pursue a fixed exchange rate regime than earlier. Of course it was never the intention that interventions would be the sole instrument for defending an exchange rate. However, there are limits to how high interest rates can be forced upon the business sector to defend the fixed exchange rate.

It shoud be possible to devise better reciprocal intervention arrangements. Adjustments of fixed exchange rates are perhaps more problematic.

Under the Basle–Nyborg agreement, exchange rates can and should be adjusted if necessary, and before market pressures arise. It has been proposed that confidential discussions on the need for exchange rate realignments should be held on a regular basis. It is, however, questionable both whether a need for adjustment will be admitted by a country which the others consider exposed, and whether leakages from such meetings can be prevented so that the meetings do not by themselves expose a country.

Against this background, it is probably the last point on policy harmonization which will be decisive for the future of the ERM. The objective is to reduce the need for exchange rate realignments in the years ahead. Even if the systems for reciprocal intervention obligations are improved, the future of the ERM could be jeopardized by the failure to achieve policy harmonization and economic convergence fast enough to eliminate the need for exchange rate realignments. Larger and more volatile capital movements have made it all the more important to invoke favourable economic fundamentals as grounds for exchange rate stability.

This implies that the criteria which must be satisfied for the ERM to succeed are the same as the conditions necessary to establish a monetary union. The question then is why should monetary union not be the next step. Is there in effect any room for stage 2 between stage 1 and monetary union?

Stage 2 still involves the costs arising from the uncertainty about exchange rate realignments, and countries will still be exposed to speculative runs on currencies. Perhaps the only way to achieve a sufficient degree of policy harmonization and economic convergence is by implementing monetary union. Then politicians no longer have an alternative to keeping price and cost inflation under the necessary control. Perhaps this is also what is necessary to achieve sufficient wage flexibility. When the social partners are convinced that exchange rates cannot be adjusted, governments can hope that the disciplinary effect in wage formation will increase.

There is no assurance. The establishment of a monetary union is a bold and risky step, and bridges are being burnt. How green is the grass really on the other side of the river?

2

Trade and financial relationships between the US and Europe

H.M. Scobie

2.1 INTRODUCTION

Let me begin by thanking this University* and the Robert Schalkenbach Foundation for inviting me to give the Henry George Lecture. It is a great honour for me to be chosen for this occasion and especially to be the first woman to deliver this lecture following a series of esteemed speakers who have presented it before me. I would like to thank Professors Giacalone and Simunek for their efforts in organizing it.

When I first was given the 'area' or the title of the talk that the University wished me to speak about – 'Trade and financial relationships between the US and Europe', it struck me as a title that embraced everything and all aspects of the economy of the two continents.

I was given the subject last November in anticipation of what would be of interest to this audience this April (1993).

I thought a great deal about the broad topic of the talk and asked myself what would really be of interest to this audience? And it reminded me of a student in Oxford who was given an essay on the topic of 'Fisheries in the UK'. He was asked to investigate the implications for the government and the implications for the fishermen. At the outset the student wrote, 'let me start with the implications for the fish'!

It struck me that the most important picture to convey to you is to give you an overview of the fundamental developments in Europe today, the path it has set itself to achieve and some of the obstacles and constraints it is facing for achieving these goals.

---

* Text of a Memorial Lecture delivered at St. John's University, New York, 15 April 1993.

The European Single Market – Monetary and Fiscal Policy Harmonization.
Edited by H.M. Scobie. Published in 1994 by Chapman & Hall,
London. ISBN 0 412 57520 5

I shall then try and highlight the implications of the new United Europe for the US today and how the US can set an example for Europe to follow.

Despite the advancement of technology in communications and the rapidity of the flow of information, the 3000 miles of water between the two continents, and hence, the physical distance, still proves a big barrier for the understanding and effective communication between the economies of the two regions.

Up to a few years ago, the US/European relationship was primarily focused on NATO. And the purpose of NATO was to 'keep the US in Europe, the Germans down and the Soviet Union out'.* However, with the European Community emerging as a single block, the US has had to alter its bilateral relations with individual member states and strengthen its ties with the EC as one entity.

In my talk today, I shall first give some background as to the evolution of Western Europe on both the trade and finance side. I shall then trace the implications for the US of the different new phenomena in Europe, and discuss routes for the US to benefit from the evolution of the European economies.

I shall confine my talk primarily to Western Europe and present this lecture in that context.

2.2 BACKGROUND TO THE EUROPEAN ECONOMY

In 1957 a treaty was signed in Rome by six countries, forming the foundation for what was known at the time as The European Economic Community (EEC) and referred to as The Common Market. These founding members were Belgium, France, West Germany, Luxembourg, the Netherlands and Italy. Among the main aims of the Treaty of Rome were 'to promote throughout the Community a harmonious development of economic activities' and to increase the standard of living of the member states.

In 1972 the then EEC was enlarged by the addition of Denmark, Ireland, Norway and the UK, although Norway withdrew subsequently leaving the enlarged EEC with nine members.

In 1979 Greece joined the Community and six years later in 1985 Portugal and Spain became members, forming the current 12-nation European Community.

In 1987 the Single European Act was signed by all member states forming the foundation of the Single European Market, details of which will be explained further below.

On forthcoming events, in 1995 there are plans to admit Austria, Finland, Norway and Sweden as new members forming the enlarged EC with 16 member states.

* Andersen, C. (1992) *Influencing the EC*, Kogan Page, London.

2.3 RECENT ECONOMIC DEVELOPMENTS IN EUROPE

Undoubtedly Germany has been the leading force in Europe and its currency, the Deutschmark, continues to dominate the other European currencies, though some of the economic variables and ratios are currently more favourable in France today.

Following the liberalization of Eastern Europe, the unification of the two sides of Germany has single-handedly been the most important development in Western Europe in recent years with economic and financial consequences for all the EC member states.

Germany is now (1993) in the third year of its reunification and it is likely to continue running a current account deficit in the next year. The cost of the unification has been so colossal that it has led to a massive cash injection by the government which in turn resulted in a huge public sector debt. The rise in money supply in turn led to wage rises and price inflation.

In 1991 wage rises were 6% and inflation was 3.5%. In 1992 the consumer prices index rose 4.5% and average wages 5.4%. German inflation during 1993 is likely to have averaged 3.5%. Wage rises are expected to have ranged between 2.5–3.0%, though public sector pay rises could go as high as 5.5%.

The German Repurchase rate ('the repro rate') was cut on 7 April 1993 by 0.04 to 8.14%. This was after the March inflation figure of 4.3%, following that for February of 4.2%. Although inflation in Germany was not what the Bundesbank desired to see, the figures on industrial production and employment in Germany released on 6 April 1993 were very weak indeed. (See Table 2.1.)

Table 2.1 German wage rises and inflation

Year	*Wage rises (%)*	*Price inflation (%)*
1991	6.0	3.5
1992	5.4	4.5
1993*	2.5–3.0	3.5
Price inflation in February 1993		4.2
Price inflation in March 1993		4.3

*Estimate

As the cost of reunification escalated and the German public expenditure increased, the Bundesbank (the autonomous Central Bank of Germany) was set to pursue compensatory policies. That is, to curb the inflationary pressures, Germany pursued a monetary policy raising their interest rate which in turn forced the other European countries within the Exchange Rate Mechanism (ERM) to maintain a high interest policy, damaging their economies and their industry, and curbing their consumer expenditure. This will be further explained below.

In short the burden of reunification added to the recessionary pressures in Europe and deepened it considerably more.

There are leads and lags in the recessionary cycles in each of the European countries. In the UK, for instance, recession began a lot earlier. A survey from the European Community forecasts that the UK will be the fastest growing country within the EC with GDP growth projected for 1993 at 1.4% and 2.7% in 1994. European growth rate during 1993 is projected at around 0.8%.

2.4 THE EUROPEAN CURRENCY SYSTEM – THE ERM

In this lecture we shall look at the European Exchange Rate Mechanism (ERM) which is a currency system limiting the movement of currency. We shall look at countries in the system and those outside such as the UK and Italy.

Prior to the formation of ERM, it was widely believed in Europe that 'a free-floating exchange rate creates an atmosphere of uncertainty which would be counter-productive to economic activity'.

Thus, one of the objectives of ERM has been the creation of stable and long-lasting exchange rate relationships. For foreign exchange affects virtually everyone. Over and above industry and financial markets, it affects public pension funds, those going on vacation, and so on.

Conventional wisdom has it that 'private agents assume that once a given state becomes a member of the ERM, the authorities are obliged to keep and support the exchange rate within the agreed band.

Businesses are eager to have the advantage of security of exchange rate in their overseas trade (i.e., selling and buying their goods to and from abroad).

Two bands were introduced, the 2.25% and the 6% band. Once a given currency joined the system, it was not permitted to oscillate outside its band. The options open to a government under ERM, once their currency falls below the bottom of the band, are: (1) using the reserves; (2) raising interest rate; (3) realignment, and (4) (only in emergency conditions) enlarging the band.

There can emerge a shift, due to exogenous developments, in the value of certain currencies within EMS. This may reflect the longer term nature of the problems in these economies which becomes the basis of the market expectations. It can make the system highly unstable.

In the run up to 'Black Wednesday', 16 September, 1992 (or 'White Wednesday' in some circles), it was first Finland, then Sweden, then Italy, who experienced their currency crises and it culminated in the UK withdrawing from the ERM on that date.

High rates of interest to support a currency clearly cannot be maintained indefinitely because of the damage they cause to the rest of the economy. Occasionally the instrument of high interest rate can simply act as a buffer in the short term, giving the national bank some breathing space. If, however, the market loses confidence, no matter how high the level of interest is pushed to, it fails to prevent the outflow of currency.

If speculators perceive that a realignment is inevitable, no sensitivity towards movements in interest rate will be shown, as indeed when the UK raised its rate by 5% on 16 September, it did not alter the market view. That is, the interest elasticity of the market falls sharply, and in effect it becomes interest inelastic.

Indeed Sweden raised its money rate to 500% in September 1992 to defend its currency, and the speculators were not averted by the rise in interest rate.

What the market percieves is the key variable in today's foreign exchange market. Thus, when it doubts the authorities' ability to defend the currency is the crucial point when the fragility of a currency system such as the ERM is put to test.

The market speculator would be aware that there are limits to the size of a central bank's reserves. Thus, the huge losses that can result for the government in question supporting its currency cannot go on ad infinitum. In short, to hold up a currency artificially is both costly and tends to be ultimately unsuccessful.

Indeed, attempts made in Britain, Sweden and Italy, for example, to defend their currencies have been on a far greater scale than have been known in the previous crises. For example, during September 1992 not only did the Italian authorities use up all of their foreign reserves, they were left with a loan of 24 billion Deutschmarks from the German government. This loan was to be repaid to the Bundesbank towards the cost of the latter's intervention for supporting the lira.

While there are limits on the size of foreign reserves of a given country, the limits are much higher (almost to the point of invisibility) on the size and volume of speculative flows. That is to say, since barriers to currency movements have been lifted by the authorities globally and deregulations have been introduced in different financial markets, the size of flows has increased substantially. This in turn has limited the ability of central banks to defend their currencies.

An imbalance has been thus created between the instruments of economic policy such as interest rate and intervention (which may include borrowing) and the world financial environment in which the instruments are to be put to force. That is, the two have become out of line due to the volume and speed of currency flows. Thus, by increasing interest rates 5 percentage points on 16 September 1992 (as in the case of the UK), no effective response was possible to achieve. Even when it was raised to 75% as in the case of Sweden, no effective response was achieved. This imbalance is also manifest with regard to intervention and borrowings by the government. In September 1992 Sweden was willing to borrow up to 25% of GDP to defend the krona.

As long as the window of free currency flow, no matter how narrow the band, exists, it is the markets and not the governments that will decide the effective value of any currency, be it lira, sterling or French franc.

The question is, how far can a currency go down at any given time? Is the decisive point when the market is short of the particular currency?

When a currency is at the floor level of its ERM band, the risk of devaluation increases. So the currency dealers try to get out of their position and sell the currency in question at the floor of ERM thereby minimizing risk. They even borrow for this purpose as was the case before the French 29 March 1993 election – anticipating a fall in the franc.

Furthermore, the dealers, once they have sold the currency, after the devaluation, can repurchase the currency for a lesser sum and they thereby achieve a net gain on the difference.

There are guidelines laid down by the central banks which limit the level of speculation that retail banks are permitted to undertake. In other words limits are imposed by, say, the Bank of England that constrain the size of currency transactions. This is because a retail bank (such as Barclays) is not allowed to take huge risks as it has a responsibility to its depositors. However, global currency transactions are not limited to retail banks and there are various ways and means of currency transactions.

If there is a devaluation of a given currency, importers will have to pay more, for they would have to offer more of that currency, say sterling, for the same good. For instance, if at the old exchange rate of, say, £1 = FF9 the importer has to pay £100 (if the price of the good were FF900), the same importer would have to pay £120 for that transaction after devaluation.

The principal way in which currencies that are oscillating within a given band differ from those that are freely floating, lies in the fact that the latter have no floor and their movements tend to be influenced by the so-called 'support levels'. Such 'support levels' are dictated more or less by the forces of the market. It appears that the collective action of all currency dealers faced with the risk of a currency at the floor* of the fixed-band ERM becomes a force in itself driving the currency in question into devaluation. This force, with such vehemence, would not operate in exactly the same way under a free-floating exchange rate.

The main question is to what extent the ERM would have to be revamped. What are the costs and benefits of the system? Clearly the ERM has helped with inflation control. That is, in the absence of gradual devaluation which can occur with a floating currency, and in the absence of the fixed bands, *ceteris paribus*, there emerge inflationary pressures imposed by lowering of the currency.

Given the scale of currency movements, in response to the overwhelming currency outflows in Sweden during the period 17–23 September, Sweden attempted to raise overnight their borrowing rate to 500% to curb the flow of the currencies out of the country – attempting to resist devaluation. By Monday 21 September the overnight rate was reduced to 50%.

This was possible because only a minority of mortgages in Sweden are advanced on a variable interest rate.

The Central Bank of Ireland after 25 September tightened exchange control by requiring advance approval in any swap activity in Irish Punts by those who are not resident in Ireland.

* The absolute floor of the ERM before the UK pulled out was DM2.77 to the pound. FTSE 100 fell to 2370 the night before.

For a period of time (up to Summer 1992) the European Monetary System had appeared as if it had a reasonable performance in ensuring monetary stability.

There were three realignments within ERM between September and December 1992, each time forcing others to raise their interest rates.

No matter what the determination of the authorities responsible to defend the currency, the market forces them to either devalue or pull out. Indeed France devalued many times. Just before a devaluation there tends to be a heavy outflow and the speculators gradually return after a devaluation.

After a devaluation the short-term money rate drops sharply. In Ireland, for example, on 1 February 1993 it dropped from 100% to 14% and interbank rates fell from 40% to 16%.

Once an economy joins a fixed-band system such as the ERM, there is a worry that if they devalued or pulled out, it would nullify all their efforts. In that sense, they are prepared to raise the interest rate (usually money rate except in the case of the UK) to whatever is necessary. But the continuing influence of very high money rates is bound to penetrate the retail market – influencing overdraft rates, mortgage rates and one-month money rates.

To ask for a group support from all the EC central banks is still not feasible, given the overall size of the reserves of all the central banks and the volume of the trade in currencies and the flow of the currency worldwide – something in the region of trillions of dollars per day versus the total reserves of a central bank which is in the region of hundreds of trillions of dollars.

2.5 MAASTRICHT AND THE SINGLE CURRENCY

Currently the earliest date set for the monetary union in the Maastricht Treaty is 1997. This may or may not materialize by the end of the century when the prime goal has been set as an irreversible move to a single currency. Not only is there a great deal of opposition to it on all fronts, the members have to meet insurmountable convergence criteria set for EMU.

France and many other European countries such as Spain are seeking to press legislation to make their central banks autonomous – so that the ambitions of politicians do not get in the way of the conduct of monetary policy, e.g. for changing interest rates, such as prime rate etc.

Many commercial bankers in Europe have sought an earlier move to monetary union by a smaller number of EC countries, for they believe that there is a misconception that convergence of the exchange rate can only occur once economic convergence has materialized.

Some argue that more realignment may be necessary before a single currency can be established. However, no realignment is likely to bring about harmony as long as the 'window' of the free movement of currency within the band exists. That is, as long as a currency is allowed to move within a given band against the other European currencies, the system is unsustainable, and if there has to be frequent realignment, what is the merit of a fixed band? The currency might as well float.

Edmond Alphandéry, French Opposition leader said on 10 February 1993 (in an address to a conference in Paris by *Les ECHOS*) that for reducing the franc's fluctuation band against the Deutschmark there has to be 'some right to co-manage such a Deutschmark Zone'.

2.6 US/EC TRADE INTERRELATIONSHIP

Before discussing the direct US/EC trade relations, I shall briefly outline the global trade scene.

The General Agreement on Tariffs and Trade (GATT) was first established in 1947. Since then global trade has risen by a factor of 12 and tariffs have fallen by some 40%.

The Uruguay Round of trade talks have been going on for over six years, headed by Arthur Dunkel. The 1993 GATT deal was negotiated by some 117 nations. Over time the Uruguay Round has come very close to being successfully concluded. Indeed on 19 January 1993 it was thought that only a few minor parts needed to be solved. But the negotiations are still continuing.

As far as direct US/EC trade relations are concerned, the key element in the two regions' trade talks and perhaps the main stumbling block lies in the area of public sector related projects. This includes both intervention in the form of subsidies – involving tens of billions of dollars – to, say, the agricultural sector, or public purchases. Until Clinton's administration the US has been a strong advocate of free trade and against trade barriers.

Clearly, the Bush administration was in favour of radically liberalized international trade. On 1 February 1993 Washington attempted to freeze out EC companies for the award of public contracts.

However, shortly after President Clinton came into office, the US unilaterally introduced stiff duties on 60% of US steel imports. This was equivalent to $2.6 billion worth of steel imports. The dumping duties have been levied provisionally of course. Moreover, 11 days after Clinton took office, his administration introduced sanctions against 'certain discriminatory purchases by the European Community'. This was in response to the Utilities Directive which enables EC states to turn down tenders for certain contracts, i.e. when more than 50% of the value of the products has non-EC content. This part of the contract affected specifically US equipment supplied to telecommunications and power generation in the European Community.

The dispute on public procurement started in 1990 when the EC introduced its 'Utilities Directive' which took effect in January 1993. This Directive is viewed quite differently from each side. The EC sees it as a market opening initiative and Washington views it as blocking US companies.

The US Administration liked all those aspects of the Utilities Directive that further opened the EC market to the US, but was unwilling to admit the restrictions that are still left in the Directive. Washington maintained that this Directive contained an element of discrimination against the US.

Whereas currently the EC exercises some form of protectionism in the area of telecommunication and power generating equipment, within the US federal and local laws there is a bias in favour of 'Buy American'.

There is for the US the threat of an evolving United Europe. Clearly the new Clinton administration has shown its keenness to 'get tough on trade' and is set to take decisions unilaterally to rectify any imbalance.

The trade partners of the US can, however, tolerate the decisions of the new administration only up to a point and thereafter, some form of retaliation would be inevitable. Following some of the recent measures, i.e. the increase on tariffs on steel and the tightening on imports of telecommunication and generating equipment for use by the Federal Government, there has been some form of effort to reach a state of truce.

The current state of the art is that there is a strive towards some form of 'horse trading'. The EC would drop a trade provision for US companies in return for the US allowing EC companies access to public sector projects in the areas of telecommunication, energy, water and transportation.

The US/EC deal struck late in 1992 called for a 21% decrease in the size of subsidized exports, using 1986–90 as the base period. The Europeans felt it demanded much higher sacrifices on the Community. For the US the subsidy scheme grew more rapidly than that of the EC. The agreement reached in November 1992 between the US and the EC involved reducing subsidies in the agricultural sector.

On 29 March 1993 the US and EC attempted to pursue a face-saving alternative. Micky Kantor came to a meeting in Brussels and tried to seek a compromise solution.

There were internal divisions both in the US and EC regarding the trade negotiations.

The trade negotiations and quibbling are likely to continue. For even if a compromise is reached and agreements are signed there are always new areas of disagreement that emerge which call for renegotiation of terms.

2.7 US/EC FINANCIAL INTERRELATIONSHIP

It has to be stressed that monetary cooperation between Europe and the US has to increase. Indeed many believe that the absence of monetary cooperation among the US and the Europeans was partly responsible for September 1992's European currency crisis and the ensuing turmoil in global foreign exchange markets.

Over the 1992/93 period, a substantial deviation has existed between European and US interest rates, with European rates substantially exceeding those of the US. This has been partly responsible for the turbulences in the currency market over the past year.

Suffice it to say the high German interest rate has attracted a great deal of US funds into the Deutschmark.

If the US introduced some element of fiscal stimulus, it is estimated to bring about a 0.5% addition to the aggregate EC growth in 1993.

If the European Single Currency materializes in due course and a hard ECU is used as the single currency, then the major market play and force becomes ECU versus the dollar. That is, all the currency arbitrage takes place between the ECU and the dollar. If the ECU becomes expensive against the dollar, Europe as a whole would have to devalue against the dollar.

2.8 IMPLICATIONS OF THE NEW EUROPE FOR THE US

The implications of the new United Europe for the US can be summarized as follows:

1. US competitive position will be reduced against member countries.
2. If a single European currency, i.e. a hard ECU materializes, currency transactions will require fewer hedges against individual currencies.
3. There will emerge some reallocation of resources as a result of the single market.

Equally, there is a danger for Europe to build trade walls around itself and prevent US products from entering the community.

There are persistent pressures towards some form of protectionist measures from the local industries in different regions. Economic theory tells us that protectionism brings about inefficiency – which in turn leads to higher prices and lower output and, hence, unemployment. And then one looks at the Japanese economy that has prospered while imposing trade barriers. Japan 'appears' to give commitment to free trade and to opening its markets. Yet the real evidence proves otherwise. By setting up the so-called 'standards' that have to be met for imported goods, Japan has managed to prevent free entry of goods into the country.

Furthermore, when it comes to restricting their car imports to, say, the EC or elsewhere, Japan puts out forecasts about the shrinkage or expansion of the future market that differs radically from the importing nations. This in turn prolongs the curb on Japanese exports.

There is continual evidence of a closed market in Japan. There is no evidence that the active protectionist policies pursued by Japan, caused inefficiency in Japanese industry. Indeed, Japanese goods have penetrated world markets more intensely over time. This is clearly demonstrated by the magnitude and the growth of their trade surplus. Equally the reverse of the argument is not true – that is by protecting, industries do not necessarily become more competitive. It is the quality of Japanese goods or for that matter any good and the ability of their industry to penetrate and capture part of the world market that is responsible for their success.

2.9 CONCLUSION

In the final analysis it is the quality of the product, the strategy of manufacturing, and the marketing and sales that will ensure the prosperity of that industry.

There can doubtless be gains in the very long term from free trade, if one treats the world as a single entity. At the same time, it should be noted that the process of achieving this long-term prosperity, particularly while production shifts to low-labour-cost economies, can be a costly route for many regions of the world.

In short, there are both opportunities and difficulties in free trade. It is 'creative' trade that will ensure the success of an industry.

REFERENCES

Andersen, C. (1992) *Influencing the EC*, Kogan Page, London.

Brooke, M. and Buckley, P. (1988) *Handbook of International Trade*, Macmillan, London.

Budd, S. A. (1987) *The EEC, a Guide to the Maze*, Kogan Page, London.

Department of Trade and Industry (1991) *The Single Market: the Facts*, HMSO, London.

Dost, G. and Soete, L. (1990) *The Economics of Technical Change and International Trade*, Harvester Wheatsheaf, Brighton.

Dudley, J. (1990) *1992: Strategies for the Single Market*, Kogan Page, London.

Dunford, C. (1991) *The Handbook of International Trade Finance*, Woodhead-Faulkner, Cambridge.

Economist Intelligence Unit (1989) *European Trends, Key Issues and Developments in the EC, EFTA and the Single Market, Background Supplement 1989–90*, London.

El-Agraa, A. and Agraa, A. (1989) *International Trade*, Macmillan, London.

Euromoney Publications (1990) *International Finance Yearbook*, London.

Euromonitor Publications (1990) *1992, The Single Market Handbook*, London.

Goodman, S. (1990) *The European Community*, Macmillan, Oxford.

Great Britain, National Audit Office (1991) *Single European Market, Report*, HMSO, London.

Greenaway, D. (1990) *Current Issues in International Trade: Theory and Policy*, Macmillan, London.

Grimwade, N. (1989) *International Trade: New Patterns of Trade, Publication and Investment*, Routledge, London.

Hopkinson, N. (1991) *The European and US Economies, Business Strategies for the New European Single Market*, HMSO, London.

Kane, D. (1988) *Principles of International Finance*, Croom Helm Routledge, London.

Kreimin, M. (1974) *Trade Relations of the EEC: An Empirical Investigation*, Praeger, London.

Leslie, J. (1987) *International Finance and Developing Countries*, Longman, London.
Levi, M. (1988) *International Finance* (5th ed.), McGraw-Hill, Singapore.
Locksley, G. (1992) *The Single European Market*, Belhaven Press, London.
Masera, R. (1987) *An Increasing Role for the ECU: A Character in Search of a Script*, Princeton University, New Jersey.
Mehnert, R. (1992) *User's Guide to the ECU*, Graham & Trotman, London.
Melvin, M. (1992) *International Money and Finance* (3rd ed.), HarperCollins, New York.
Moore, L. (1985) *The Growth and Structure of International Trade since the Second World War*, Harvester Wheatsheaf, Brighton.
Morris, B. (1991) *The European Community, 1991/2*, Macmillan, London.
Motamen-Scobie, H. (1988) (ed.) *Economic Modelling in OECD Countries*, Chapman & Hall, London.
Motamen-Scobie, H. (1992) 'The gap between the practitioner and the theoretical and applied economist'. *Economic Modelling*, **9**, No. 3, 306–12.
Motamen-Scobie, H. (1992) 'Timing of entry into the European economic system' in (eds H. Motamen-Scobie and C. Starck, *Economic Policy Coordination in an Integrating Europe*, Central Bank of Finland, Helsinki, 127–39.
Motamen-Scobie, H. (1993) *The Stock Exchange: Dealing Practices and Regulatory Environment*, McGraw-Hill, London, (in press).
Motamen-Scobie, H. and Starck, C. (1992) (eds), *Economic Policy Coordination in an Integrating Europe*, Central Bank of Finland, Helsinki.
Nevin, E. (1990) *The Economics of Europe*, Macmillan, London.
O'Brien, R. (1992) *Finance and the International Economy: The AMEX Bank Review Prize Essays*, 6, AMEX Bank Review and Oxford University Press, New York.
Papaconstantinou, H. (1988) *Free Trade and Competition in the EEC Law, Policy and Practice*, Routledge, London.
Pilbeam, K. (1992) *International Finance*, Macmillan, London.
Pippenger, J. (1984) *Fundamentals of International Finance*, Prentice-Hall, New Jersey.
Pomfret, R. (1991) *International Trade: An Introduction to Theory and Policy*, Basil Blackwell, Oxford.
Poniachek, H. (1989) *International Corporate Finance: Markets, Transactions, and Financial Management*, Unwin Hyman, London.
Ronent, A. (1991) *The European Community Fact Books*, Chamber of Commerce and Industry, London.
Servais, D. (1988) *The Single Financial Market*, Office for Official Publications of the European Communities, Luxembourg.
Stewart, F. and Sengupta, A. (1982) *International Financial Cooperation: A Framework for Change*, Frances Pinter, London.
Stoll, H. (1990) *International Finance and Financial Policy*, Quorum, Distopia Ltd, London.
Terry, B. J. (1990) *International Finance and Investment, Multinational Corporate Banking*, Bankers Books, London.
Tsoukalis, L. (1992) *The New European Economy*, Oxford University Press, New York.
United Nations Conference on Trade and Development (1987) *Handbook of International Trade and Development Statistics, Supplement*, UNCTAD, Geneva.
Washington D.C. International Finance Corporation (1990) *Annual Report-International Finance Corporation*, Washington.
Watson, A. (1990) *Finance of International Trade*, Bankers Books, London.
Waxman, L. (1985) *Finance of International Trade*, Graham & Trotman, London.
Williams, A. (1991) *The European Community*, Basil Blackwell, Oxford.

3

What might explain the September 1992 speculative attacks on the French franc?

P.P. Moutot

3.1 INTRODUCTION

The large but unsuccessful speculative attacks launched against the French franc during the September 1992 EMS (European Monetary System) crisis at a time when the fundamentals of the French economy were widely considered as satisfactory have often prompted the following question: were these speculative attacks the manifestation of a speculative bubble or can they be explained rationally, if not fundamentally?

The view of this paper is that the dilemma suggested by this question is only superficial. For the concept of 'bubbles,' at least as understood in theoretical models, does not offer any micro- or macroeconomic basis to the birth and burst of such bubbles. First, these models, which are usually built under the hypothesis of rational expectations, represent bubbles as special solutions and do not give any explanation for their particular and sudden emergence. Second, they do not take into account recent findings (Frankel and Froot, 1991, for example) concerning the exchange rate expectations of economic agents. For, far from being perfectly rational and therefore based on a common and true model, these expectations are usually heterogeneous and, even for the same economic agent, may not be consistent in the short and long term. Finally, the change over time of the relative weight given by market participants to alternative views of the future is often instrumental in explaining abrupt market movements (Orléan, 1990).

Therefore understanding speculative attacks and the so-called 'bubbles' can only be done under three conditions. First, one has to identify those alternative and competing views of the future. Second, one has to understand what factors

The European Single Market – Monetary and Fiscal Policy Harmonization.
Edited by H.M. Scobie. Published in 1994 by Chapman & Hall,
London. ISBN 0 412 57520 5

might have forced market expectations to shift from one view of the future to the next at some definite point in time. Finally, one has to show how the homogenization of expectations, which has to take place for this shift to happen, occurs through the speculative attack and, in the case of the French franc, its subsequent containment.

It is this three-step strategy that will be followed when discussing the September 1992 unsuccessful speculative attacks on the French franc. For pretending that this bubble deserves no explanation on the ground that its birth and burst were so close would not be satisfactory. However, this three-step strategy will inevitably run the risk of getting oversimplistic, given that market expectations are difficult to observe and measure and that perfect objectiveness is impossible when attempting to reconstruct and classify other people's thoughts into a few competing views of the future. Consequently, this risk was minimized by ensuring that this reconstruction remains in line with opinions recorded in discussions held with market participants during and after the speculative attacks.

We will therefore show first that, coexisting with the very positive view of the French economy held by most macroeconomists on the basis of the good economic results of recent years, some points of gloom possibly leading to a competing view remained until the speculative attack. Then we will examine why this competing view became exclusive of the more positive one in the light of international developments around the time of the French referendum and how it may have led to the speculative attack on the French franc. We shall also show the response of the French and German authorities, how it led to the abandonment of this competing view, brought a satisfactory answer to the interrogations of the market and was finally successful in making the more positive view prevail. As a conclusion, we will try to draw some lessons from this episode for the stability of the EMS during the coming phase of transition to European Monetary Union.

3.2 TWO ALTERNATIVE VIEWS OF THE FRENCH ECONOMY

A positive view of the French economy gained increasing credibility as a result of prudent economic and financial policies over the period 1987–92. However, some remaining uncertainties have presented a potential but, until September 1992, subdued challenge to this positive view in the opinion of some market participants.

3.2.1 The long-term positive view

This view holds that the economic performance of France is getting increasingly close to – and even better than – the performance of Germany, due to a policy of exchange rate stability *vis-à-vis* the Deutschmark, to restrictive monetary and fiscal policies, to the opening of the French economy following the removal of credit and capital controls (in 1987 and 1990 respectively), and to the simultaneous development of efficient capital markets. This is reinforced by the fact that France already satisfies the convergence criteria required by the Maastricht Treaty to enter the EMU and is backed by substantive achievements at the level of policies, the real economy, and market prices.

At the level of policies (see Table 3.1) the yearly money growth progressively declined from 9.8% in 1987 to about 4.2% over the last 12 months; the French budget deficit remained among the lowest in Europe despite a cyclical increase in 1992; and the low ratio of public debt to GDP compares favourably with most other European countries.

Table 3.1 France: Main financial indicators

	1987	*1988*	*1989*	*1990*	*1991*	*1992*(*)(+)
Money growth (M3)	9.8	8.4	9.6	8.9	2.5	4.2(+)
Budget deficit (as percent of GDP)	2.28	2.03	1.74	1.81	1.93	2.45(*)
Public debt (as percent of GDP)	40.7	42.66	41.25	40.42	41.44	
GDP growth	2.20	4.5	4.1	2.2	1.10	2.0
Trade balance (in FF billions)	−52.2	−50.7	−68.1	−73.7	−56.4	22.0(+)
Current account (in FF billions)	−30.0	−28.8	−29.8	−52.7	−33.4	−3.17(+)
Unemployment (%)	10.5	10.0	9.4	8.9	9.3	10.2(*)
Inflation rate	3.12	2.7	3.5	3.4	3.1	2.57(+)
Average 3-month interest rate differential with Germany	4.28	3.66	2.33	1.89	0.43	0.37(+)

*Most recent official forecast at the date of the speculative attack.
+Last 12 months period.

As to the real economy the GDP growth has remained positive despite the slowdown experienced in other countries in 1991 and was close to 1.4% in 1992. The trade balance and the current account have steadily improved. For the first time since 1986 they are both positive over the last 12 months as a result, not only of cyclical factors, but also of increased market shares due to a simultaneously improved price and non-price competitiveness (Aglietta and Bauland, 1992).

This positive view is also backed by developments in market prices.

- The inflation rate, 2.6% over the last 12 months, is markedly lower in France than in Germany.

- The 3 month interest rate differential with Germany, which still attained a 4% in 1987, was less than 0.4% on average over the 12 months preceding the speculative attack.

Finally, the credibility of the French franc *vis-à-vis* the Deutschmark could also be observed through exchange rates. Beyond the absence of any exchange rate crisis between January 1987 and September 1992, it is worth noting that the temporary tensions between the French franc and the lira in 1990 or the peseta in 1991 subsided quickly. Moreover, the expectations of devaluations measured either through methods derived from the Target Zone literature (Svensson, 1992) or by the movement of forward exchange rates against the Deutschmark relative to the official band decreased steadily (Figures 3.1a–f). They became almost insignificant from mid-1990 on (Figures 3.2a–f), as the forward exchange rates for maturities up to 12 months entered the band and became increasingly close to each other.

3.2.2 The remaining uncertainties

However, some uncertainties over the ability of the French authorities to pursue the same policy of 'franc fort' in the long term remained. The first point of gloom came from the persistence of a high level of unemployment at the highest point of the business cycle in 1990 followed in 1991 and 1992 by an increase to over 10% of the workforce. This unemployment had long-term structural causes and its increase was slower than in other countries. Nevertheless its very existence entailed the risk that the French authorities would eventually yield to domestic expansionary pressures, casting doubts on the sustainability of rigorous macroeconomic policies in the face of adverse shocks.

A second related point of interrogation came from the risk that the objective of exchange rate stability would conflict with the often perceived desire of French monetary authorities to lower interest rates. Although such conflict had been easily avoided up to October 1990 (Figures 3.3a and 3.3b) as long as the interest rate differential with Germany was substantial, it remained to be seen what the true priority of the French authorities was once this differential became small. For the decrease of the day-to-day differential had been pursued between October 1990 and October 1991 at the cost of a clear upward movement of the exchange rate inside the band. This movement had been reversed over the first quarter of 1992 after the French Minister of Finance had indicated in November 1991 that the primary objective of the French authorities would be, from now on, the attainment of a satisfactory exchange rate position inside the EMS band. The willingness of the French authorities, however, to increase this differential in order to defend the exchange rate parity had not been seriously tested yet because the December 1991 increase in the intervention rate (*taux des appels d'offre*) had been more limited than the correspondent German increase and the July 1992 increase of the German discount rate had not been accompanied by similar measures on the French side.

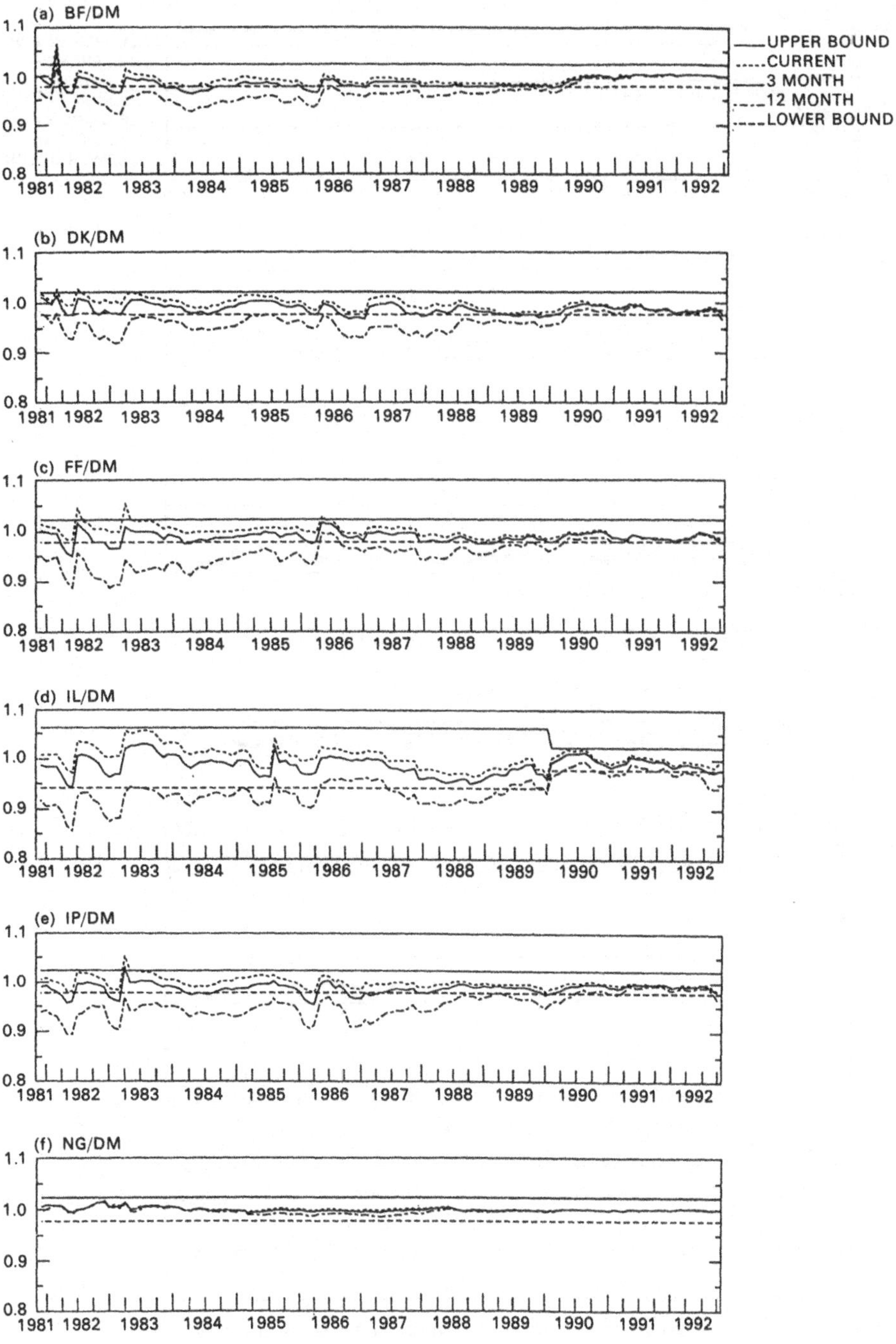

Figure 3.1 Current and forward exchange rates: (a) BF/DM; (b) DK/DM; (c) Ff/DM; (d) IL/DM; (e) IP/DM; (f) NG/DM

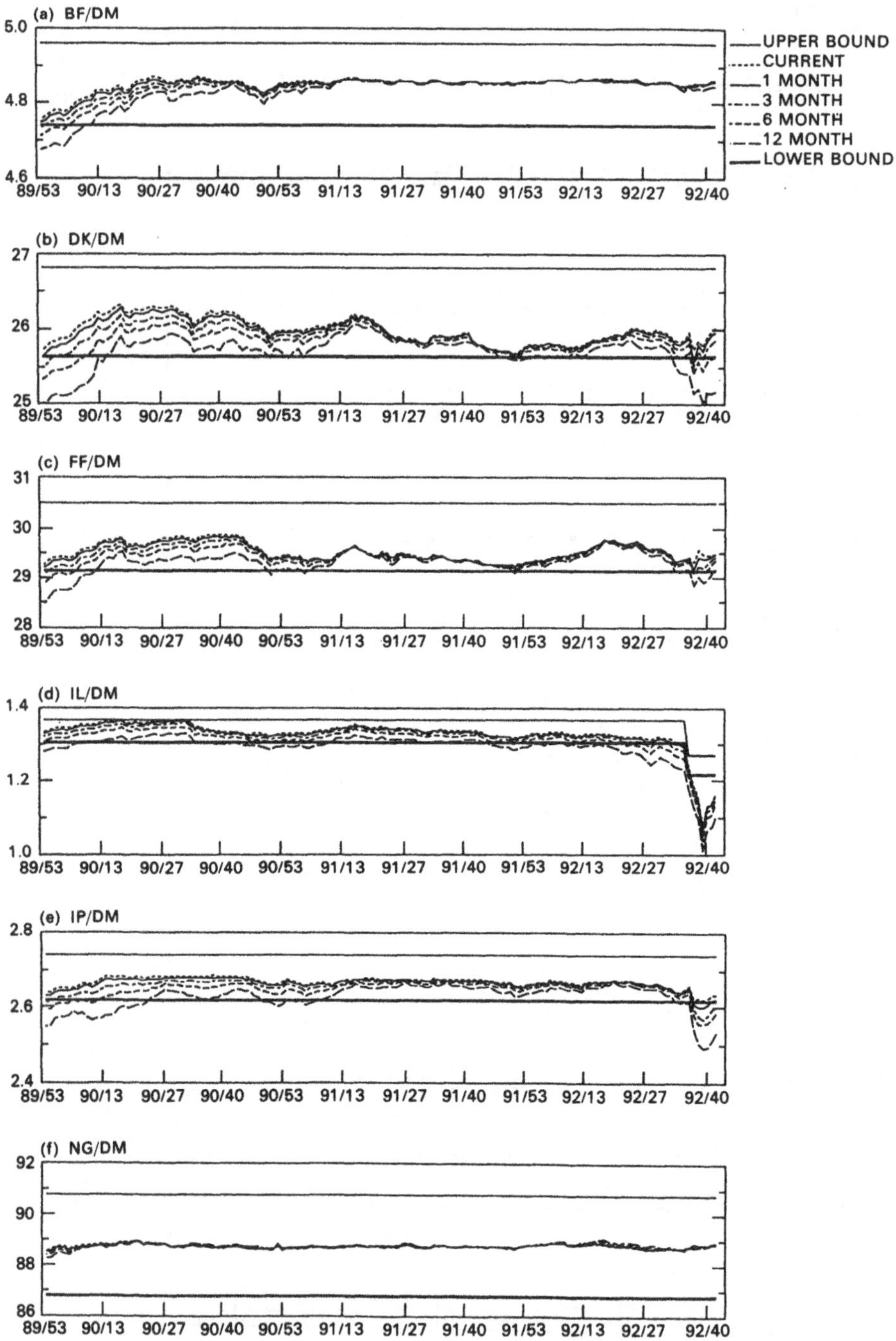

Figure 3.2 Current and forward exchange rates: (a) BF/DM; (b) dK/DM; (c) FF/DM; (d) IL/DM; (e) IP/DM; (f) NG/DM

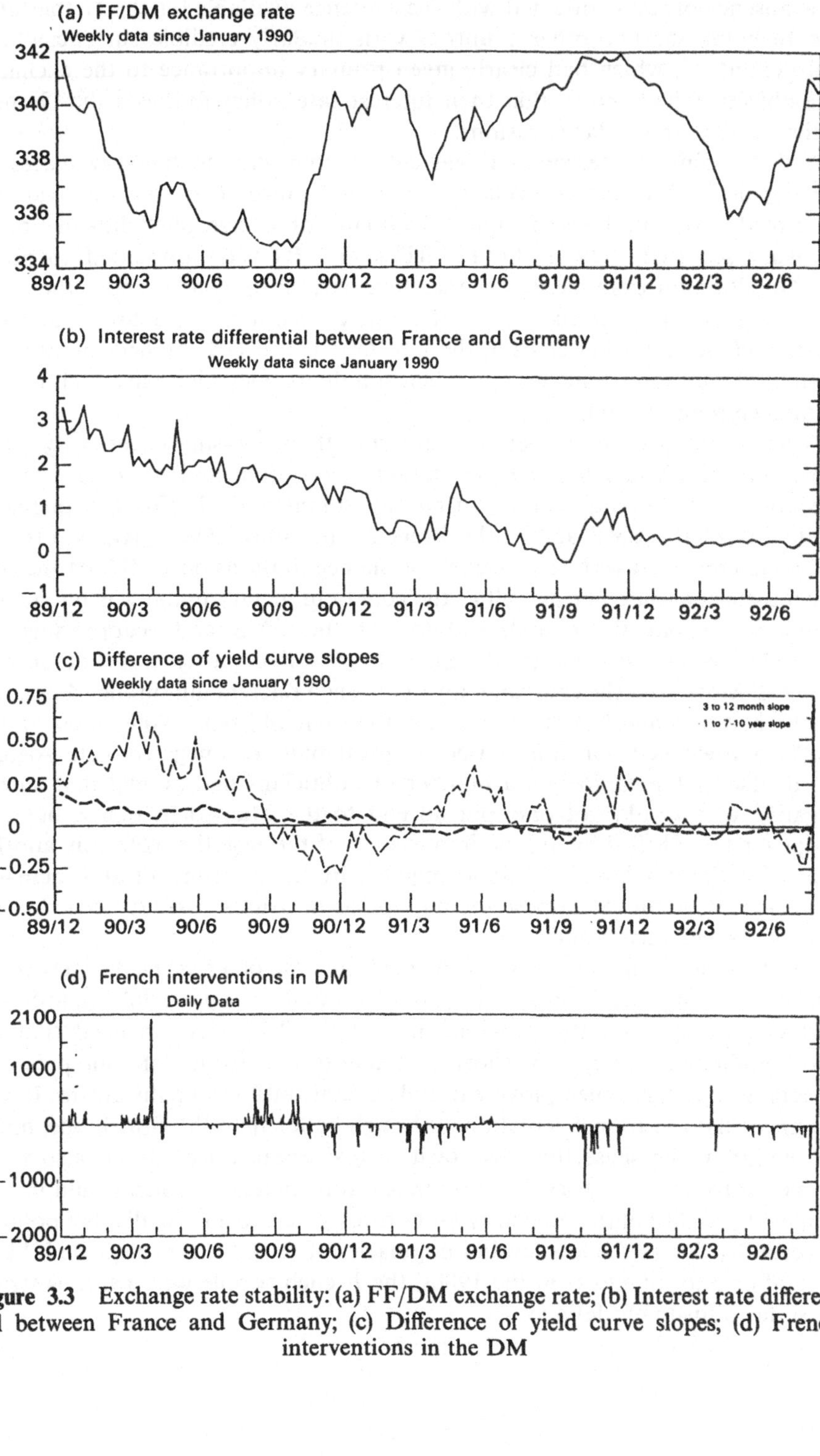

Figure 3.3 Exchange rate stability: (a) FF/DM exchange rate; (b) Interest rate differential between France and Germany; (c) Difference of yield curve slopes; (d) French interventions in the DM

This absence of test contrasted with the evidence available for the Netherlands and Belgium, the two other countries with similarly credible currencies. For these countries, which had clearly given primary importance to the exchange rate objective, had shown that their interest rate policy followed the German policy closely on similar occasions.

A third point of interrogation was closely connected to the very success of the capital and credit controls removal in France. For this removal had prompted strong in-flows of capital. Estimates of foreign portfolios in French Treasury securities (OATs, ORTs, BTFs and BTANs) amounted to about FF550 billion for example. It was therefore natural to wonder about the depth of foreign investors' confidence in the French economy at a time when real estate and stock market crisis in the US, Japan, and UK implied the need for fresh funds in those countries and when simultaneously Germany itself needed to finance reunification.

A fourth point of interrogation came from the increasing uncertainty about the future of EMU following the Danish referendum and its impact on the position of the French franc during the summer 1992. For the increased credibility of the EMS and of the French franc since 1990 (Figures 3.1c and 3.2c) had coincided with the progress of the negotiations on EMU. At the time when their final outcome as well as the goal of monetary union was put at risk, wondering about the overall stability of the EMS and reappraising the credibility of the French commitment to a stable parity was not entirely illogical. Moreover, the campaign for the French referendum on the Maastricht Treaty had begun and polls showed that the share of French voters in favour of the Treaty declined, which increased the probability of a negative vote. Also, in the course of the campaign, a number of politicians had argued that such a negative vote would not only put an end to the Maastricht treaty, but also endanger the EMS. Finally, the importance of the negative vote was another proxy for the low level of support enjoyed by the government and increased doubts on its ability to impose the unpopular measures possibly needed in the case of a speculative attack.

All these uncertainties, therefore, formed the base of a pessimistic view of the French economy shared mainly by a limited number of powerful Anglo-Saxon market participants until mid-September 1992. This view assumed that the good fundamentals might be short-lived due to the strong domestic pressures to reflate that high unemployment and capital outflows might create. It also assumed that the French situation, although better than the British one, might be similar in the sense that the crash of real estate prices would also make French consumers very sensitive to interest rate increases, which would in turn impair the ability of the monetary authorities to use them. Finally, the political uncertainty due to the low level of popularity of the government made it likely that, after a lot of efforts in the 1980s, the French people were perhaps struck by some 'adjustment fatigue'.

Nevertheless, this pessimistic view could not gain much credence as long as other countries with less favourable fundamentals remained inside the ERM and that good results, in particular foreign trade surpluses, kept accumulating in France. Also, no external shock had put to the test the ability of French authorities to enforce restrictive policies and what counted most, at least in the eyes of most European market participants, was the excellent results obtained up to that point. It therefore remained only a potentially alternative model of the French economy up to September 1992.

3.3 HOW THE TWO VIEWS BECAME EXCLUSIVE OF EACH OTHER

It is now time to see why the positive and negative models or views became exclusive of each other around the time of the French referendum, i.e. why the expectations of market participants suddenly shifted from the positive to the negative view of the French economy. For this, one has to take two facts into account. First, although the EMS is a system of 'fixed, but adjustable parities,' it was never immune to some dynamics of expectations and therefore to sharp movements. Second, the accumulation of factors increasing the likelihood of the negative view made more probable such a sudden shift.

3.3.1 The dynamics of expectations in the EMS

It is worth indicating at this stage, that some dynamics of expectations were common inside the EMS and that variations in the credibility of the exchange rate bands not only explained a large part of exchange rate and interest rates variability but were also swift and significant in some instances.

Let us map the deviation from parity of the French franc/Deutschmark exchange rate against the day-to-day interest rate differential between France and Germany since January 1987, date of the last general realignment (Figure 3.1). According to Bertola and Svensson (1993) and considering a day as an infinitely small maturity, the day to day interest rate differential is the sum of two terms:

$$\delta(x, g) = \tilde{\delta}(x) + g \tag{3.1}$$

where:
x is the deviation of the exchange rate from parity,
$\tilde{\delta}(x)$ is a negatively sloped function of x, i.e. $\tilde{\delta}'(x) < 0$, and g is the expected rate of devaluation and therefore a measure of the credibility of the band.

Therefore, when the band is fully credible, g should be nil and Figure 3.4 should show a negatively sloped cloud of points (Svensson, 1990), the movement of interest rates being inversely correlated to the movements of exchange rates. For, whenever the French franc depreciates and the exchange rate

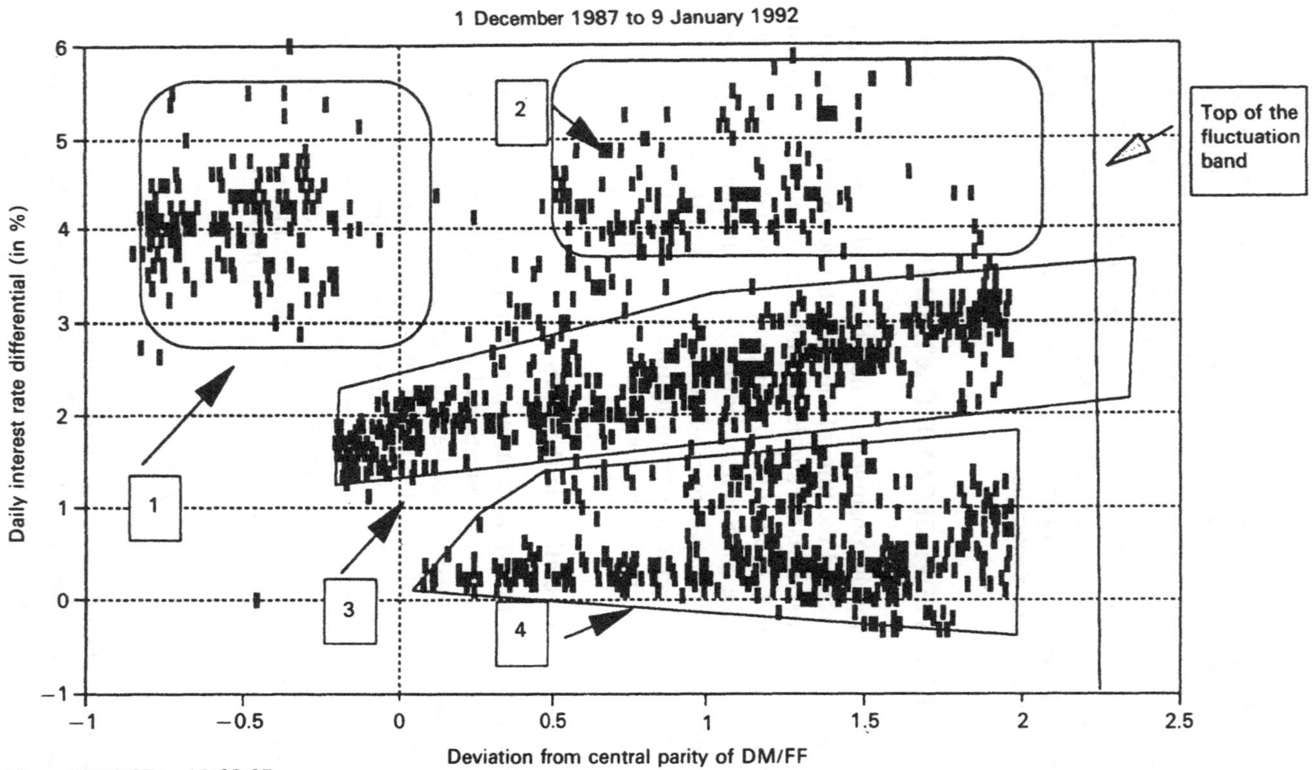

1: Period from 01/12/87 to 10/28/87
2: Period from 10/28/87 to 06/24/88
3: Period from 06/24/88 to 10/12/90
4: Period from 10/12/90 to 09/01/92

Figure 3.4 France and Germany (from 1 December 1987 to 9 January 1992)

against Deutschmark increases, markets should anticipate a subsequent appreciation of the French franc, justifying a decrease of the interest rate differential.

However, Figure 3.4 shows a cloud of points which, astonishingly enough, can easily be separated into four subclouds, each corresponding to a definite subperiod and none of them being negatively sloped. On the contrary, the two most recent ones, which form a first set of subperiods, show either a positive or nil slope. Therefore, according to the Bertola and Svensson model, movements in expected rates of devaluation have explained most of the French franc–Deutschmark exchange rate variations. This phenomenon became particularly clear over the two last subperiods, which form a second and clearly different set of subperiods. As the jump between the first and the second set of subperiods took place in June 1988, when a very significant loosening of French exchange rate controls was decided and followed by substantial capital inflows, it is probable that the more limited dependence of exchange rate variations on expectations of devaluation inside the first set of subperiods was partly due to capital controls.

Moreover, the variation of the expected rate of devaluation, i.e. of credibility, looks at the same time strongly autocorrelated and capable of very sudden jumps connected to major economic or political events when moving from one subcloud to the next. The jump (from subperiod 1 to subperiod 2) observed in October 1987 closely followed the October crash and the appreciation of the Deutschmark *vis-à-vis* the US dollar. The June 1988 jump (subperiod 2 to 3) corresponded both to a loosening of capital controls and to an episode of US dollar strength accompanied by concerted interventions; it was also achieved in a matter of days. Finally, the December 1990 jump (subperiod 3 to 4) took place at a time when the negotiation of the Maastricht Treaty was gathering pace. It was a time when markets perceived the need for high interest rates in Germany as a consequence of reunification more clearly and reacted to the decrease of the interest rate differential with Germany by a return of the French franc to lower levels against the Deutschmark. Although a little longer than the earlier jumps, this jump was a matter of weeks.

Finally, the quasi-linear shape of the two most recent subclouds as well as their positive or nil slope imply that the correlation between the expected rate of devaluation, g, and the level of the French franc/Deutschmark exchange rate inside the band was high. For the quasi-linearity suggests that:

$$\delta(x, g) = \delta(x) \quad \text{and} \quad \delta'(x) \geqslant 0 \tag{3.2}$$

which implies

$$dg/dx = \delta'(x) - \tilde{\delta}'(x) > 0 \tag{3.3}$$

This is in line with the feeling often disclosed by market participants that the closer the French franc comes to its ceiling, the higher the expectations of devaluation become. This behaviour is also in line with recent theoretical models incorporating some market participants' uncertainty about the true level of commitment of monetary authorities to the defence of their exchange rate band (Cukierman, Kiguel and Liederman, 1992).

In the same line of reasoning, the nil slope of the most recent subcloud could be interpreted as a sign that this link, although still significant, has weakened since December 1990, perhaps as a result of an increased likelihood of EMU. For, assuming that $\tilde{\delta}(.)$ is constant across subperiods, eq. (3.3) implies that:

$$dg/dx_{[\text{Third subperiod}]} \geqslant dg/dx_{[\text{Fourth subperiod}]} \tag{3.4}$$

This nil slope would then reveal the higher level of confidence of market participants in the commitment of French authorities to the maintenance of the parity to the Deutschmark since December 1990 in accordance also with the positive view of the French economy and the high hopes generated by the negotiation of the Maastricht Treaty.

Therefore the dynamics of opinions and the sudden shifts of expectations which are associated play an important role in the EMS, even in periods without realignments. It is not surprising under such conditions that, at the end of August, the doubts on EMU as well as the stretching of the lowest subcloud to the right – to its limits – may have prompted the question of a return to a former subcloud implying either higher interest rates or a realignment.

3.3.2 The factors behind the shift

In this overall context, several factors gradually increased the relative likelihood of the pessimistic view at the time of the French referendum.

First, the opinion of market participants as well as market prices and especially yield curves showed a weakness of the French franc and some likelihood of tensions during the summer (Figures 3.2a–d). This did not mean that a large speculative attack was expected, but simply that some similitude with other periods of tensions like October 1990 or October 1991 existed. This was particularly apparent when observing a specific type of financial spreads, the differential of slopes between 3- and 12-month maturities of the French and German yield curves. For, each time the French yield curve becomes less inverted than the German, it is likely that markets do not expect interest rates in France to decrease as fast as in Germany. This may explain why, close to the periods when such a situation happened (see Figure 3.3a, 3.3c, and 3.3d), exchange rate tensions and outflows of reserves were observed in France. The pessimistic view was therefore reinforced by the fact that, according to yield curve data, tensions could be expected.

Second, during the 1992 summer, the general interests of France in the international debate on the adequate level of interest rates came to be perceived by markets as different from German interests and closer to British or Italian interests. For the divorce between the level of short-term interest rates in the US and Japan on one hand and in Germany on the other hand was responsible for an appreciation of the Deutschmark which strongly reduced the competitiveness of the UK and Italy while making the financing of the very indebted private sector in the UK and public sector in Italy more difficult. These developments, although much less important in France due to a much sounder financial health, were often interpreted by Anglo-Saxon market operators as a sign that France may encounter difficulties too. Although this analysis was contradicted by the existence of a substantial financing capacity of French private firms in 1992 (as a result of an export-led demand and reduced investment by firms), this feeling was reinforced by numerous declarations from the French Goverment in favour of lower interest rates.

Third, the devaluation of the lira, and the floating of the sterling and lira, soon followed by the devaluation of the peseta, designated the French franc as a likely candidate for devaluation. This was not solely due to the fact that the French franc was the only remaining major currency to attack. It was also linked to the following.

1. The presence of long-time correlations between the evolution of the French franc/Deutschmark crossrate and the Lira/Deutschmark as well as Sterling/Deutschmark cross rates on a daily basis which implied pressures on the French franc.
2. The belief that the French export industry could not handle the loss of competitiveness implied by the British and Italian floating, although calculations would show that the impact on Germany was probably similar and that this loss left France still more competitive than in 1987, whether the real effective exchange rate was calculated with reference to consumer prices, producer prices, or unit labour costs and in relation to EMS or OECD countries.

Fourth, a large uncertainty on the functioning of the EMS and on the quality of the cooperation between central banks concerning interventions emerged after the British decision of floating.

Fifth, at the beginning of September, markets were impressed by the results of polls indicating that French voters might reject the Maastricht Treaty. Consequently, they became uncertain concerning the impact of such a vote on the French political situation. Therefore the referendum focused the dynamics of expectations, as it offered a precise date on which to unite the different views of market operators and, by its result or by the margin of the Yes vote, gave a supplementary indication on the likelihood of EMU and therefore on the support for monetary and exchange rate stability.

Sixth, the profits derived from successful speculative attacks on the lira and sterling strongly encouraged speculators to launch a new attack on the French franc despite the strong quality of its fundamentals. It is likely that this decision was encouraged by two particular biases of foreign exchange market-markers. First, as they play the two partially conflicting roles of speculators and of clearing house of the information generated by their customers' orders, they are sometimes induced in underweighting fundamental information when making their own trades (Lyons, 1991). Second, as they also play the role of advisors to numerous investors, they are sometimes tempted to dramatize shifts that may increase their trading and broking fees: this behaviour may have prompted the sudden publishing in September of several studies warning investors of devaluation risks. One may therefore argue that the shift of beliefs which took place after 17 September was only partly related to the evolution of fundamentals and was a largely endogenous consequence of previous EMS developments and of foreign exchange markets organization. It was certainly profitable for market participants with market power to encourage such a shift of beliefs.

Lastly, the messages given by French authorities were probably wrong and/or late. Before the referendum, the French Minister of Finance had indicated that an interest rate decrease was likely in the case of a Yes vote in the referendum. Moreover, in the wake of the referendum, while substantial outflows had already begun, any increase in interest rates was ruled out for fear that it might affect the results of the vote. Finally, as the positive effect hoped from the victory of the Yes vote after the referendum did not make exchange rate tensions subside, one more full day, 21 September, passed without any interest rate increase. As a consequence, at least during that day, the pessimistic model looked as if it could be borne by facts.

3.4 THE CRISIS AND THE HOMOGENIZATION OF EXPECTATIONS

However, the ultimate failure of the speculative attack and the major reflow of funds into France that followed showed that the positive view finally prevailed. This out-turn is largely explained by the way the crisis was managed. Taking place mainly between the 17 and 24 September, it can be separated into three parts: the days preceding the increase in French interest rates and the common declaration with the German authorities, the days immediately following them, and the reflow of funds into France that marked the end of the speculative attack.

3.4.1 The beginning of the crisis

From the 17–22 September, the French authorities limited themselves to interventions on the foreign exchange market without recourse to interest rate increases, for such increases could have influenced the vote for the referendum. In that context, the main aim of the interventions was to prevent the exchange rate from reaching its limit of 3.43 against the Deutschmark. This was felt important, for reaching this limit would have simultaneously increased expectations of devaluation, as shown by eq. (3.3), and facilitated the homogenization of market expectations around the negative view, each market participant expecting all the others to bet against the franc.

On the contrary, not reaching the limit and making discrete interventions had the advantage of making the market participants who were already aware of the speculative attack more uncertain of the time when a possible devaluation would take place and obliged them to speculate on the moment when this limit would be reached. The Banque de France tried therefore to hold the exchange rate close to 3.42 while letting the rate move around this level during the day.

This strategy can be contrasted with the strategy followed by the Bank of Denmark which did not attempt to limit against its exchange rate against the Deutschmark, but was nevertheless successful at resisting speculative attacks. As apparent in Figure 3.5, this is probably due to a different relationship between the deviation from parity of the Danish Krone and the expected rate of devaluation of this currency. For the scope of the relation between the interest rate differential with Germany and the deviation from parity of the Danish Krone has become clearly negative since end-March 1990. Therefore

$$dg/dx = \delta'(x) - \tilde{\delta}'(x)_{\text{or close to } 0}^{\text{either} < 0} \qquad (3.5)$$

Consequently, the risk taken by the Bank of Denmark when letting the Krone approach its limit appears more limited than a similar risk taken by the Banque de France. Given the pre-eminent role played by non-residents in the speculation against the French franc, this difference may be the consequence of the larger role of the French franc and of the internationalization of Paris as a financial centre.

However, this technique of interventions could only be used in order to buy time while voters prepared for the referendum in the hope that a positive referendum would calm the markets down. However, as outflows abated only on the morning of the twenty first after the referendum and regained momentum at the end of that day, more measures became necessary.

3.4.2 The Franco–German communiqué and the increase of interest rates

The 23 and 24 September were the turning point of the crisis, for they brought a satisfactory answer to most of the uncertainties forming the base of the negative scenario.

First, the official repurchase rate (*taux des prises en pension*), the highest of the two official rates, was increased to 13% from 10.5% to convince the market that the stability of the exchange rate remained the primary objective of French authorities.

Second, a joint statement by the Banque de France, the Deutsche Bundesbank and the French and German Finance Ministries indicated that 'no change in the central rate is justified'. This cleared uncertainties concerning the solidarity of Germany. Moreover, the Bundesbank was seen buying French francs against Deutschmarks at intramarginal rates several times, which was considered by market participants as a strong sign of commitment.

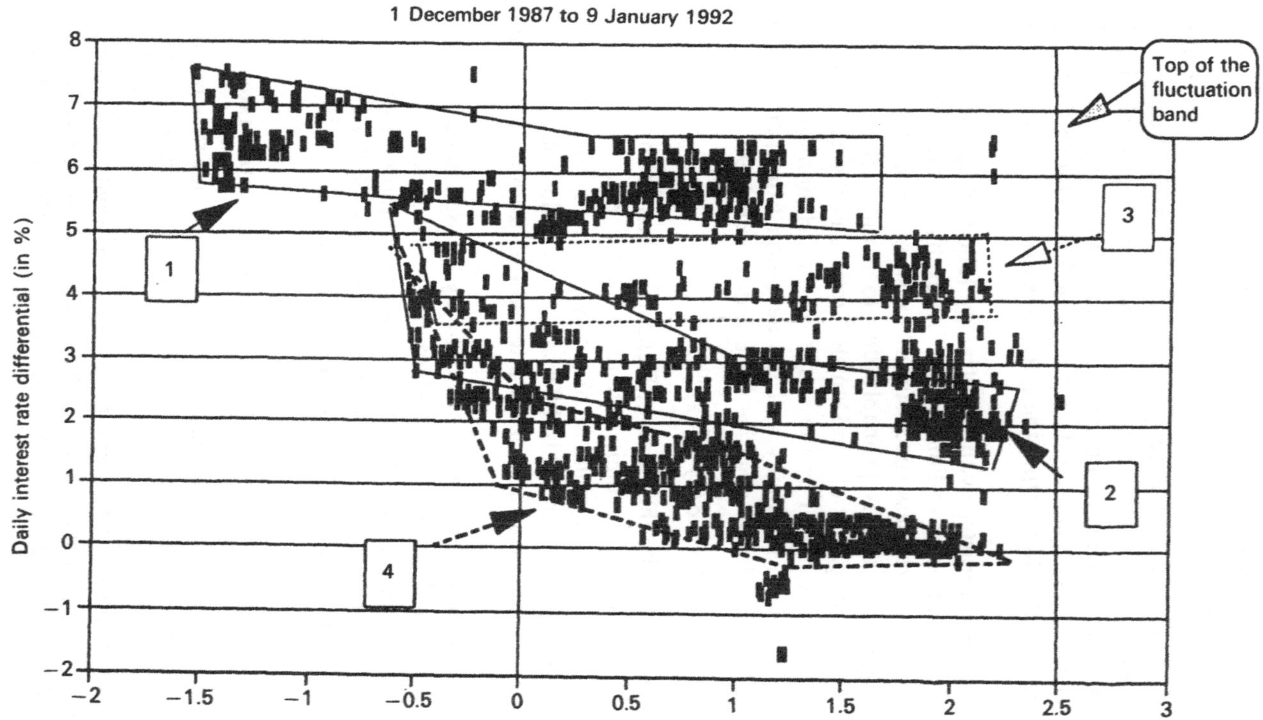

1: Period from 01/12/87 to 10/28/87
2: Period from 10/28/87 to 06/24/88
3: Period from 06/24/88 to 10/12/90
4: Period from 10/12/90 to 09/01/92

Figure 3.5 Germany and Denmark (from 1 December 1987 to 9 January 1992)

Third, short-term interest market rates were pushed up to more than 20%, due to the increasing scarcity of collaterals (Treasury bills and first grade commercial paper) requested by the Banque de France from banks benefiting from the official repurchase rate. As a consequence of this scarcity, the Banque de France had to ease its requirements for collaterals somewhat. However, this scarcity as well as the limitation of the access to the official repurchase rate to resident banks (this practice is common in most countries) worked in favour of the French franc: the interest rates not only soared on the domestic money market but also an interest rate differential between the domestic and the Euro market appeared shortly afterwards as a result of the differentiation made by lenders between resident banks benefiting from this access and other banks. The determination of French authorities to fight speculation and their ability to impose high interest rates in the face of domestic criticism was therefore clearly proven and the slope of the short-term end of the French yield curve became markedly more inverted that the German one (Figures 3.6b and c), indicating that markets expected a rapid decrease of French interest rates.

Fourth, the consistency of short-term interest rate developments with the long-term positive view was kept alive due to the stability of French long-term rates from the 1- to 10-year maturity. For residents and French banks did not speculate against the French franc, as shown by balance of payments figures. Moreover, they did not attempt to sell French securities. As for non-residents with long-term portfolios, they remained confident in the French economy and sold only a very limited share (about FRF 50 billion) of their total portfolio, with some of them hedging their exchange rate risk by borrowing and selling French francs. Therefore these limited sales of securities were absorbed without major difficulties by market makers who, due to the Treasury bills naturally supplied by their own trade, were able to finance a large part of their positions at official rates instead of high short-term market rates. Hence the very organization of the French money market management worked in favour of the franc by helping differentiate the economic agents supporting the long-term favourable view of the French economy from short-term speculators. This was made clear by the limited contagion of the short-term rates to the rest of the yield curve (Figure 3.7). Combined with the support of the Bundesbank, it gave the French monetary authorities a much longer horizon than the 10 to 30 days horizon of the speculation which, encouraged by the floating of the lira and sterling, had anticipated a quick victory.

3.4.3 The reflow

This set of measures quickly convinced the markets that the positive scenario was borne by facts. Speculation subsided and reflows were observed. At the end of September, a significant part of the FRF160 billion official reserves sold during the crisis had been bought back. At the end of October, official reserves reached again their pre-crisis level.

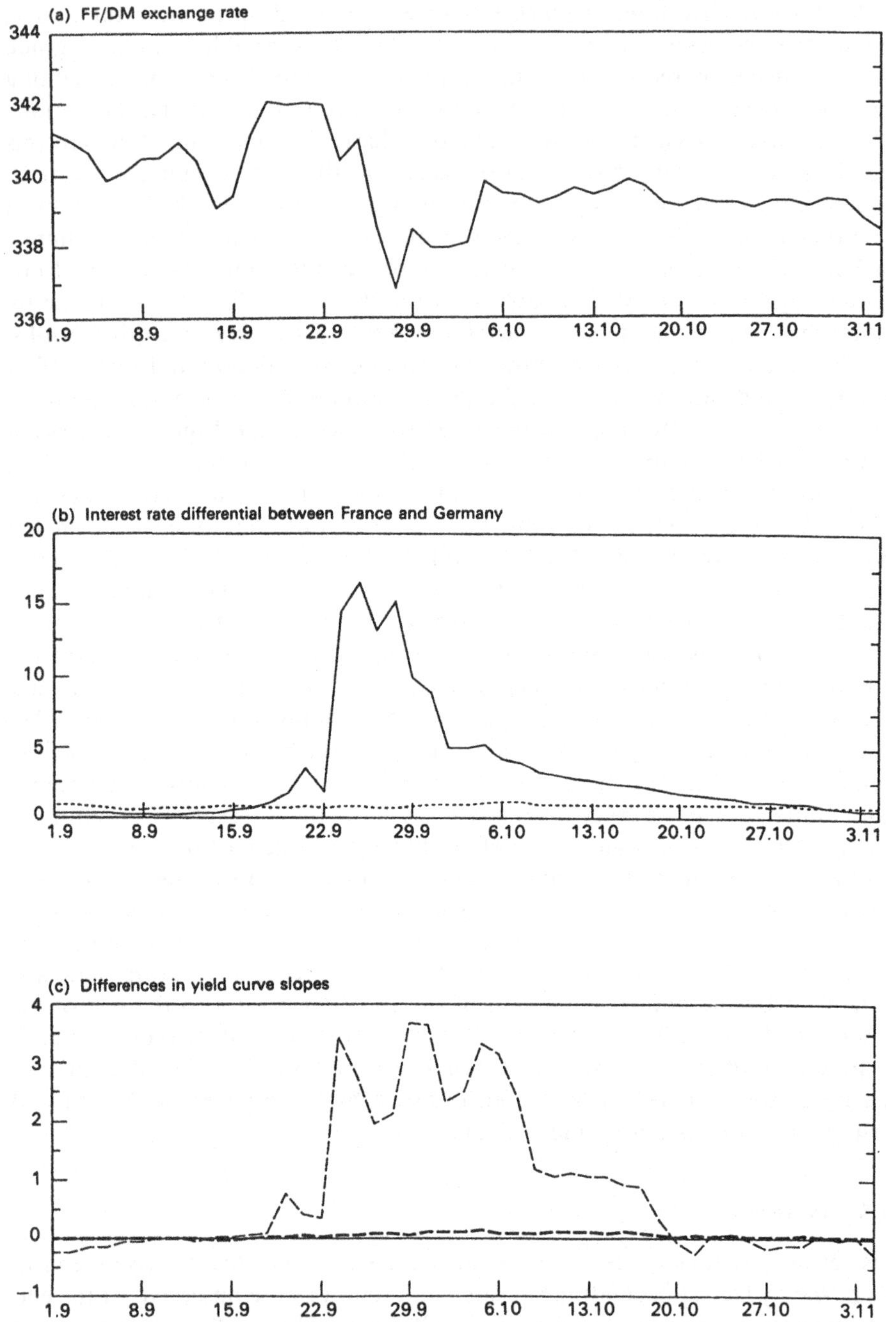

Figure 3.6 Domestic French franc interest rates: (a) FF/DM exchange rate; (b) Interest rate differential between France and Germany; (c) Differences in yield curve slopes

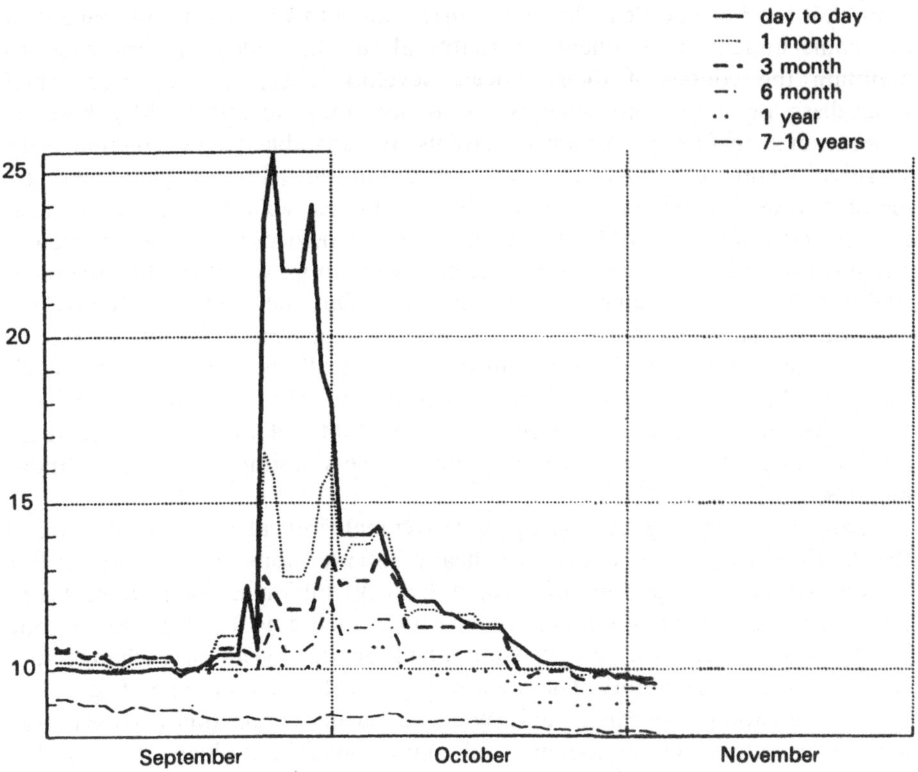

Figure 3.7 Domestic French franc interest rates

This fast reflow was the result of a prudent management of interest and exchange rates. Interest rates were lowered in a progressive manner to convince markets of the firmness of French authorities. As to the exchange rate, its appreciation was progressive. For, although it was important that markets felt that the crisis had ended, an excessive appreciation might have made the unwinding of positions taken against the French franc more difficult. Finally, a return of official rates to their pre-crisis level was decided in order to show that the crisis was over.

3.5 CONCLUSION

Beyond the crisis, several lessons for the second phase of EMU and the stability of expectations inside the EMS can be drawn from the turmoil undergone by the EMS in September 1992. They deal with the factors at the origin of speculative attacks, the size of these attacks, and the ability of the EMS to contain them.

First, it has become clear that even currencies with very sound fundamentals can come under attack whenever doubts about the ability of authorities to maintain the course of their policies develop. These doubts, even when groundless or based on debatable evidence, may spread rapidly because expectations on foreign exchange markets are unstable, autocorrelated, very sensitive to endogenous dynamics and sometimes biased by the gains made by major market participants as a result of a higher volatility. They are also heavily influenced by political and institutional developments like referenda and must be envisaged in a context encompassing more variables than the most traditional macroeconomic variables. In particular, the opinion that markets have on the sustainability and time consistency of economic policies play a central role. In that sense, the September 1992 speculative attack on the French franc may be better understood as a test proposed by the markets and passed by the French monetary authorities on the ability of the latter to increase interest rates rather than as a judgement on the soundness of French fundamentals.

Second, the very large size of capital movements indicates that the defence of the EMS parities may necessitate heavy interventions in the future. For unprecedented interventions of around US$ 30 billion in value have taken place in several of the countries under attack including France. On the one hand, such interventions may be amplified by the biases of exchange rate markets towards instability. These biases have probably been magnified by the freedom of capital movements and by an increasing connection between large foreign exchange market makers and major portfolio holders in a market where the daily volume of transactions reaches about US$ 1000 billion. On the other hand, the size of those interventions should not be deemed abnormal considering that a similar context of free capital markets did not exist in Europe in the past. Furthermore, to the extent that such capital movements can also be envisaged as the equivalent for national central banks of 'bank runs' on commercial banks, one may argue that their size was not disproportionate. In relation to the size of central bank balance sheets or to national monetary bases, they were probably smaller than the credit lines commonly negotiated by private banks to protect themselves against such runs which often amount to a higher percentage of their balance sheets.

Third, these new developments need to be accommodated by EMU structures and institutions if a smooth transition of Community countries to EMU is to take place. Therefore it will be necessary in the future to correct exchange rate disequilibria as a result of insufficient economic convergence sooner and more fully than was the case when the lira was realigned at the beginning of September 1992. Moreover, realignments should not be piecemeal but concern all currencies likely to come under pressure.

However, even if this is done, it will also be necessary, if brutal shifts are to be avoided, to anticipate and analyse the different and competing views of the future held even on the soundest economies by markets' participants. This pleads for the development, at the level of EMU and as a part of the European monetary cooperation, of a very thorough following of market developments and expectations so that movements can be anticipated at best. The question raised is therefore: how to adapt and organize the institutions in charge of this cooperation so that they perform that task at best?

Finally, the speculative attacks on the French franc led to some questioning about the optimal size of the anchor country if the transition to EMU is to be stable. For the size of the support offered by the anchor country to other EMS currencies, especially if several of them possess good fundamentals, may become excessively large as a share of its monetary base. In the case of Germany, this support reached up to one third of the monetary base last September, was difficult to sterilize promptly, and certainly influenced the domestic monetary situation.

Under these conditions, one may wonder whether the transition to EMU would be sustainable with several large converging economies like France or whether markets might endanger the stability of the EMS whenever a shift of opinions generates a speculative tide. In the absence of an anchor country able to fully play the role of an efficient, powerful, and well-informed 'lender of last resort', the latter option might prevail even when this shift of opinions is not justified. A collective anchor, which would result from a close cooperation and coordination of the monetary policies of strongly converging countries, might therefore be the answer. Whether such a solidarity can be established remains to be seen.

ACKNOWLEDGMENTS

I am grateful to M. Aglietta, A. Robert, J. P. Redouin, N. de Sèze, Y. Nachbaur, C. Gaujour, A. Magnier, and others for numerous and helpful discussions and comments. However, the views expressed in this paper are solely the responsibility of the author and should not be interpreted as reflecting those of the Banque de France or of members of its staff.

REFERENCES

Aglietta, M. and Bauland, C. (1990) Le Franc: de l'Instrument de Croissance à la Recherche de l'Ancrage Nominal. Colloque Du Franc Poincaré à l'Ecu, Working Paper.

Bertola, G. and Svensson, L. E. O. (1993) Stochastic devaluation risk and empirical fit of target zone models. *Review of Economic Studies*, in press.

Cukierman, A., Kiguel, M. A. and Leiderman, L. (1992) The Choice of Exchange Rate Bands: Balancing Credibility and Flexibility, mimeo November 1992.

Frankel, J. A. and Froot, K. (1991) Exchange rate forecasting techniques, survey data, and implications for the Foreign Exchange Market, NBER Working Paper no. 3470.

Lyons, R. K. (1991) Private Beliefs and Information Externalities in the Foreign Exchange Market, NBER Working Paper no. 3889, October 1991.
Orléan, A. (1990) Le Rôle des Influences Inter-personnelles dans la Détermination des Cours Boursiers, Rapports et Documents du CREA, no. 9001A, February.
Svensson, L. E. O. (1990) The Term Structure of Interest Rates in a Target Zone: Theory and Swedish Data, Working Paper, Institute of International Economic Studies, University of Stockholm.
Svensson, L. E. O. (1992) Assessing Target Zone Credibility: Mean Reversion and Devaluation Expectations in the ERM, Institute for International Economic Studies, University of Stockholm.

4

Interest rate determination across the maturity spectrum in a small open economy: the case of Switzerland*

F. Ettlin and M. Bernegger

4.1 INTRODUCTION

According to UIP (uncovered interest parity) the domestic interest rate for a given maturity equals the interest rate on the comparable asset denominated in foreign currency plus the expected rate of depreciation of the local against the foreign currency. In this original and most simple form the hypothesis is not only based on the absence of restrictions on international capital movements, but also builds on strong assumptions of risk neutrality and homogeneity of exchange rate expectations. The measurement of exchange rate expectations has already posed problems in the early stages of research: the forward premium turned out to be an inadequate predictor of actual and expected exchange rate changes. The addition of a constant risk premium factor to the strict version of UIP did not help much to resolve the issue, so a time-varying risk premium has become a favoured supplementary variable for explaining interest rate differentials.

In our view, the mainstream literature relying on UIP has two main shortcomings: the basic hypothesis is too incomplete, and the usual operationalization of expected exchange rate changes does not seem to work in practice. In the UIP-formulation of the international linkage of interest rates a

---

* The article is an updated and revised version of the paper presented at the Workshop on Economic Policy Coordination held at the Netherlands Bank, Amsterdam, 4–6 November 1992.

The European Single Market – Monetary and Fiscal Policy Harmonization.
Edited by H.M. Scobie. Published in 1994 by Chapman & Hall,
London. ISBN 0 412 57520 5

key explanatory variable – the domestic day-to-day rate – is omitted. Monetary policy influences interest rates mainly through that rate. Interest rates for longer maturities tend to reflect expectations about the average day-to-day interest rate in the relevant time span and thus about the future course of monetary policy. If this very important factor is disregarded, empirical studies of international interest rate linkages are severely misspecified and therefore misleading. This further implies that the frequently applied residual method of deriving empirical estimates of the exchange rate risk premium is likely to yield unreliable and distorted results. The distortion gets accentuated as in the literature most of the empirical work deals with short-term money market rates for one or three months, for which the influence of the neglected domestic day-to-day rate has been shown to be particularly strong (see Ettlin and Bernegger, 1992).

Concerning the operationalization of expected exchange rate changes, it appears that the widespread recourse to the ex-post realized changes on the basis of rational expectations arguments is unhelpful. The rational expectations approach implies not only that prices are determined on the basis of a commonly shared view of the fundamental determinants, but also that the market participants' forecasts of those determinants are, on average, unbiased. In view of such far-fetched and restrictive assumptions, it is not surprising that the corresponding empirical results tend to be rather poor. Thus a search for a better alternative is called for.

This chapter is an attempt to deal with these shortcomings in modelling international interest rate linkages. The study represents an extension of some earlier work by the authors on the domestic and international determinants of interest rates (Bernegger and Ettlin, 1991; Ettlin and Bernegger, 1992).

4.2. MODELLING STRATEGY FOR INTEREST RATE DETERMINATION

The movement of interest rates in different countries reflects to varying degrees the influence of domestic and foreign factors. It is the contention of the authors that the major domestic influence on the whole spectrum of interest rates is well represented by the day-to-day money market rate, whereas the direct foreign influence should be gathered through one or more foreign interest rates of corresponding maturity and other matching attributes.

In modern financial systems with binding reserve requirements and developed interbank money markets, central bank policy directly influences the domestic day-to-day interest rate. The transmission mechanism of monetary policy effectively starts with this rate, whereas under previous monetary arrangements it started with the central bank's discount rate. If reserve requirements have to be fulfilled on a daily basis, obviously every day the one-day rate is determined by central bank policy. If reserve requirements have to be fulfilled as an average within a longer reserve period, some longer rates may also be directly influenced by central bank policy. In practice, reserve periods are short – two weeks or a month in most countries. In this case central bank policy mainly determines the average day-to-day rate during the specific reserve period. Moreover, most central banks control the day-to-day rate through operating procedures which keep the rate within a narrow range. Changes of that range, or more precisely of the mean of the range, correspond to policy changes of the central bank. Thus, the development over time of the day-to-day rate reflects the central bank's policy reaction function.

In a purely domestic context interest rates for longer maturities reflect expectations about the future one-day rate in the corresponding time span. A three-month rate thus contains the market's expectation of the day-to-day rate set or influenced by central bank policy during the coming three months. So money and bond market participants, in fact, mainly have to guess about future central bank policy. Of course, various deviations from the pure expectations theory of interest rates may occur. Thus, longer maturities normally include term premia to compensate for the loss of liquidity; regulations or investors' preferences might result in other distortions.

In the more representative context of an open economy with international capital mobility, interest rate determination becomes more complex. Domestic intertemporal substitution then interacts with international optimization considerations. Therefore, the domestic interest rate for a given maturity is mainly determined by the expected day-to-day rate for the corresponding time span, foreign rates for the same maturity, and the expected rate of change of the domestic currency value of foreign currencies over the relevant time horizon.

These contentions are partly contrary to the UIP-hypothesis which stresses the international optimization aspects, but completely neglects any consideration of intertemporal optimization in the domestic money and bond markets. According to UIP there is no independent role for the domestic day-to-day rate in interest rate determination. It implies, moreover, that the matching foreign interest rate should make itself felt with a unit coefficient all along the maturity spectrum.

The interest rate model should, of course, also include a representative measure of the expected change of the exchange rate over the appropriate maturity span. However, as these expectations are usually not observed and recorded, they can in most cases be included in the model only on the basis of the specific supplementary assumptions. UIP-models relying on rational expectations often take the ex-post realized exchange rate changes as proxy series for the ex-ante expected changes. The results based on that approach, however, tend to be not at all satisfactory.

An alternative way of dealing with exchange rate expectations is to make use of some time series properties of actual exchange rates. Flexible exchange rates exhibit intermediate and longer term stochastic trends. These trends probably reflect the fact that underlying economic fundamentals of the exchange rate, such as the relative price level or the accumulated current account balances, also exhibit such trends. Given such intermediate stochastic trends and the high variance of exchange rates in the short run, it seems reasonable for market participants to rely to a certain extent on a continuation of intermediate-run exchange rate movements. Past changes of exchange rates are thus introduced as an errors-in-variables measure of expected exchange rate changes in the empirical models below. In contrast to similar empirical procedures in the literature, which until now have not proved successful, this approach summarizes not short-run but intermediate-run past developments.

The proposed model is applied to Swiss franc interest rates. In accordance with our composite hypothesis, the interest rate for a given maturity is determined by the domestic day-to-day rate expected over the relevant time span, foreign interest rates for the same maturity, the expected rate of depreciation of the appropriate exchange rates, and a term premium for holding the longer maturities.

4.3 EMPIRICAL IMPLEMENTATION

The set of interest rates analysed in the following empirical study consists of Euromarket deposit rates with maturities of one month, three, six and twelve months as well as three and five years. Since the government debt in Switzerland is quite low, and the issue and exchange of financial titles is subject to considerable special taxation, the country lacks a liquid secondary market for government bonds as well as a developed onshore domestic money market. The interest rate structure therefore can most appropriately be assessed from Euromarket rates.

The Eurodeposit markets for the shorter-term deposits are very liquid. For maturities in excess of 12 months they are not quite as liquid. (This is indicated, for example, by larger bid-ask spreads and fewer intra-day adjustments to the market conditions for the longer-term deposits. Actually, for the longer-term maturities, the swap markets represent the more liquid segments. As they have become increasingly important only during the 1980s, it was not possible to get a hold of sufficiently long time series for this study. The longer term Eurodeposit rates are nevertheless closely connected with the corresponding swap rates, which determine their pricing. Because of our use of monthly averages of daily data, however, liquidity considerations are not as important, so that the Eurodeposit rates also offer a good picture of the structure of interest rates.) Nevertheless, they provide good indications on the structure of interest rates in Switzerland. Corresponding time series are also available for other currencies, such as the US dollar, pound sterling or the Deutschmark. These interest rates are internationally comparable.

The sample period for the ordinary least squares (OLS) regressions spans from January 1980 to December 1991. The starting date was chosen so that the immediately preceding interlude, when, for more than a year, the Swiss National Bank had switched from money supply to exchange rate targeting, was excluded in order to have a more homogeneous data set. Actually, even the limited sample of 144 observations is affected by significant institutional changes. (In this chapter we mention only a few of these institutional details; for a more complete description see Bernegger and Ettlin, 1991.) It is to be pointed out, that the use of a short distributed lag rather than just the current value of the Swiss day-to-day rate is primarily motivated by the peculiarity of extreme end-of-month rate jumps. Under the liquidity regulations which were in force until the end of 1987, the banks actually had to fulfill the requirements only at the end of the month, the so-called 'ultimo'. The Swiss National Bank thus had leverage over the banking system mainly on those occasions. As a result, the day-to-day rates tended to be extremely high – up to 100% per annum – at the 'ultimo' and mostly very low during the preceding days of the month. Therefore, market participants were able to get an accurate assessment of the monthly average of that rate only at the end of the month. Their respective expectations thus had to be formed mostly on the preceding month's outcome. In addition, the ultimo rate – the day-to-day rate at the end of the month – was quite volatile.

It therefore seems appropriate to smooth the monthly data of the day-to-day rate when using it as a regressor for explaining the level of Swiss franc interest rates. Actually, for this purpose two- and three-month moving average filters seem to be appropriate. This also helps to smooth the end-of-quarter rate peaks in the data which have not been seasonally adjusted. Until 1987 such a pattern of rate peaks occurred because of an increased cash liquidity demand by the banks for window dressing purposes, which was not fully accommodated by the Swiss National Bank. At the year-ends such seasonal peaks used to appear not only in the day-to-day rate, but also in some other short-term rates.

The variable intended to reflect the expected exchange rate change is formed as a moving average of the annualized monthly changes of the exchange rate. The lags regarding the starting point of these measures were introduced to decrease simultaneity problems between the Eurodeposit rates, exchange rates and domestic day-to-day rates. In spite of their lack of sophistication, these rolling proxy measures of exchange rate expectations based on the intermediate-run past experience prove to be useful in explaining the level of all the Swiss franc Eurodeposit rates considered in this chapter. In fact, polynomial lag distributions in place of the simple moving average lag distributions would have yielded even better results.

With regard to statistical methodology, use is made of Engle and Granger's two-stage OLS estimation procedure for time series which consists of $I(1)$, i.e. a first-order integration and therefore nonstationary in levels, as well as $I(0)$ which is stationary in first difference form (Engle and Granger, 1987). For the data series in the study, this univariate characterization of $I(1)$ for the levels and $I(0)$ for the first differences of the data series cannot be rejected on the basis of augmented Dickey–Fuller tests. But the proposed null hypothesis – like in principle also the hypothesis of uncovered interest parity – calls for a relationship where the levels of interest rates are to be combined with first difference measures of the exchange rate. From the point of view of time series analysis this means that the regression vector consists of $I(1)$ level data in combination with one (or more) $I(0)$ first difference variable(s) for the exchange rate change. This is certainly not the standard case of a cointegrated relationship. Since the vectors of interest rate levels used in the study are cointegrated by themselves (see for example Bernegger and Ettlin, 1991) and thus jointly $I(0)$, the addition of one or more $I(0)$ variable(s) is nevertheless acceptable.

In the error-correction equations for the first differences of the Euromarket rates, however, $I(0)$ variables appear jointly with one or more $I(-1)$ variables, which indicates overdifferencing. In contrast to underdifferencing, overdifferencing will not lead to nonstationary results.

4.4. RESULTS OF ESTIMATION

Detailed empirical results are presented in Table 4.A.1–4.A.6 in the Appendix. The summary Tables 4.1 and 4.3 provide a convenient overview of the point estimates of the coefficients in the level and first difference equations, respectively. From the viewpoint of our proposed hypothesis, the level equations contain the more relevant information. All the equations show only one foreign interest rate among the explanatory variables. For the determination of any Swiss Eurodeposit rate considered it is the matching German rate which dominates the foreign influence. This effect is relatively limited at the short end of the interest rate spectrum and gets stronger for the longer maturities. The estimated coefficients vary from 0.29 to 0.67. All of them appear to be not only significantly different from zero but also significantly below unity, at least if the unknown nonstandard distribution of the corresponding t-values is disregarded. This

Table 4.1 Summary of estimated values from the level equations in the appendix tables

	Constant term	*Domestic day-to-day rate*	*D-Mark rate for same maturity*	*Past exchange rate changes*	*Past rate of inflation*	*Durbin–Watson statistic*	*Standard error of estimate*
R1MSF	0.24	0.70	0.29	0.11		1.28	0.45
R3MSF	0.41	0.56	0.40	0.16		0.84	0.44
R6MSF	0.49	0.50	0.43	0.17		0.76	0.40
R1YSF	0.67	0.40	0.54	0.13	−0.15	0.93	0.32
R3YSF	0.92	0.27	0.61	0.16	−0.21	0.61	0.38
R5YSF	0.67	0.24	0.67	0.13	−0.25	0.64	0.34

interpretation is confirmed by the estimated first-difference results, where standard t-tests are valid. The alternative assumption of a unit coefficient for the foreign rate, as presumed by the uncovered interest parity hypothesis, can therefore be considered as a doubtful restriction with regard to all six maturities.

Also in accordance with the basic hypothesis of the chapter a strong influence of the domestic day-to-day rate is confirmed. As expected, that coefficient is largest with regard to the one-month Eurodeposit rate, where it is estimated to be 0.70. A consistent pattern of declining values can be seen across the rate spectrum; the coefficient of the five-year rate is the lowest with a value of 0.24. According to the alternative uncovered interest parity hypothesis all the coefficients of the domestic day-to-day rate should be zero. The alternative seems to be clearly rejected also in this regard.

The estimated level coefficients of the domestic day-to-day rate and of the foreign rate tend to sum to about unity for all the maturities. This suggests that the Swiss Eurodeposit rates are approximately linearly homogeneous with regard to the Swiss day-to-day rate and the appropriate Deutschmark Eurodeposit rate. However, it should be mentioned that in the initial results for the two longest maturities the values of the domestic and foreign interest rate coefficients only added up to about 0.7. We interpreted this as an indication of potential misspecification. With regard to the long maturities, in particular, the future day-to-day rates expected over the corresponding time periods are not adequately approximated by the current (and recent) day-to-day rates alone. The monetary policy and business cycle context is, of course, also taken into consideration by the market. Therefore cyclically high or low day-to-day rates will not be interpreted without modification as an indication for corresponding rates in the intermediate- and longer-term future. To account for cyclical swings in the day-to-day rate, a measure of lagged inflation is included in the regression specification for the longer-term rates. The simple two-year moving average of inflation chosen as an additional regressor in the level equations yields negative coefficients. Thus, with relatively high (low) levels of recent inflation rates, the current domestic day-to-day rates tend to be above (below) their expected average level for the respective maturity span. This, of course, is in agreement with the known reaction pattern of the Swiss National Bank to the development of inflation. After allowing for such an effect in the estimated equations, the long rates also exhibit approximately the linear homogeneity property for the sum of the coefficients of the domestic day-to-day rate and the foreign interest rate.

The estimated coefficients of the three-year moving average term for the annual rate of change of the Swiss franc exchange rate for the Deutschmark are all positive. Their magnitudes in the level equations range from 0.11 to 0.17. With a coefficient of 0.17, for example, a one percentage point decrease in the moving average measure of exchange rate changes – indicating an appreciation of the Swiss franc against the Deutschmark – would lower Swiss Eurodeposit rates by 17 basis points. This does not make any allowance for monetary policy reactions through the day-to-day rate in response to exchange rate changes.

The estimated constant terms listed in Table 4.1 show a tendency to increase with the maturity span. This represents a part of the implied term premia for holding the longer maturities. Additional, time-dependent term premium effects can be extracted if the coefficient of the Deutschmark rate is multiplied by the difference between the Deutschmark interest rate and the domestic day-to-day rate. Because of the presence of the exchange rate and inflation measures in the model equations the full-term premia and their movements over time would be more complicated to extract and interpret. Instead, average term premia for the sample period, calculated in the usual naive way as the simple difference between the average interest rate level for a given maturity and the average day-to-day rate, are listed in Table 4.2.

Although the sample included periods with flat, humped or inverse yield curves, the positively sloped normal yield pattern quite clearly dominates the picture, both in Switzerland and in Germany. For Swiss franc deposits the average premium ranges from 0.73 percentage point for the one-month maturity to 1.42 percentage points for the five-year maturity.

For Deutschmark deposits the corresponding numbers are 0.04 and 1.21 percentage points. The Swiss yield curve is initially very steep and rather flat between six months and five years. The German yield curve in comparison is decisively higher for all maturities, but shows a more even curvature. The peculiar shape of the Swiss average yield curve reflects the decreasing impact of the day-to-day rate as the maturities increase and the very low average level of the Swiss as compared to the German day-to-day rate.

The estimated values of the Durbin–Watson statistic in Table 4.1 would be too low if judged in the traditional manner against an ideal value of 2.0. However, in the first stage of the Engle–Granger procedure for nonstationary $I(1)$ level variables, the Durbin–Watson value should primarily be interpreted as an indication of the stationarity of the regression residuals. For that purpose it is sufficient if the Durbin–Watson statistic differs significantly from zero. As this seems to be true according to the relevant nonstandard criteria, cointegration – i.e. a valid stationary long-run relationship among the regression variables – can be presumed. This presumption is supported by the values of

Table 4.2 Average levels of Eurodeposit rates and term premia 1980–91

Interest rate	*Swiss franc denominated*		*Deutschmark denominated*	
	Average level	*Term premium*	*Average level*	*Term premium*
Day-to-day	4.69	0	6.73	0
One month	5.42	0.73	6.77	0.04
Three months	5.65	0.96	6.89	0.16
Six months	5.86	1.17	7.05	0.32
One year	5.80	1.11	7.13	0.40
Three years	5.91	1.22	7.60	0.87
Five years	6.11	1.42	7.93	1.21

Table 4.3 Summary of estimated values from the first-difference equations in the Appendix

	Domestic day-to-day rate	*D-Mark rate for same maturity*	*Past exchange rate changes*	*Past inflation rate*	*Durbin–Watson statistic*	*Standard error of estimate*
R1MSF	0.60	0.55	0.11		2.04	0.34
R3MSF	0.48	0.66	0.12		1.85	0.31
R6MSF	0.36	0.69	0.11		1.75	0.28
R1YSF	0.33	0.74	0.07		1.89	0.25
R3YSF	0.17	0.56	0.14	−0.35	1.73	0.26
R5YSF	0.17	0.60	0.13	−0.34	1.73	0.23

the augmented Dickey–Fuller statistic, ADF, estimated on the regression residuals for the respective level equation. The corresponding results are shown in the bottom line of Tables 4.A.1–4.A.6. These values should be interpreted on the basis of test criteria given in Engle and Yoo (1987).

The estimation results for the first differences of the Swiss franc deposit rates are shown in the Appendix together with the corresponding results for the level of these rates. The coefficients of the error correction term are all negative and strongly significant, thus confirming cointegration between the variables in the level equations. Table 4.3 offers a summary of the first-difference results which can be compared with the level results in Table 4.1.

The declining impact of the domestic day-to-day interest rate is also clearly apparent also from the first-difference coefficients; they range from 0.60 for the one-month to 0.17 for the three- and five-year rates. However, the complementary rising influence of the Deutschmark rates seen in the level equations now only appears for the set of maturities up to one year. Nevertheless, the relative strength of the domestic as compared with the foreign interest rate effect also decreases across the entire maturity spectrum in the first-difference equations. Although in Table 4.3 the same type of influence emerges from the past exchange rate changes, as in Table 4.1, the coefficients are somewhat smaller than in the level equations. The corresponding *t*-values in Tables 4.A.1–4.A.6 range from 2.0 to 4.3.

The error correction equations for the changes in the Swiss franc Euro-deposit rates account for between 51% and 76% of the total variance of the dependent variable. The standard errors of the estimated equations range from 23 to 34 basis points.

4.5 TESTS OF THE ALTERNATIVE UIP-HYPOTHESIS

For an overall assessment of the authors' composite interest rate hypothesis, it also seemed appropriate to take a closer direct look at the evidence regarding the alternative UIP-hypothesis. The results of cointegration tests on the same sample of Swiss franc and Deutschmark Eurodeposit rates are most unfavourable to this stock-in-trade of international and monetary macroeconomics. The results for the one-year rate are illustrated in Table 4.4. The estimated values of the Cointegration Regression Durbin–Watson statistic of the first six listed equations are all much too close to zero to reject nonstationarity of the regression residuals. This applies for several alternative specifications of UIP: regressions of the interest rate differential between Swiss franc and Deutschmark deposits on a constant risk premium factor without and with inclusion of a further variable for the actual exchange rate changes over the relevant future time horizon as well as regressions of the Swiss interest rate level on a constant and the corresponding German rate with and without the ex-post realized future exchange rate changes added as an additional regressor.

However, the results improve substantially with the addition of the three-year moving average measure of the intermediate-run past exchange rate changes. The latter respresents, according to the authors' interpretation, an empirical proxy for exchange rate expectations. Non-cointegration between matching Swiss and German interest rates and this measure of exchange rate change can, in fact, be rejected. The estimated coefficients of this exchange rate variable are surprisingly high, when the Swiss Eurodeposit rates are regressed on the matching German rates, the proposed indicator of exchange rate changes and a constant. In the case of the one-year rates illustrated in Table 4.4, the second-last row indicates a corresponding coefficient of 0.38. In fact, in the one-month maturity case that coefficient would be as high as 0.5, and for the five-year maturity it would still amount to 0.3. These results are in sharp contrast to the estimated coefficients for the ex-post realized exchange rate change in Table 4.4 – they are essentially zero.

It appears that our exchange rate variable gives UIP a first chance to survive the pertinent stationarity tests. But the results still violate the unit coefficient assumption of the UIP-hypothesis. All the estimated coefficients for the foreign interest rate are considerably less than unity. When, in accordance with the authors' preferred hypothesis, the domestic day-to-day rate is also added as a further regressor, the results improve once more quite dramatically. However, with these modifications the specification in the last row of Table 4.4 definitely corresponds more to the authors' model than to the UIP-hypothesis.

When the day-to-day rate is included as a regressor, the estimated coefficients for the past changes of the exchange rate are less than half as large as when it is excluded. For example, according to the two last rows of Table 4.4, the coefficients are 0.16 and 0.38 respectively. This finding points to neglected simultaneity problems, which are a substantial weakness remaining in the present study. Due to the Swiss National Bank's behaviour pattern there also seems to be a substantial similar response of the day-to-day rate to the exchange rate variable. The single equation interest rate models in this study should therefore be complemented by a second equation for the day-to-day

Table 4.4 Summary of cointegration regressions concerning UIP for the one-year maturity

	Constant	*R1YDM*	*R1DSF*	*Actual future change of exchange rate*	*Past change of exchange rate*	*Adjusted coefficient of deter-mination*	*Durbin–Watson statistic*	*Standard error of estimate*
	−1.34					0	0.08	1.13
(R1YDM	−1.31			−0.01		0.16	0.11	1.04
–R1TSF)	−1.01			−0.00	0.36	0.54	0.22	0.77
	−0.99				0.40	0.52	0.22	0.79
	0.62	0.73				0.76	0.11	0.94
	0.38	0.76		0.01		0.78	0.14	0.89
R1YSF	0.74	0.75		0.00	0.37	0.92	0.43	0.54
	0.77	0.75			0.38	0.92	0.43	0.54
	0.71	0.47	0.40		0.16	0.97	0.82	0.35

rate in form of a reaction function of the central bank. There is, moreover, a further missing equation for the exchange rate, which in part responds to interest rate differentials. These deficiencies should be corrected in future work by building on an appropriate simultaneous equation system containing, at least, those three equations.

4.6 SUMMARY AND POLICY IMPLICATIONS

In the literature, international interest rate linkages are mostly discussed within the framework set by the hypothesis of uncovered interest parity (UIP). Since the empirical results from UIP-models usually are not very satisfactory, presumably large time-varying risk premia have been invoked in trying to explain international interest rate differentials. This mainstream literature, relying on UIP, has essential shortcomings. The UIP-hypothesis implies severe mis-specification as a most important explanatory variable, the domestic day-to-day rate of interest, is omitted. In modern financial systems – with binding reserve requirements for the banks and with developed interbank money markets – monetary policy affects interest rates mainly through that rate. In a purely domestic context interest rates for maturities of more than one day would – apart from term premia – primarily reflect expectations about the average day-to-day interest rate in the relevant time span and thus about the future course of monetary policy. With international capital mobility, interest rate determination is more complex because of the additional impact of matching foreign interest rates and of expected changes of the corresponding exchange rates.

The empirical results in the paper provide strong support for the suggested role of the day-to-day rate. In fact, with regard to the shorter-run money market rates the coefficient for the impact of the domestic day-to-day rate exceeds that of the matching foreign, i.e. German, interest rate. However, the longer the maturity span gets, the smaller the coefficient of the domestic day-to-day rate becomes while the coefficient of the foreign interest rate increases accordingly. The assumption of a unit coefficient for the foreign interest rate implied in UIP was in no case confirmed. The corresponding coefficient estimates are all positive, but substantially below unity, as suggested by the basic hypothesis of the paper.

To operationalize exchange rate expectations, a three-year moving average of past exchange rate changes was applied. This proxy variable shows a substantial direct impact of past exchange rate changes on Swiss interest rates. This is in contrast to results with a rational-expectations-based approach whereby the ex-post realized exchange rate changes are taken as proxy indicators of the unobserved expected exchange rate changes.

According to the results presented the Swiss National Bank, Switzerland's monetary authority, can influence the short-money market rates relatively well through the day-to-day rate. As the term to maturity lengthens, however, this direct leverage of domestic monetary policy on interest rates gets successively weaker, and the influence of the matching German rate gets correspondingly stronger. Swiss monetary policy, moreover, has to contend with a considerable influence of SFr–DM exchange rate changes on domestic interest rates. Therefore, monetary policy also affects Swiss interest rates indirectly through its leverage on the exchange rate. Since the exchange rate is affected by other domestic and by foreign determinants as well, it represents in principle a second constraint limiting the autonomy of the National Bank in determining Swiss interest rates.

In international comparisons of interest rates, the level of Swiss rates are generally found to be very low. This characteristic pattern can, according to the results of the present chapter, mainly be explained by the very low level of the domestic day-to-day rate of interest. The Swiss National Bank was able to permit such low interest rates because other factors, in particular the large cumulative current account surpluses and the relative price stability, supported the foreign exchange value of the Swiss franc in the long run.

APPENDIX: ESTIMATION RESULTS

Table 4.A.1 Estimated equations for the one-month interest rate on Swiss franc Eurodeposits

Sample space	*1980 M1–1991 M12*		*1980 M2–1991 M12*	
Explanatory variables	*Level equation*		*Difference equation*	
constant		0.243		
		(2.14)		
R1MDM(t)		0.294		0.554
		(11.69)		(7.05)
M2R1D(t)		0.703		0.603
		(23.32)		(14.89)
M3YSFDM(t-4)		0.110		0.113
		(4.36)		(2.47)
D12C(t)				0.501
				(5.65)
e(t–1)				−0.470
				(6.74)
Summary statistics				
R^2		0.959		0.762
SEE		0.446		0.345
F(.,..)	(3, 140)	1129.4	(5, 137)	91.1
DW		1.284		2.037
ADF(0)		−8.199		

R1MDM Interest rate on one-month Euromarket deposits in Deutschmarks, monthly average of daily data.
R1D Interest rate on day-to-day money (tomorrow-next) in Swiss francs, monthly average of daily data.
M2R1D Two-month moving average of *R1D*.
M3YSFDM Three-year moving average of the annualized monthly percentage change of the SFr-DM exchange rate.
D12C Constrained seasonal dummy variable: 1 for December and −0.091 for the other months until 1987M12 and 0 thereafter.
e Error correction term, derived from the estimated level equation.
R^2 Coefficient of determination
SEE Standard error of estimate.
F(.,..) *F*-statistic for the joint significance of the explanatory variables, the relevant degrees of freedom are indicated in the parentheses.
DW Durbin–Watson statistic (in the level equations to be interpreted as Cointegration Regression Durbin–Watson value).
ADF(.) Augmented Dickey–Fuller test statistic, with the number of autoregressive terms indicated in parentheses.

Table 4.A.2 Estimated equations for the three-month interest rate on Swiss franc Eurodeposits

Sample space	*1980 M1–1991 M12*		*1980 M2–1991 M12*	
Explanatory variables	*Level equation*		*Difference equation*	
constant		0.409		
		(3.64)		
R3MDM(t)		0.405		0.664
		(16.26)		(9.75)
M2R1D(t)		0.555		0.422
		(18.48)		(10.89)
M3YSFDM(t-4)		0.157		0.117
		(6.29)		(2.81)
D12C(t)				0.234
				(2.82)
R1D(t–2)				0.055
				(2.26)
e(t–1)				−0.354
				(5.78)
Summary statistics				
R^2		0.959		0.686
SEE		0.438		0.308
F(.,..)	(3, 140)	1110.8	(6, 136)	52.1
DW		0.843		1.854
ADF(1)		−6.30		

R3MDM	Interest rate on three-month Euromarket deposits in Deutschmarks, monthly average of daily data.
R1D	Interest rate on day-to-day money (tomorrow-next) in Swiss francs, monthly average of daily data.
M2R1D	Two-month moving average of *R1D*.
M3YSFDM	Three-year moving average of the annualized monthly percentage change of the SFr–DM exchange rate.
D12C	Constrained seasonal dummy variable: 1 for December and −0.091 for the other months until 1987M12 and 0 thereafter.
e	Error correction term, derived from the estimated level equation.

Table 4.A.3 Estimated equations for the six-month interest rate on Swiss franc Eurodeposits

Sample space	*1980 M1–1991 M12*		*1980 M2–1991 M12*	
Explanatory variables	*Level equation*		*Difference equation*	
constant		0.492		
		(4.68)		
R6MDM(t)		0.501		0.693
		(21.16)		(11.12)
M2R1D(t)		0.427		0.312
		(15.15)		(8.81)
M3YSFDM(t-4)		0.175		0.112
		(7.55)		(3.08)
D12C(t)				0.133
				(2.01)
R1D(t–2)				0.050
				(2.21)
e(t–1)				−0.330
				(5.37)
Summary statistics				
R^2		0.964		0.683
SEE		0.401		0.284
F(.,..)	(3, 140)	1239.6	(6, 136)	51.4
DW		0.847		1.749
ADF(1)		−6.088		

R6MDM	Interest rate on six-month Euromarket deposits in Deutschmarks, monthly average of daily data.
R1D	Interest rate on day-to-day money (tomorrow-next) in Swiss francs, monthly average of daily data.
M2R1D	Two-month moving average of *R1D*.
M3YSFDM	Three-year moving average of the annualized monthly percentage change of the SFr–DM exchange rate.
D12C	Constrained seasonal dummy variable: 1 for December and −0.091 for the other months until 1987M12 and 0 thereafter.
e	Error correction term, derived from the estimated level equation.

Table 4.A.4 Estimated equations for the one-year interest rate on Swiss franc Eurodeposits

Sample space	*1980 M1–1991 M12*		*1980 M2–1991 M12*	
Explanatory variables	*Level equation*		*Difference equation*	
constant		0.674		
		(7.67)		
R1YDM(t)		0.542		0.741
		(21.64)		(13.54)
M3R1D(t)		0.403		0.330
		(15.69)		(7.52)
M3YSFDM(t-5)		0.134		0.067
		(6.74)		(2.05)
M2YINF(t)		−0.147		
		(5.31)		
D12C(t)				0.124
				(2.17)
e(t–1)				−0.389
				(5.48)
Summary statistics				
R^2		0.972		0.690
SEE		0.320		0.247
F(..,..)	(4, 139)	1239.8	(5, 137)	63.4
DW		0.927		1.888
ADF(0)		−6.373		

R1YDM	Interest rate on one-year Euromarket deposits in Deutschmarks, monthly average of daily data.
R1D	Interest rate on day-to-day money (tomorrow-next) in Swiss francs, monthly average of daily data.
M3R1D	Three-month moving average of *R1D*.
M3YSFDM	Three-year moving average of the annualized monthly percentage change of the SFr–DM exchange rate.
M2YINF	Two-year moving average of the annual rate of inflation
D12C	Constrained seasonal dummy variable: 1 for December and −0.091 for the other months until 1987M12 and 0 thereafter.
e	Error correction term, derived from the estimated level equation.

Table 4.A.5 Estimated equations for the three-year interest rate on Swiss franc Eurodeposits

Sample space	*1980 M1–1991 M12*		*1980 M2–1991 M12*	
Explanatory variables	*Level equation*		*Difference equation*	
constant		0.922		
		(5.95)		
R3YDM(t)		0.607		0.556
		(14.72)		(8.57)
M3R1D(t)		0.270		0.165
		(8.96)		(3.69)
M3YSFDM(t-5)		0.164		0.145
		(6.53)		(4.26)
M2YINF(t)		−0.213		
		(5.79)		
M3YINF(t))				−0.346
				(2.54)
e(t–1)				−0.341
				(6.03)
Summary statistics				
R^2		0.931		0.517
SEE		0.380		0.261
F(.,..)	(4, 139)	487.1	(6, 136)	42.8
DW		0.613		1.726
ADF(2)		−5.65		

R3YDM Interest rate on three-year Euromarket deposits in Deutschmarks, monthly average of daily data.
R1D Interest rate on day-to-day money (tomorrow-next) in Swiss francs, monthly average of daily data.
M3R1D Two-month moving average of *R1D*.
M3YSFDM Three-year moving average of the annualized monthly percentage change of the SFr–DM exchange rate.
M2YINF Two-year moving average of the annual rate of inflation
M3YINF Three-year moving average of the annual rate of inflation.
e Error correction term, derived from the estimated level equation.

Table 4.A.6 Estimated equations for the five-year interest rate on Swiss franc Eurodeposits

Sample space	*1980 M1–1991 M12*	*1980 M2–1991 M12*
Explanatory variables	*Level equation*	*Difference equation*
constant	0.669	
	(3.45)	
R5YDM(t)	0.668	0.601
	(15.77)	(9.03)
M3R1D(t)	0.242	0.175
	(9.56)	(4.27)
M3YSFDM(t-5)	0.132	0.128
	(5.85)	(4.10)
M2YINF(t)	−0.250	
	(7.55)	
M3YINF(t))		−0.335
		(2.69)
e(t–1)		−0.348
		(5.83)
Summary statistics		
R^2	0.925	0.550
SEE	0.337	0.234
F(.,..)	(4, 139) 440.7	(5, 137) 34.0
DW	0.645	1.734
ADF(1)	−5.378	

R5YDM	Interest rate on five-year Euromarket deposits in Deutschmarks, monthly average of daily data.
R1D	Interest rate on day-to-day money (tomorrow-next) in Swiss francs, monthly average of daily data.
M3R1D	Three-month moving average of *R1D*.
M3YSFDM	Three-year moving average of the annualized monthly percentage change of the SFr–DM exchange rate.
M2YINF	Two-year moving average of the annual rate of inflation.
M3YINF	Three-year moving average of the annual rate of inflation.
e	Error correction term, derived from the estimated level equation.

REFERENCES

Bernegger, M. and Ettlin, F. (1991) 'Zinsbestimmung und Transmission monetärer Impulse im Geldmarkt', *Schweizerische Zeitschrift für Volkswirtschaft und Statistik*, September, 579–615.

Engle, R. F. and Yung, S. Y. (1987) 'Forecasting and testing in co-integrated systems', *Journal of Econometrics*, May, 143–59.

Ettlin, F. and Bernegger, M. (1992) 'Interest rate determination in the Eurocurrency Market', in *Economic Policy Coordination in the Integrating Europe*, Bank of Finland, Series C8, C. Starck and H. Motamen-Scobie (eds).

FURTHER READING

Bank for International Settlements (1989) *International Interest Rate Linkages and Monetary Policy*, Basle.

Béguelin, J.-P., Ettlin, F. and Schiltknecht, K. (1985) 'Swiss interest rates and savings: some considerations', in *Nominal and Real Interest Rates: Determinants and Influences*, Bank for International Settlements, Basle, 249–58.

Cumby, R. and Obstfeld, M. (1984) 'International interest rate and price level linkages under flexible exchange rates: a review of recent evidence', in *Exchange Rate Theory and Practice*, (eds) J. Bilson and R. Marston, Chicago, University of Chicago Press, Chicago.

Dickey, D. A. and Fuller, W. A. (1979) 'Distribution of the estimators for autoregressive time series with a unit root', *Journal of the American Statistical Association*, June, 423–31.

Engle, R. F. and Granger, C. W. J. (1987) 'Co-integration and error correction: representation, estimation and testing', *Econometrica*, **55**.

Frankel, J. (1982) In search of the exchange risk premium: a six currency test assuming mean-variance optimization. *Journal of International Money and Finance*, **1**, 255–74.

Hermann, W. and Rich, G. (1988) 'Zinssätze und Wechselkurs in der Schweiz–McKinnons unsichtbare Hand', in *Wechselkursstabilisierung, EWS und Weltwährungssystem*, (ed.) O. Issing, Hamburg, 163–87.

Kirchgässner, G. (1985) 'Die Schweiz im internationalen Zinszusammenhang: Eine zeitreihenanalytische Untersuchung für die Zeit von 1974–1983', *Schweizerische Zeitschrift für Volkswirtschaft und Statistik*, **121**(4), 329–51.

Kirchgässner, G. and Wolters, J. (1987) 'US–European interest rates linkages: a time-series for West Germany, Switzerland and The United States', *Review of Economics and Statistics*, **69**(4), 675–84.

Mishkin, F. S. (1984) 'Are real interest rates equal across countries: an empirical investigation of international parity conditions'. *Journal of Finance*, **39**, 1345–57.

Stock, J. H. and Watson, M. W. (1988) 'Testing for common trends'. *Journal of the American Statistical Association*, December, 1097–1107.

5

Credibility of exchange rate policies: the Belgian experience

J. Michielsen

5.1 REGAINING CREDIBILITY

In the early 1980s Belgium was the sick man of Europe. In 1981 the gross public borrowing requirement amounted to 16% of the GDP and the current account deficit to 4%. There were huge capital outflows and the spread between the official and free exchange rate contained an implicit BEF-depreciation of nearly 10%.

In such a context a devaluation was deemed unavoidable as a shock therapy in order to restore competitiveness and to ensure the political and social acceptability of unpopular measures.

It is not the intention here to give a detailed description of the Belgian adjustment policy during the 1980s. The author only wants to demonstrate that the credibility of the exchange rate has been restored through a rather long and gradual process with interrelated measures and adjustments in four areas: economic; financial; monetary; and exchange rate policy.

The first and most urgent action was economic adjustment or the correction of fundamental imbalances. In the period subsequent to the devaluation, priority has been given to the reduction of the external deficit and to the restoration of external competitiveness and business profitability. The budgetary problem was tackled with some delay which reflected the concern to avoid a simultaneous overdose of restraint. Moreover, this delay does not explain the persistence of a budget deficit which is still well above the magic threshold enshrined in the Maastricht criteria. What counts more is that Belgium – as well as some other countries – has missed the opportunity of strong economic growth in the late 1980s for an acceleration of budgetary adjustment. Economists will point in this respect to the concept of cyclically adjusted budgets, the

The European Single Market – Monetary and Fiscal Policy Harmonization.
Edited by H.M. Scobie. Published in 1994 by Chapman & Hall,
London. ISBN 0 412 57520 5

use of which was at a given moment even suggested for the definition of the Maastricht budgetary criteria, but overriding technical as well as political objections were raised in the course of the discussions.

Once the Belgian authorities felt that the correction of the economic fundamentals was well under way, they devoted more attention to the adjustment of the financial system. The basic reasoning for the external monetary policy was that the phenomenon of sizeable net capital outflows is as much a problem of insufficient inflows as of excessive outflows. To a certain extent capital outflows are a natural consequence of portfolio diversification by residents operating in an environment of free capital movements and increasingly integrated markets. With a credible exchange rate policy and free access to national capital markets, there is no compelling reason for excluding corresponding inflows from non-residents. In this spirit Belgium has successively reduced the witholding tax on fixed capital income, abolished the dual exchange market and modernized the financial system and securities industry.

A third contribution to exchange rate credibility has been the adjustment of the monetary policy framework. Before the monetary reform – which became operational in January 1991 – the conduct of monetary policy in Belgium was rather simple. The main instrument of that policy was the fixing by the Bank, in consultation with the Minister of Finance, of the interest rate for very short-term Treasury certificates. Owing to the importance and characteristics of these public debt securities, their interest rates were the guiding rates of the money market in Belgian francs.

Since 29 January 1991 the National Bank has been conducting monetary policy through its own operations. The instruments of a regulatory nature have been replaced by market-oriented procedures. By fixing the terms on which it lends to the financial intermediaries, the Bank influences the marginal financing cost of those institutions and can send signals to the market indicating the desired orientation of short-term interest markets. In addition to modernizing the money market, the reform has strengthened policy credibility in two important ways. First, interest rate changes are more directly related to money market developments which facilitates their justification.

Second, the reform has been accompanied by the phasing out of direct monetary financing of the budget. Draft legislation now provides for the completion of this process within a few months time.

A fourth area of credibility building has been exchange rate policy itself which has become more and more ambitious. Following the 1982 devaluation, the exchange rate objective as formulated at the time of the realignments of the central rates of the EMS, has gradually advanced from keeping the exchange rate for the Belgian franc steady *vis-à-vis* the average rate for the currencies of the partner countries to maintaining the rate against the currency which is regarded as the stability anchor. In June 1990, the Belgian Government confirmed this development by publicly undertaking to peg the Belgian franc to the most stable EMS currency in the present circumstances, the Deutschmark.

The Belgian authorities believe that the credibility of such a strong currency policy has to be secured by a strategy of tracking the value of the Deutschmark more closely inside the ERM-band. A persistent weak position in the band would risk undermining the credibility of the declared policy aim. Even the acceptance of a significant negative spread *vis-à-vis* the anchor currency – which is deemed to be only temporary – is not without risks as adverse conditions may always hamper a subsequent reversal of positions inside the band.

The official communication of the Belgian franc – Deutschmark was designed to remove the remaining risk premium in the setting of Belgian interest rates. The elimination of this risk premium has made it easier for the political authorities to accept an increased margin of manoeuvre for the monetary authorities in using interest rate policy for exchange rate purposes.

5.2 LESSONS TO BE LEARNED

Are there lessons to be learned from the Belgian experience? Belgium is a small country which, at the international and European level, is not a policy maker but a policy taker. Moreover, the economic and monetary imbalances were so severe that emergency measures were required which were often tailored to specific problems in the Belgian economy. Markets have long memories and once credibility has been lost or severely shaken, it may take much time to restore it.

There are some points gleaned from the Belgian experience which are worthy of note. First, economic policy coordination starts at home and the best contribution which each country can make is to put its own house in order. This also applies to small countries especially in the ERM where each member may become a source of systemic tension. Although the EMS constitutes a useful policy framework and EC-commitments and international organizations offer external constraints and advice, national authorities are themselves responsible for the implementation of their adjustment policies.

Second, in a small open economy an exchange aim is a more efficient way to achieve price stability than fixing standards for the expansion of monetary aggregates. In Belgium no use is made of quantitative monetary targets. Past research has shown that given the volatility of international capital flows and shifts between monetary and non-monetary aggregates, the corridor around the monetary norm should be too large to serve as a useful policy instrument. Moreover, through the exchange rate as an intermediate target, one borrows its monetary policy from the anchor country.

Despite the uncertainties surrounding German policy, there seems to be no suitable alternative anchor to the Deutschmark in the absence of a genuine European monetary policy.

In any case, averages such as the ECU do not provide a solid anchor and can only be a 'second best' or transitional solution. They are not compatible with the aim of optimal stability because of their definition unless there is a high degree of convergence which would, however, make the use of averages as a yardstick for policy coordination redundant. Moreover, averages do not contain a concrete, identifiable and coherent policy framework. Finally, averages as a yardstick for exchange rate policy do not eliminate the payment of risk premiums.

Third, pegging to an anchor currency increases the degree of exchange rate rigidity. This does not constitute a threat to the system provided the fundamentals are good and there is enough flexibility in interest rate policy.

The tendency towards rigidity in a system such as the ERM is mainly attributed to the politization of the exchange rate which becomes a matter of national prestige. There are, however, other determining factors relating to the nature of the exchange rate as an adjustment instrument. In order to act as a shock therapy and a trigger for unpopular measures, exchange rate changes have to be sufficiently large which implies the previous build-up of fundamental imbalances and thus a malfunctioning of the system.

Small adjustments which might accommodate monetary policy dilemmas also have their drawbacks and limitations. They are seldom accompanied by other policy measures; they are not an efficient deterrent against speculative flows; and they do not remove risk premiums in the currencies of these countries which proceed to small devaluations.

Nevertheless, one of the items which will probably come out of an assessment of the last crisis is the need for more rapid exchange rate adjustments in order to avoid a build-up of imbalances and a breakdown of the system. The author remains sceptical about the practical implementation. Should one elaborate and officialize a set of indicators which would offer a presumption of the need for parity changes? What should we do in case of a disagreement given the impossibility of submitting exchange rate decisions to majority voting instead of unanimity? Or should we simply continue to rely on the outcome of crisis situations?

Even if no practical solutions are found for ensuring more timely realignments, Ministers should at least return to clear and unambiguous realignment decisions – once these have become necessary – in order to avoid the confusion which has characterized recent decision-making.

Fourth, the public debt ratio has got an excessive weight in the Maastricht criteria especially in comparison with the external current account balance.

This proposition is directly inspired by the actual peculiar situation that a country with the highest public debt ratio in the Community has one of the strongest currencies. This situation would be less remarkable in a period of calm when, in the absence of exchange risk, the ranking of positions in the ERM-band is often determined by the level of nominal interest rates belonging to countries with poor inflation records. This is the so-called 'EMS-paradox'. However, during crises, markets are expected to look at the fundamentals.

It would be wrong to ignore or underestimate the policy constraint of a public debt ratio in the order of magnitude of 125% of GDP. Such a ratio means that interest payments absorb a significant part of budgetary receipts and that an important and persistent primary budget surplus is needed in order to reduce the deficit and the debt ratio itself. However, if at the same time the country concerned experiences a current account surplus in its balance of payments, it covers at least its budgetary needs with its own savings while exporting the surplus.

In a monetary union with capital flows the concept itself of current account balances may be questioned. Moreover, one could argue that current account disequilibria should be reflected in the interest rate differentials which are themselves a Maastricht criterion. However, even during the final stage the union members may remain sensitive to the flow of savings and the perception or presumption of important disequilibria could become an element of friction and fragility. It would therefore be wise to devote attention to the distribution of savings on the eve of the passage to Stage Three. Moreover, the current account deserves at least as much importance as the debt ratio in assessing the fundamentals underlying the currency positions in the EMS during the preparatory stage.

It is not surprising that, in the course of the Treaty negotiations, the Belgian representatives have argued in favour of an upgrading of the current account in the set of criteria for access to the third stage. However, on this point, only a compromise solution was reached whereby the current account is listed as a secondary criterion to be considered in a global assessment together with the development of the ECU, market integration and wage cost and price indicators.

6

EMU – The issues for banks

A. Gubitz

6.1 INTRODUCTION

The private sector on the whole has contributed relatively little to the analysis and public discussion of the European Monetary Union (EMU), one exception being the financial sector, banks in particular. Its special interest can hardly be explained just by the size of its share in total value added in Europe, which is roughly 7% – not that large. It is rather that banks are affected by practically all kinds of economic activity. Thus their performance is significantly related to the development of macroeconomic aggregates. The implementation of EMU is probably the most demanding structural change banks have to digest by the end of this decade. While EMU promises a range of advantages to the non-financial sector, none of them is certain for banks and some are directly to their detriment.

Banks are affected by EMU in three different ways: first on the microeconomic level, second by changes in the overall financial variables and third by the effects on the real economy. The paper will briefly address these issues.

6.2 MICROECONOMIC ASPECTS

One of the most obvious gains discussed in detail in the European Commission's study 'One Market, One Money' (1990) is the reduction in transaction costs. There will be no need to buy foreign exchange inside Europe and fees for cross-border payments are likely to be substantially reduced. For banks this simply means that some of its forex trade (including derivatives) will die, although the stronger the new European currency is, the more the dominant position of the US dollar in international transactions will be eroded (Barclays Group Treasury, 1991 and NatWest, 1992).

The European Single Market – Monetary and Fiscal Policy Harmonization.
Edited by H.M. Scobie. Published in 1994 by Chapman & Hall,
London. ISBN 0 412 57520 5

With the implementation of EMU at Stage Three, monetary policy instruments will have to be standardized. This will affect the spread for banks. As higher interest rates in Germany are likely, the structure of balance sheets will have to be adjusted. With exchange rate risks and national interest rate differentials disappearing, the supply of deposits as well as the demand for loans will be affected by intensified competition among European banks.

Furthermore, the choice of security will become much larger. Diversification in stock portfolios is likely to increase, while the need to diversify in the bond market will be reduced. All in all rating will play a more prominent role in portfolio selection. Banks will accordingly have to supply more and different kinds of information to their customers, especially with respect to the European stock markets. No doubt there will be winners and losers in the course of this adjustment process, but a larger and more efficient capital market will also create growth effects, especially if price stability throughout Europe can be successfully defended.

The European banking sector is still very much disintegrated into national markets. Most banks have a competitive advantage in the business related to the currency of their home country. The single market for financial services and a gradual move to fixed exchange rates will to a large extent remove these barriers, but a complete erosion of differences in competitiveness will probably be reached only via a single currency. Issuing business will be most significantly affected. Needless to say the German banks will lose their Deutschmark-specific competitive advantage.

While costs and benefits of a single currency in Europe are complementary with respect to the financial and the non-financial sector, the period of transition will probably prove to be costly for both. Changes have to be made on the grounds of a high degree of uncertainty with respect to the probability of reaching Stage Three at all, the timetable of implementation, the size of EMU, and the length of time, when more than one legal tender will circulate. The costs involved are briefly these: training staff, changing computer systems, running dual accounting systems, reforming cross-border payment systems, and meeting the large demand for information for customers. Under cost considerations a rapid switch to one legal tender at Stage Three is desirable.

Although most banks face similar adjustment needs, gains and losses are hard to quantify. What can be fairly safely said is that it is not so much the loss of certain types of business but the fiercer competition that will affect the banking sector most. The high degree of uncertainty will prove to be an additional burden.

6.3 FINANCIAL MARKETS AND EMU

Today, most market participants are more sceptical about the timely implementation of EMU within the next six years than a year ago, not to mention an increasing number of people who believe that EMU will never become reality.

This is not just the result of the Danish 'No' vote, which revealed more criticism elsewhere, most notably in the UK. The recent crisis in the EMS and its outcome have demonstrated how fragile the path of convergence is. Only a few countries will be able to pass the Maastricht criteria within a few years. Two countries have suspended their currencies from the exchange rate mechanism (ERM). This damaged not only their own credibility, but also that of the whole EMS. While realignment risks have persisted in the past, the additional risk of a regime switch has to be taken into account as well.

According to simulations which were carried out with the National Institute's Global Econometric Model (NIGEM), the devaluation of the pound and the lira together with the interest rate measures taken so far in Germany, France, Italy and the UK, increase inflation in Italy and the UK by an amount probably big enough to carry them out of the critical range defined in the Maastricht Treaty for a number of years (Table 6.1).

Table 6.1 Summary of simulation results

	Year 0[a]	*Year 1*	*Year 2*	*Year 3*	*Year 4*	*Year 5*
3-month interest rate[b]						
Germany	−0.225	−0.875	−0.075	0.0	0.0	0.0
Italy	0.387	0.0	0.0	0.0	0.0	0.0
UK	−0.625	−2.550	−1.350	−0.225	0.0	0.0
Effective exchange rate[c]						
Germany	0.760	3.388	3.729	3.691	3.687	3.687
UK	−2.823	−10.080	−8.488	−7.724	−7.660	−7.660
Italy	−2.877	−12.036	−12.312	−12.358	−12.362	−12.362
Inflation[b,d]						
Germany	−0.008	−0.163	−0.241	−0.215	−0.200	−0.179
UK	0.312	1.558	1.636	1.647	1.384	1.014
Italy	0.248	1.958	1.551	1.267	1.120	1.021
GNP[c]						
Germany	−0.003	0.000	0.109	0.024	−0.073	−0.134
UK	−0.028	1.113	2.076	2.084	1.562	0.883
Italy	−0.030	1.181	1.912	1.927	1.668	1.313
Current account[e]						
Germany	0.108	0.157	0.001	0.005	−0.010	−0.029
UK	−0.449	−1.651	−1.445	−0.926	−0.502	−0.256
Italy	−0.322	−0.298	0.280	0.473	0.537	0.551

[a]Shock in the fourth quarter;
[b]Difference from base level;
[c]Percentage difference from base level;
[d]As measured by the consumption deflator;
[e]In percent of GNP, difference from base level.

In particular it was assumed that short-term interest rates in the UK decline substantially faster than in the baseline, while they are temporarily higher in France and Italy. German short-term rates are reduced somewhat faster after the realignment. Nominal short-term interest rates remain – by assumption – low, even after inflation substantially accelerates both in Italy and the UK, i.e. monetary aggregates grow accordingly. The depreciation of the pound sterling and the lira *vis-à-vis* the Deutschmark that took place between the end of August and mid-October amounted to roughly 14%. This translates into an effective devaluation of both currencies of around 11 and 12% respectively in the first year after the EMS crisis. For the exchange rate a backward-looking open interest rate parity was assumed. Thus the depreciation of the pound is somewhat reversed after the shock.

In this rather expansionary scenario GNP improves for a number of years in both Italy and the UK with a maximum effect of 2% in the third year after the EMS shock. The price to be paid, however, is higher inflation, especially in Italy, despite the absence of an interest rate reduction. Furthermore the growth effect is more sustained in Italy. As Germany faces a real appreciation, a modest decrease in interest rates, and some improvement in its export market growth, the total effect on GNP is almost zero. The current accounts of all countries show a significant J-curve effect; for the UK it is a particularly prolonged one. The simulation results depend heavily on the assumption of a permanent decrease in interest rates in the UK and Germany and of a permanent devaluation of the pound and lira. If forward-looking expectations are assumed for the exchange rates, the depreciation is quickly reversed and growth effects occur only temporarily. Details of the results are given in the Appendix.

The obvious question as of today is whether sterling and the lira should return to the ERM soon. In the UK the question of leaving the ERM had been raised well before the actual suspension. It was generally argued that the pound had entered the ERM at a central rate too high to ensure competitiveness with its European trading partners. Despite the inflationary shock in Germany due to unification, the UK's price stability never outperformed Germany's. The gap in the long-term interest rate narrowed to one percentage point at minimum in early summer, but widened again thereafter (Figure 6.1).

If it is true that the risk premium on long-term rates cannot fall below a certain minimum due to the realignment and the devaluation risk inside the ERM-band, this premium will have to increase once the pound returns to the ERM. This could only be compensated by reducing inflationary expectations. At times when it is decided to stimulate growth this is a more than delicate task. If membership of the ERM and eventually EMU has been the ultimate goal, a timely realignment would have been preferable to suspending membership. Now that the cost of leaving the ERM is already taking effect, the additional degree of freedom in monetary policy might as well be kept for some time.

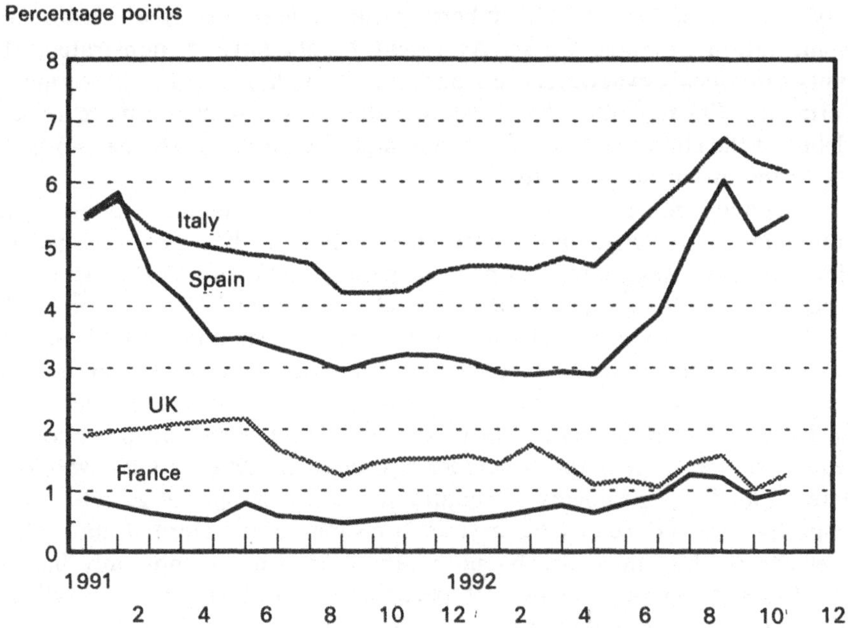

*10-year government bond yields, end-of-period; last value: 23 November 1992

Figure 6.1 Long-term interest rate differential* in the ERM

Italy is even more a clear case for staying out of the ERM, whatever the government might have announced in the recent past. Not only is the inflation rate substantially higher than in most other EMS countries, but the long-term interest rate differential compared with Germany has never fallen below four percentage points and is sharply increased after the Danish referendum. While a high risk premium would be necessary to defend whatever is the fixed exchange rate, the effort to escape the public debt trap would lose credibility at the same time. Therefore Italy is an obvious case where domestic stability has to be restored first before external stability is superimposed. In order to avoid speculative attacks with inflationary shocks on the lira, the government could adopt a crawling peg.

To sum up the above discussion, a realignment in the EMS was on the agenda long before September 1992 and an early adjustment of the parities would have been better. The exit of two currencies from the ERM did more harm than necessary. Even stable currencies came under severe pressure and the whole system is suffering from a setback in credibility. With more flexibility within the EMS likely, the issue to be discussed now is whether the chances for EMU have worsened or improved in the course of events. The Maastricht

Treaty requires stable ERM membership for at least two years before the implementation of Stage Three. As recent events have demonstrated, this stability can quickly evaporate even for countries with a sound macroeconomic performance. On the other hand, the devaluations revealed a more reliable guideline of the choice of countries which might be able to participate in EMU at the beginning of Stage Three.

The disintegration of the ERM has revived the discussion of a two-speed Europe, now somewhat more accurately called a 'Europe of concentric circles'. There are suggestions to proceed with a 'hard-core EMU' faster than envisaged in the Maastricht Treaty. The idea seems to be premature at this stage. First of all, there is still some tension in the remaining ERM. Second, what will happen to those countries which would participate in a single currency now, but do not fulfil the convergence criteria later? One of the basic ideas of the Maastricht Treaty, namely to give each European country an equal chance to pass the convergence criteria in 1996 or later, would be violated. Third, the problems of running a quasi-fixed exchange rate system have partly been induced by the asymmetric shock of the German unification. The effects of this shock are by no means over. Fourth, not only has the recent ERM crisis put the aim of participating in EMU into the distant future, the overly ambitious goal of EMU within a very limited number of years has itself contributed to disruptions on European foreign-exchange markets.

6.4 EMU – GAINS FOR GROWTH AND EMPLOYMENT?

The aim of a monetary union in Europe is not within easy reach. Why then all that trouble? The proponents of EMU argue that the benefits of the single-market programme can only be fully reaped if the latter is augmented by a single currency. Without entering into discussions of whether there are 'residual' gains, doubts have frequently been raised as to whether these are big enough to justify the costs in the transitional period as well as thereafter. Of the expected gains created by a combination of the single market and EMU that can be quantified, the largest share is due to the single market, at least from the perspective of the banking industry.

Many banks hope that the efficiency gains of EMU will free capacity to extend business in other areas, one of which could be Eastern Europe. Therefore the chances of EC enlargement versus EMU deserve more attention in the future. If policy priorities are adjusted accordingly, a two-speed Europe with EMU as its core might follow smoothly by itself. However, it should not be forced into existence. Historical examples of single markets have shown that they are beneficial over a long period of time without a single currency.

REFERENCES

European Commission (1990) One market, one money. *European Economy*, No. 44.

National Westminster Bank (1992) European Integration: The Banking Issues. *Proceedings of the NatWest Conference* held on 13 February 1992.

Barclays Group Treasury (1991) The implications for banking. Report published by Barclays Bank.

National Institute for Social and Economic Research (1992) NIGEM: National Institute Global Econometric Model, Model documentation as of November 1992.

APPENDIX

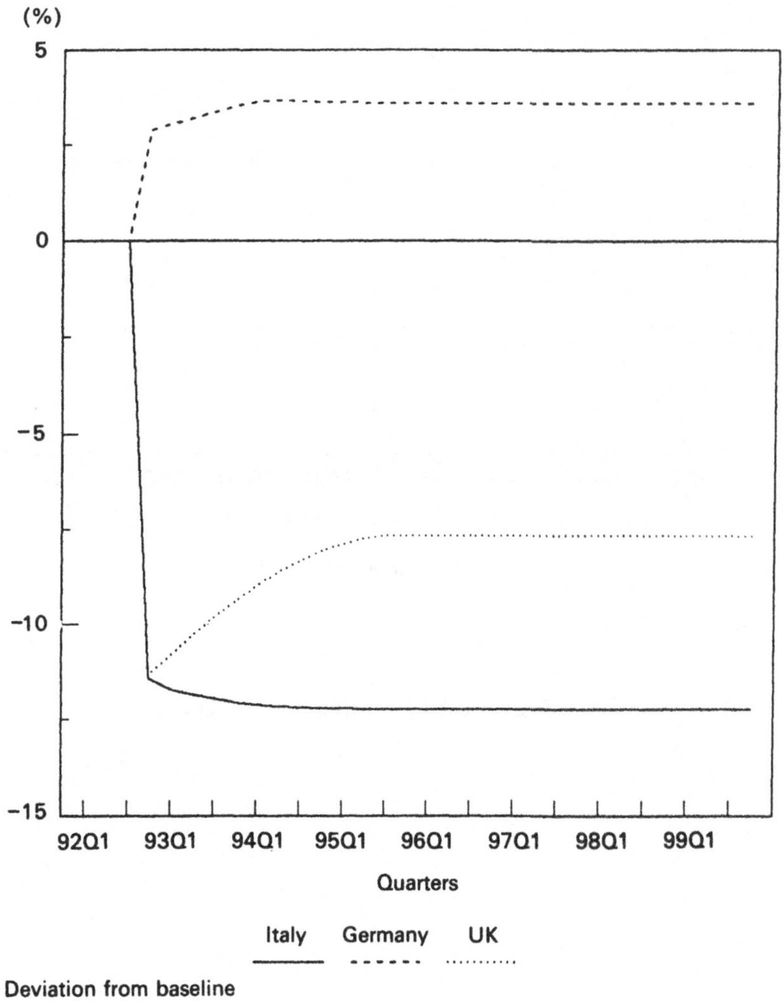

Figure 6.A.1 Effective exchange rates

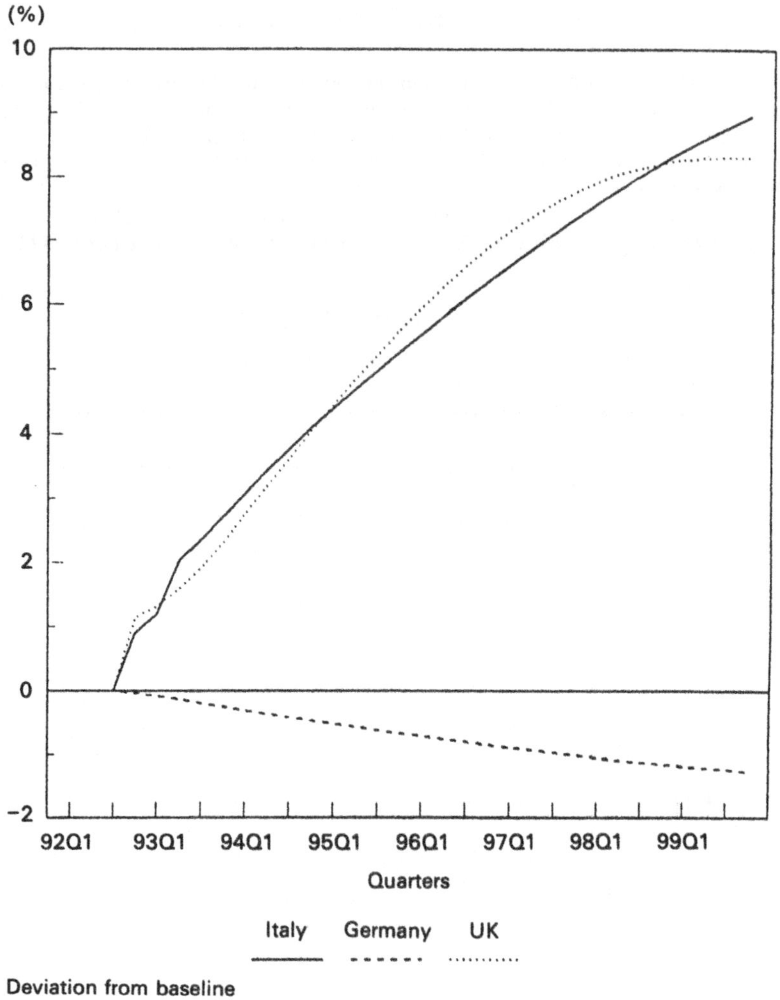

Figure 6.A.2 Consumption deflators

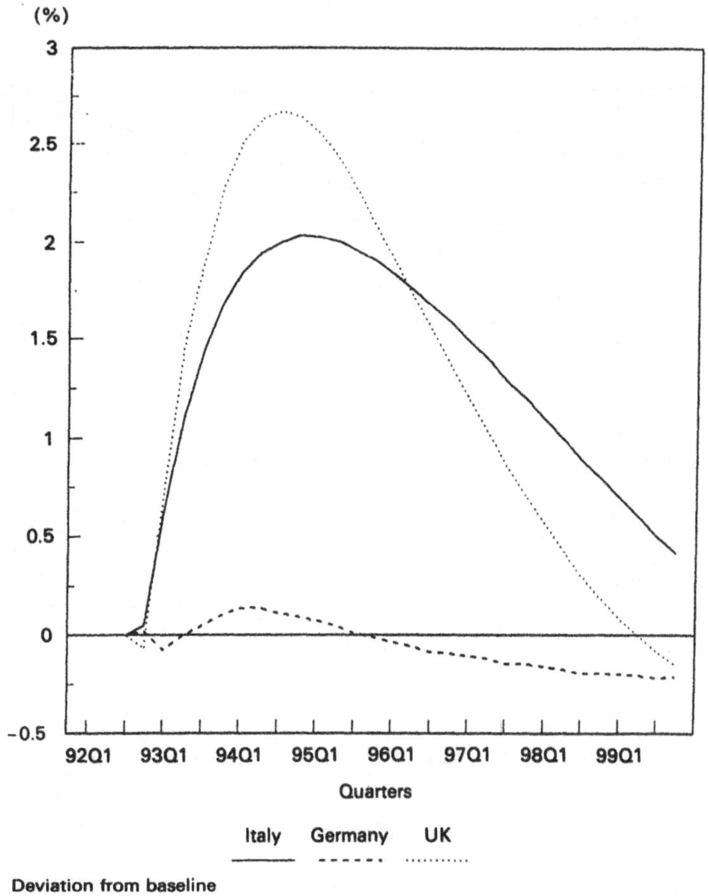

Figure 6.A.3 GNP

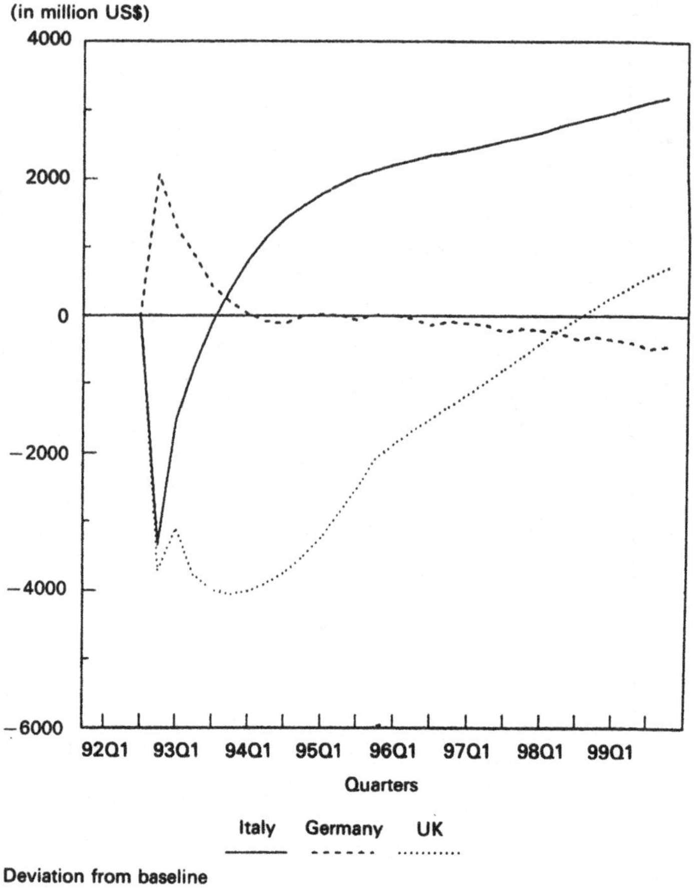

Figure 6.A.4 Current account

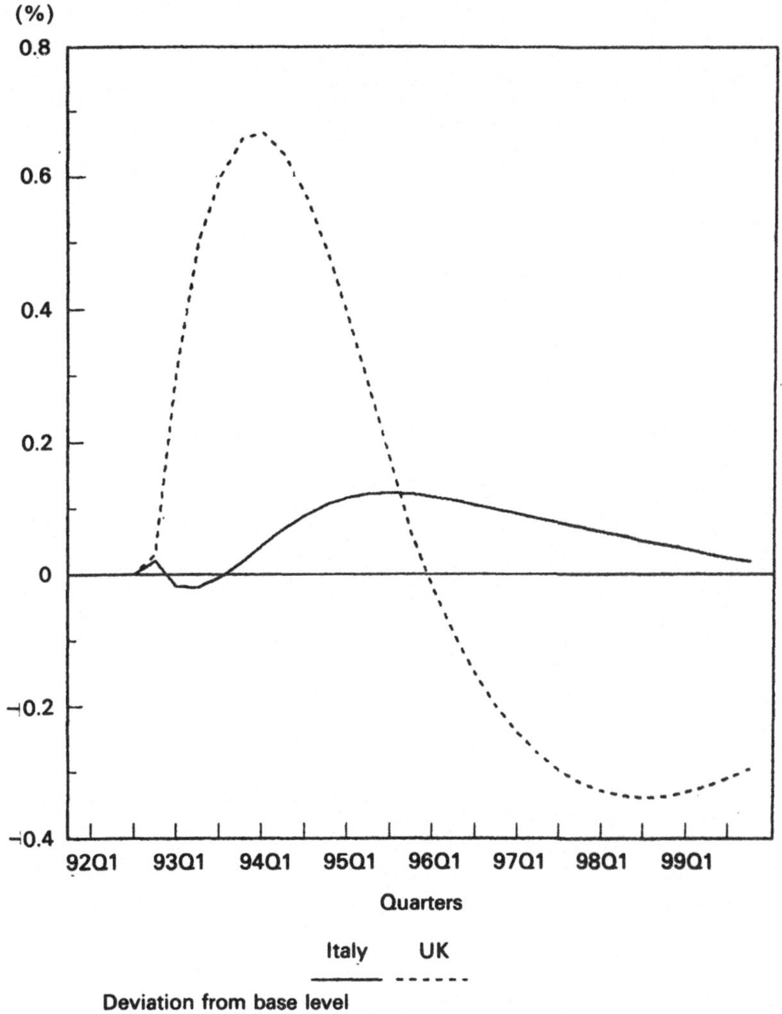

Figure 6.A.5 GNP with forward-looking exchange rates

7

Monetary and fiscal policy in a monetary union

P.S. Pollard

7.1 INTRODUCTION

In February 1992, the leaders of the European Community (EC) met in Maastricht, Holland, to sign a treaty marking the Community's determination to achieve economic and monetary union by the end of the century. Now, one year after the signing of the Maastricht Treaty, there is much less confidence that this goal will be met. The adoption of convergence programs placing limits on fiscal spending, and the *de facto* relinquishment of monetary policy control to the Bundesbank have produced substantial inflation benefits for the EC countries, but have produced no gains in the real economy. The establishment of a convergence requirement and the limits placed on fiscal policy even after the institution of a monetary union, mandated by the Maastricht Treaty, are based on the belief that restricting a country's ability to run fiscal deficits is necessary for a well functioning monetary union.

Despite this belief, our understanding of how the EC economies will be linked through a monetary union is limited. This paper attempts to improve this understanding through the development of a macroeconomic model of a monetary union that can be used to show how the monetary policy actions of the central bank and the fiscal policy actions of the member governments affect the countries in the union.

The European Monetary Union will be fundamentally different from a typical federal monetary union system, such as the US or Canada, due to the difference in the relative importance of the central government and regional authorities. Whereas the expenditures of the US federal government constitute around 20–5% of US GDP, the expenditures of the European Community government are at present only slightly more than 1% of the GDP of the EC and are not expected to exceed 3% of GDP (Lamfalussy, 1989). Furthermore,

The European Single Market – Monetary and Fiscal Policy Harmonization.
Edited by H.M. Scobie. Published in 1994 by Chapman & Hall,
London. ISBN 0 412 57520 5

the European Community goverment has no means for active fiscal policy. In the European Community, the member states will continue to be the primary fiscal policy makers. Thus, the interactions of the regional players are of prime importance in modelling the monetary union.

The model developed here is in the spirit of open economy models of Oudiz and Sachs (1984), Sachs and Wyplosz (1984), Kole (1988) and Kenen (1989, 1990). All of these models start by setting out the underlying relationships for the components of aggregate demand. The model developed in this paper takes this approach by specifying structural equations describing the goods, money and bonds markets, but also adds equations which determine the supply side of the economy – this is also done in the work by Oudiz and Sachs (1984). Open economy macro models, particularly those analysing policy coordination, typically assume that output is demand determined. In this model, output is determined by the interaction of demand and supply factors. The supply side becomes particularly important given that changes in prices in one country affect aggregate supply in both countries. Furthermore, the model incorporates interest earning terms (which are neglected in most models, an exception is Kole) as this allows last period's interest rate to have an effect on this period's consumption. As a result, the balance of payments status of a country proves to be a determinant of policy effects.

The fiscal policy pursued by a country is shown to have a greater effect on its output and inflation if it is a net debtor rather than a net creditor. However, fiscal expansion in one country is more likely to have a positive effect on output and inflation in the other country if the former country is a net creditor and the latter country a net debtor. Monetary policy undertaken by the independent central bank has a positive effect on output and inflation in both countries, but has a greater effect on the net debtor country.

Thus, the results indicate that balance of payments asymmetries can lead to dissension with a monetary union over policies pursued by the member countries. Such asymmetries have always existed within the EC, and there is evidence that the creation of a European Monetary Union will increase these asymmetries. Artis and Bayoumi (1991) found that the increase in capital integration in the world economy in the 1980s corresponded to growing capital account imbalances. An increase in capital mobility reduces the external constraints on borrowing. Thus, the European Monetary Union, which is to be characterized by full capital mobility, is likely to increase the level and persistence of current account imbalances among its member countries.

The rest of the paper proceeds as follows. Section 7.2 develops a two country model of a monetary union. Section 7.3 explains the linkages between the countries as captured in the aggregate supply and demand equations for each country. Section 7.4 gives the solution for equilibrium output and inflation in each country, and derives comparative statistics which indicate how the policies of one country or the central bank affect both countries within the monetary union. This section also examines how the existence of a monetary union changes the results of the standard two country open economy model. The final section presents the conclusions and indicates areas for further research.

7.2 THE MODEL

There are two countries, indexed by 1 and 2, which are of similar size. Each country maintains independent control over its fiscal policy, but the monetary policy for the two countries is controlled by an independent central bank. The countries produce goods which are imperfect substitutes. Goods are traded freely between the two countries. There are no transportation costs, but preferences for goods may vary across the countries. The government and the private sector in each country demand both domestic and foreign goods.

Each government issues one period bonds which are bought by the residents of each country and the central bank. The bonds are perfect substitutes, and capital is perfectly mobile. Thus, the nominal interest rate prevailing in each country at all times is the world interest rate. There are no private issues of bonds, nor is there any capital accumulation.

There is a common currency which is issued by the central bank. Money creation is controlled solely by the central bank through bond purchases. Since the money supply is determined solely by the extent of bond purchases by the central bank, it is possible that the monetary authority might be constrained in its ability to increase the money supply. Given that this constraint is unlikely to be binding except in cases of hyperinflation, and given that the central bank's primary objective is price stability, it is assumed throughout that the constraint is nonbinding. Since the real money supply is equal to the real value of bonds held by the central bank, the government makes its interest payments not in money but in goods. The central bank, however, neither purchases goods, nor turns its profits over to the national governments. Therefore, one can assume that the goods payment of interest is immediately consumed by the central bank. This assumption is made to ensure that the central bank does not have control over goods or the allocation of seignorage in the model.

All variables are measured in real terms. The deflator used to convert a country's nominal variables to real variables is its consumer price index. (See Table 7.1 for a listing of variables and parameters.) All stock variables are measured at the start of the period, which is indexed by t. Spending and portfolio decisions are made at the start of period t.

7.2.1 Country 1's economy

The equations describing country 1's economy are listed in Table 7.2. Equations (7.1)–(7.3) describe the supply side of the economy. Domestic price inflation,

Table 7.1 Notation

Variables

a = real private domestic absorption
b^{p} = real private bond holdings
b = real bond issues by the government
b_{m} = real central bank bond holdings
g = real government spending
$\imath$ = nominal world interest rate
$i = 1 + \imath$
m = real balances
nx = real net exports
p = domestic price index
p^{c} = consumer price index
R = real interest rate
$r = 1 + R$
R^{e} = expected real interest rate
t = real lump sum taxes
y = real output
y^{d} = real disposable income
$\bar{y}$ = optimal or natural level of real output.
π = consumer price inflation
π^{e} = expected consumer price inflation
d = government budget deficit

Parameters

c = marginal propensity to consume
ε = private marginal propensity to import
ε_{g} = government marginal propensity to import
λ = income sensitivity of money demand
θ = interest sensitivity of money demand
ϕ = interest sensitivity of domestic absorption
α = sensitivity of domestic price inflation to deviations of output from its natural level
γ = weight attached to domestic prices in the consumer price index

equation (7.1), is determined by the deviation of output from its natural level, and expected domestic price inflation. This gives a standard expectations augmented Phillips curve. The consumer price index is given by equation (7.2) as a weighted average of domestic and foreign prices. The weights are set in the initial period, as determined by the proportion of consumption consisting of domestic goods and imports, respectively. (As is the practice with consumer price indexes, these weights are not adjusted each period, but may be updated after a number of years. For the purpose of this paper, there is no updating.)

The demand side of the model, for country 1, is given by equations (7.4)–(7.13). Equations (7.4) and (7.5) define the ex ante and ex post real interest rate, respectively. Equation (7.6) defines $\tilde{p}$ as the ratio of country 2's to country 1's consumer prices. This term is used to convert country 2's real variables, which appear in country 1's equations, into the same units as country 1's real

Table 7.2 Equations underlying country 1's economy

Supply	
$\frac{p_{1,t}-p_{1,t-1}}{p_{1,t-1}}=\alpha\frac{y_{1,t}-\bar{y}}{\bar{y}}+\frac{E_{t-1}p_{1,t}-p_{1,t-1}}{p_{1,t-1}}, \quad \alpha>0$	(7.1)
$p^c_{1,t}=\gamma p_{1,t}+(1-\gamma)p_{2,t}, \quad \frac{1}{2}<\gamma<1$	(7.2)
$\pi_{1,t-1}\equiv\frac{p^c_{1,t}-p^c_{1,t-1}}{p^c_{1,t-1}}$	(7.3)
Demand:	
$R^e_{1,t}\equiv i_t-\pi^e_{1,t}$	(7.4)
$R_{1,t}\equiv i_t-\pi_{1,t}$	(7.5a)
$r_{1,t}\equiv i_t-\pi_{1,t}$	(7.5b)
$\tilde{p}_t\equiv\left(\frac{p^c_{2,t}}{p^c_{1,t}}\right)$	(7.6)
$y_{1,t}=a_{1,t}+g_{1,t}+nx_{1,t}$	(7.7)
$a_{1,t}=cy^d_{1,t}-\phi R^e_{1,t}, \quad \frac{1}{2}<c<1, \quad 0<\phi<1$	(7.8)
$y^d_{1,t}=y_{1,t}+r_{1,t-1}b^p_{1,t-1}-t_{1,t}$	(7.9)
$nx_{1,t}=\epsilon a_{2,t}\tilde{p}_t+\epsilon_g g_{2,t}\tilde{p}_t-\epsilon a_{1,t}-\epsilon_g g_{1,t}, \; 0<\epsilon<\frac{1}{2}, \; \epsilon_g\leqslant\epsilon,$	(7.10)
$g_{1,t}=t_{1,t}-r_{1,t-1}b_{1,t-1}+b_{1,t}$	(7.11)
$m_{1,t}=\lambda y^d_{1,t}-\theta i_t, \quad 0<\lambda\leqslant 1, \quad 0<\theta<1$	(7.12)
$b^p_{1,t}=y^d_{1,t}-a_{1,t}$	(7.13)

variables.[1] Therefore, all of the real variables in country 1's (country 2's) demand and supply equations are in terms of country 1's (country 2's) consumer price index.

Equations (7.7)–(7.11) describe the goods market. Equation (7.7) is the national income identity. Real income (output) is equal to real private domestic absorption, a_t, real government spending, g_t, and real net exports, nx_t. Real private domestic absorption, equation (7.8), depends positively on real disposable income, y^d_t, and negatively on the ex ante real interest rate, R^e_t. Real disposable income, y^d_t, is given by equation (7.9), as real income less lump sum taxes, t_t, plus real interest earnings and the repayment of bonds bought by the private sector last period (where these two terms are by definition the gross real interest earnings on private holdings of bonds, $r_{t-1}b^p_{t-1}$) – see Pollard (1993) for the derivation. Real net exports are given by equation (7.10). Neither the private marginal propensity to consume, ε, nor the government's marginal

[1] For example:

$$g_{2,t}\tilde{p}_t=\left(\frac{G_{2,t}}{p^c_{2,t}}\right)\left(\frac{p^c_{2,t}}{p^c_{1,t}}\right)=\frac{G_{2,t}}{p^c_{1,t}}$$

where $G_{2,t}$ is nominal spending by the government of country 2.

propensity to consume, ε_g, is a function of relative prices. In an earlier version of this paper, a parameter was included in the net export equations of the two countries to capture the price substitution effect. The inclusion of this parameter only alters the subsequent analysis if there is a large divergence in prices between the two countries. The government budget constraint is given by equation (7.11). Real government spending, g_t, is constrained by the real interest payments and repayments of last period's bonds; these two combined give by definition the gross real interest payments on bonds, $r_{t-1}b_{t-1}$, (see Pollard (1993) for the derivation) less tax revenues, t_t, and new bond issues, b_t. The creation of an independent central bank removes the ability of the government to finance a deficit through money creation.

Equations (7.12) and (7.13) describe the asset markets. Demand for real balances, equation (7.12), depends positively on real disposable income, via the transactions motive, and negatively on the nominal interest rate. The savings function is given by equation (7.13). All saving is through bond holdings, and real private bond demand is determined by the difference between real disposable income and real private domestic absorption – for this result see Pollard (1993).

7.2.2 Country 2's economy

The parameter values in the model for country 2's economy are assumed to be the same as those for country 1. (This assumption is made to keep the asymmetries between the two countries to a minimum.) Thus, the equations modelling country 2's economy, given in Table 7.3, are essentially the same as those for country 1. However, the variables for country 2's economy are deflated by its consumer price index.

7.2.3 Market equilibrium conditions

The conditions for equilibrium in the bond, money and goods markets are presented in Table 7.4. The bonds issued by the government of a country are held by three groups of agents: the public in each country and the central bank. Equation (7.28) shows the equality between the supply of bonds issued by country 1, and the demand for these bonds, broken down by type of demander. Equation (7.29) presents the same information for country 2. Equation (7.30) is the world bond market equilibrium condition.

The actual holdings by the residents in the two countries of the bonds issued by each government is impossible to determine. This follows from the bonds being perfect substitutes and from the assumption of perfect capital mobility. The central bank's holding of each bond is determined through the money market restrictions, as explained below.

Equation (7.31) gives the money market clearing condition. The supply of real balances is determined by the central bank's purchases of each govern-

Table 7.3 Equations underlying country 2's economy

Supply

$$\frac{p_{2,t}-p_{2,t-1}}{p_{2,t-1}}=\alpha\frac{y_{2,t}-\dfrac{\bar{y}}{\tilde{p}_t}}{\dfrac{\bar{y}}{\tilde{p}_t}}+\frac{E_{t-1}p_{2,t}-p_{2,t-1}}{p_{2,t-1}},\quad \alpha>0 \tag{7.14}$$

$$p^c_{2,t}=\gamma p_{2,t}+(1-\gamma)p_{1,t},\quad \tfrac{1}{2}<\gamma<1 \tag{7.15}$$

$$\pi_{2,t-1}\equiv\frac{p^c_{2,t}-p^c_{2,t-1}}{p^c_{2,t-1}} \tag{7.16}$$

Demand

$$R^e_{2,t}\equiv\iota_t-\pi^e_{2,t} \tag{7.17}$$

$$R_{2,t}\equiv\iota_t-\pi_{2,t} \tag{7.18a}$$

$$r_{2,t}\equiv i_t-\pi_{2,t} \tag{7.18b}$$

$$\frac{1}{\tilde{p}_t}\equiv\frac{p^c_{1,t}}{p^c_{2,t}} \tag{7.19}$$

$$y_{2,t}=a_{2,t}+g_{2,t}+nx_{2,t} \tag{7.20}$$

$$a_{2,t}=cy^d_{2,t}-\phi R^e_{2,t},\quad \tfrac{1}{2}<c<1,\quad 0<\phi<1 \tag{7.21}$$

$$y^d_{2,t}=y_{2,t}+r_{2,t-1}b^p_{2,t-1}-t_{2,t} \tag{7.22}$$

$$nx_{2,t}=\epsilon a_{1,t}\frac{1}{\tilde{p}_t}+\epsilon_g g_{1,t}\frac{1}{\tilde{p}_t}-\epsilon a_{2,t}-\epsilon_g g_{2,t}\quad 0<\epsilon<\tfrac{1}{2},\ \epsilon_g\leqslant\epsilon \tag{7.23}$$

$$g_{2,t}=t_{2,t}-r_{2,t-1}b_{2,t-1}+b_{2,t} \tag{7.24}$$

$$m_{2,t}=\lambda y^d_{2,t}-\theta\iota_t\quad 0<\lambda\leqslant 1,\quad 0<\theta<1 \tag{7.25}$$

$$b^p_{2,t}=y^d_{2,t}-a_{2,t} \tag{7.26}$$

Table 7.4 Equilibrium conditions[a]

Bond market

$$b_{1,t}=b_{11,t}+b_{12,t}+b_{1m,t} \tag{7.28}$$

$$b_{2,t}=b_{21,t}+b_{22,t}+b_{2m,t} \tag{7.29}$$

$$b_t=b_{1,t}+b_{2,t}\tilde{p}_t \tag{7.30}$$

Money market

$$m_t=m^d_{1,t}+m^d_{2,t}\tilde{p}_t \tag{7.31}$$

$$m_t=b_{1m,t}+b_{2m,t}\tilde{p}_t=b_{m,t} \tag{7.32}$$

$$b_{1m,t}=\tfrac{1}{2}m_t=\tfrac{1}{2}b_{m,t} \tag{7.33}$$

$$b_{2m,t}=\tfrac{1}{2}m_t\frac{1}{\tilde{p}_t}=\tfrac{1}{2}b_{m,t}\frac{1}{\tilde{p}_t} \tag{7.34}$$

Goods market:

$$y^d_{i,t}-a_{i,t}-d_{i,t}=ca_{i,t}\quad i=1,2 \tag{7.35}$$

[a]All world variables are deflated by country 1's price index.

ment's bonds, as given by equation (7.32). The next two equations, (7.33) and (7.34), determine the central bank's holdings of each country's bonds. For simplicity, it is assumed that the central bank buys half of its bonds from country 1 and half from country 2. (Relaxing this assumption will not affect the model.) These four equations indicate that while the initial distribution of real balances between the countries is determined by the central bank, the ultimate distribution is determined by demand conditions in each country.

Equation (7.35) gives the goods market clearing condition for either country. Real disposable income less domestic absorption and the government deficit must be equal to the real current account balance.

7.2.4 Assumptions on the parameters

It is assumed that γ, the weight given to domestic prices in the consumer price index, is greater than 0.5, which indicates that the residents of each country prefer their own goods to foreign goods. The marginal propensity to consume domestic goods out of disposable income, c, is assumed to be greater than 0.5, and thus the marginal propensity to consume imported goods, ε, must be less than 0.5. These two assumptions also correspond to the preference for home goods over foreign goods in each country. Furthermore, the government's marginal propensity to import, ε_g, is constrained to be not greater than the private marginal propensity to import, ε. This restriction is made since in practice a large portion of government spending goes towards the salaries of government workers, and governments generally do not have a weaker preference for domestically produced goods over foreign goods than do their citizens.

7.3 Aggregate supply and aggregate demand

Using equations (7.1)–(7.3) and (7.14)–(7.16) one can derive the aggregate supply equations for country 1 and country 2 (for the derivations see Pollard, 1993):

$$y_{1,t}=\bar{y}+\frac{\bar{y}}{\alpha(\gamma_1\gamma_3-\gamma_2\gamma_4)}[\gamma_3(\pi_{1,t-1}-\pi^e_{1,t-1})-\gamma_2(\pi_{2,t-1}-\pi^e_{2,t-1})] \quad (7.36)$$

$$y_{2,t}=\frac{\bar{y}}{\tilde{p}_t}+\frac{\bar{y}/\tilde{p}_t}{\alpha(\gamma_1\gamma_3-\gamma_2\gamma_4)}[\gamma_1(\pi_{2,t-1}-\pi^e_{2,t-1})-\gamma_4(\pi_{1,t-1}-\pi^e_{1,t-1})] \quad (7.37)$$

where:

$$\gamma_1=\frac{\gamma p_{1,t-1}}{\gamma p_{1,t-1}+(1-\gamma)p_{2,t-1}},\ \gamma_2=\frac{(1-\gamma)p_{2,t-1}}{\gamma p_{1,t-1}+(1-\gamma)p_{2,t-1}}$$

$$\gamma_3=\frac{\gamma p_{2,t-1}}{\gamma p_{2,t-1}+(1-\gamma)p_{1,t-1}},\ \gamma_4=\frac{(1-\gamma)p_{1,t-1}}{\gamma p_{2,t-1}+(1-\gamma)p_{1,t-1}}$$

Each country's aggregate supply is determined by the natural level of output and unanticipated inflation in both countries. Given the restriction $\gamma > \frac{1}{2}$, it follows that:

$$\gamma_1\gamma_3 - \gamma_2\gamma_4 > 0$$

and thus the coefficients on the inflation terms in each aggregate supply equation are positive. An increase in a country's own inflation rate, holding inflationary expectations constant, has a positive effect on its output which implies that the short-run aggregate supply curve is upward sloping in inflation-output space. The long-run aggregate supply curve for each country is vertical.

An increase in inflation in one country decreases short-run aggregate supply in the other country. This result can be easily explained by solving equation (7.36) for $\pi_{1,t-1}$.

$$\pi_{1,t-1} = \frac{\alpha(\gamma_1\gamma_3 - \gamma_2\gamma_4)}{\bar{y}\gamma_3}(y_{1,t} - \bar{y}) + \pi^e_{1,t-1} + \frac{\gamma_2}{\gamma_3}(\pi_{2,t-1} - \pi^e_{2,t-1}).$$

Suppose domestic prices in country 2 ($p_{2,t}$) increase. This raises inflation in country 2 and in country 1. In country 2, the increase is represented by a movement along the aggregate supply curve. In country 1, since $y_{1,t}$ is unchanged, the increase in $\pi_{1,t-1}$ is represented by a decrease in aggregate supply.

The process of solving for aggregate demand indicates clearly the links between the two countries through the goods, money and bond markets. The first step in solving for aggregate demand in each country is the derivation of output in country i as an explicit function of output in country j and exogenous variables. (See Pollard (1993) for this derivation.) The result of this process for country 1 is given below:

$$\begin{aligned} y_{1,t} = & \left[\frac{[(1-\epsilon_g)-(1-\epsilon)c]2\theta + \lambda\phi}{(1-(1-\epsilon)c)2\theta) + \lambda\phi}\right] g_{1,t} \\ & + \left[\frac{(1-\epsilon)2c\theta - \lambda\phi}{(1-(1-\epsilon)c)2\theta + \lambda\phi}\right] b_{1,t} + \left[\frac{(1-\epsilon)2c\theta\phi}{(1-(1-\epsilon)c)2\theta + \lambda\phi}\right] \pi^e_{1,t} \\ & + \left[\frac{2c\epsilon\theta - \lambda\phi}{(1-(1-\epsilon)c)2\theta + \lambda\phi}\right] y_{2,t}\tilde{p}_t \\ & + \left[\frac{(\epsilon_g - \epsilon c)2\theta + \lambda\phi}{(1-(1-\epsilon)c)2\theta + \lambda\phi}\right] g_{2,t}\tilde{p}_t \\ & + \left[\frac{2c\epsilon\theta - \lambda\phi}{(1-(1-\epsilon)c)2\theta + \lambda\phi}\right] b_{2,t}\tilde{p}_t + \left[\frac{2\epsilon\phi\theta}{(1-(1-\epsilon)c)2\theta + \lambda\phi}\right] \pi^e_{2,t}\tilde{p}_t \end{aligned}$$

$$+\left[\frac{\phi}{(1-(1-\epsilon)c)2\theta+\lambda\phi}\right]b_{m,t}$$

$$+\left[\frac{2c\theta(1-2\epsilon)}{(1-(1-\epsilon)c)2\theta+\lambda\phi}\right]r_{1,t-1}(b_{21,t-1}\tilde{p}_{t-1}-b_{12,t-1})$$

$$+\left[\frac{\lambda\phi-c\theta}{(1-(1-\epsilon)c)2\theta+\lambda\phi}\right]r_{1,t-1}b_{m,t-1} \qquad (7.38)$$

Equation (7.38) can be used to determine the direct and feedback demand linkages between the two countries, a process which is lost when one begins with a reduced form demand equation.

The coefficients on the exogenous variables in equation (7.38) show the direct effects of these variables on aggregate demand in country 1. For example, real government expenditures in country 2 directly affect country 1, to the extent that they increase country 1's exports, and to the extent that they increase the world interest rate. The export effect is itself comprised of two parts: a positive effect due to the increase in spending on imports by the government in country 2, as measured by ε_g, and a negative effect resulting from a decline in private spending on imports in country 2 which occurs given that the increase in government spending was financed by an increase in taxes. (Since the government's budget constraint given in equation (7.11) must be met, an increase in g_{2t} holding b_{2t} constant implies that taxes, t_{2t}, are increased.) This latter effect is measured by εc. Thus, the overall direct impact of an increase in government spending by country 2 on aggregate demand in country 1 is indeterminate.

The term y_{2t} in equation (7.38) captures the feedback effects of the exogenous variables on output in country 1. A change in any of the exogenous or predetermined variables in equation (7.38) not only has a direct effect on output in country 1 but also has a feedback effect on aggregate demand in country 1 resulting from the effect on aggregate demand in country 2. Returning to the example of an increase in government spending by country 2, this not only directly affects country 1, as explained above, but also affects country 1 through its impact on demand in country 2. An increase in spending by the government in country 2 will increase income in country 2 which in turn will have spillover effects on country 1 by increasing trade and the world interest rate.

Thus, there are two channels of influence through which an exogenous variable affects aggregate demand in country i: a direct one through the initial effects on the markets in country i and an indirect one through the impact on output in country j which in turn works through the market linkages to affect demand in country i. This indirect, or feedback effect will be negative if $\lambda\phi > c\theta$.

Solving for output in country 2 as an explicit function of output in country 1, and substituting the resultant equation into equation (7.38), then using equation (7.5b) to replace $r_{1,t-1}$ gives the final form of the aggregate demand equation for country 1. Substituting equation (7.38) into the output equation for country 2, and using equation (7.18b) to replace $r_{2,t-1}$ gives the final form of the aggregate demand equation for country 2. These two aggregate demand equations are given below.

$$y_{1,t}=A_1g_{1,t}+A_2b_{1,t}+A_3\pi^e_{1,t}+A_4g_{2,t}\tilde{p}_t+A_5b_{2,t}\tilde{p}_t+A_6\pi^e_{2,t}\tilde{p}_t$$
$$+A_7b_{m,t}+i_{t-1}Y_1-\pi_{1,t-1}Y_1 \tag{7.39}$$

$$y_{2,t}=A_1g_{2,t}+A_2b_{2,t}+A_3\pi^e_{2,t}+A_4g_{1,t}\left(\frac{1}{\tilde{p}_t}\right)+A_5b_{1,t}\left(\frac{1}{\tilde{p}_t}\right)$$
$$+A_6\pi^e_{1,t}\left(\frac{1}{\tilde{p}_t}\right)+A_7b_{m,t}\left(\frac{1}{\tilde{p}_t}\right)+i_{t-1}Y_2-\pi_{2,t-1}Y_2 \tag{7.40}$$

where

$$Y_1=A_8(b_{21,t-1}\tilde{p}_{t-1}-b_{12,t-1}+A_9\tfrac{1}{2}b_{m,t-1}$$

$$Y_2=A_8\left(b_{12,t-1}\frac{1}{\tilde{p}_{t-1}}-b_{21,t-1}\right)+A_9\tfrac{1}{2}b_{m,t-1}\left(\frac{1}{\tilde{p}_{t-1}}\right)$$

and A_1–A_9 are given in Table 7.5.

The slope of each country's aggregate demand curve $(-1/Y_i)$ in period t depends on the net debtor/creditor status of each country in period $t-1$. Given that this is a two country model, both countries can not be net creditors. Furthermore, given the existence of a common independent central bank, one country must be a net debtor. In this system the sum of the balance of payment accounts of two countries does not equal zero, but instead equals the central bank's holdings of bonds less its real interest earnings from last period's holdings of bonds. When country 1 is not a net debtor, the amount of country 2's bonds held by the residents of country 1 must be greater than the amount of country 1's bonds held by the residents of country 2 $(b_{21}\tilde{p}>b_{12})$. Likewise, when country 2 is not a net debtor, $b_{12}>b_{21}\tilde{p}$. If both countries are net debtors, the absolute value of the difference between the cross border bond holdings of country 1 and country 2 is restricted to be less than half the bond holdings of the central bank $(|b_{21}-b_{12}|<1/2\, b_m)$.

These conditions indicate that the ability of one country alone to be a net borrower is constrained by the willingness of the residents of the other country to be lenders. This indicates that even if the central bank is unwilling to finance the expansionary policies of a country, it can still pursue these policies as long as the residents of the other country are willing to lend to it. That is, given the lack of capital controls between the two countries, as long as the residents of one country are willing to finance the deficit spending of the other, neither the central bank nor the other government will be able to prevent or constraint the expansionary policies of one government. The central bank will still be able to constrain one government to the extent that it is willing to use restrictive

Table 7.5 Coefficients in the aggregate demand equation

$$A_1 = 1 - \frac{\epsilon_g}{1-c+2c\epsilon} > 0$$

$$A_2 = \frac{2\theta c(c-1+\epsilon-2c\epsilon)+\lambda\phi(1-2c+4c\epsilon)}{2(1-c+2c\epsilon)(c\theta-\theta-\lambda\phi)} \gtrless 0$$

$$A_3 = \frac{2\phi\theta(c-1+\epsilon-2c\epsilon)+\lambda\phi^2(2\epsilon-1)}{2(1-c+2c\epsilon)(c\theta-\theta-\lambda\phi)} > 0$$

$$A_4 = \frac{\epsilon_g}{1-c+2c\epsilon} > 0$$

$$A_5 = \frac{\lambda\phi-2c\epsilon\theta}{2(1-c+2c\epsilon)(c\theta-\theta-\lambda\phi)} < 0$$

$$A_6 = \frac{\phi(\lambda\phi-2\epsilon\lambda\phi-2\epsilon\theta)}{2(1-c+2c\epsilon)(c\theta-\theta-\lambda\phi)} \gtrless 0$$

$$A_7 = \frac{\phi}{2(\theta-c\theta+\lambda\phi)} > 0$$

$$A_8 = \frac{c(1-2\epsilon)}{1-c+2c\epsilon} > 0$$

$$A_9 = \frac{c\theta-\lambda\phi}{c\theta-\theta-\lambda\phi} > 0$$

$$A_1 + A_2 = \frac{2\theta(1-c)(1-\epsilon_g)+2\theta c\epsilon+\lambda\phi(1-2\epsilon_g)}{2(1-c+2c\epsilon)(\theta-c\theta+\lambda\phi)} > 0$$

$$A_4 + A_5 = \frac{2\epsilon_g\theta+2c\theta(\epsilon-\epsilon_g)-\lambda\phi(1-2\epsilon_g)}{2(1-c+2c\epsilon)(\theta-c\theta+\lambda\phi)} \gtrless 0$$

monetary policies which will affect both countries. There are several issues to consider in this regard. The first is the relative impact of restrictive monetary policies on both countries, versus the impact of the expansionary fiscal policies on both countries. The second is the relative impact of the two policies on the country pursuing expansionary fiscal policies. A third issue is the willingness of the 'errant' country to challenge the central bank and to engender the disdain of its neighbours. All of these factors are likely to be significant in determining policy outcomes. The first two issues are considered further below. (Another issue which is outside the realm of this model is whether such expansionary policies will cause the residents of the two countries to view the bonds of the expansionary government as risky, and require a risk premium, which will drive a wedge between interest rates on the bonds. Such a premium depends on the belief that the government in question is likely to default on its debt.)

In order for a country's aggregate demand curve to be downward sloping, it is necessary that $\lambda\phi > c\theta$. This is the same condition which indicates that the feedback effect in equation (7.38) is negative. (Even with this condition, it is possible that when one country is a net debtor and the other a net creditor, the aggregate demand curve for the net debtor country could be upward sloping. This result does not change the comparative static analysis in the section 7.4. To simplify the discussion, it is assumed that both countries' aggregate demand curves are downward sloping.) This condition is also useful in determining the signs of some of the coefficients in the aggregate demand equations. These coefficients (see Table 7.5) indicate the overall effect of changes in the policy and exogenous variables on aggregate demand in each country.

The direct, feedback and overall effects of an increase in the variables in the aggregate demand equation for country i are given in Table 7.6. An increase in real expenditures by country 1's government, financed by taxes, directly increases aggregate demand in country 1. The increase in aggregate demand in country 1 triggers an increase in the exports of country 2 resulting in a positive spillover effect on aggregate demand in country 2. This increase in aggregate demand in country 2 has a net crowding out effect, and thus contracts aggregate demand in country 1. Although this feedback effect is negative, it is not strong enough to offset the initial increase in aggregate demand in country 1. The increase in country 1's aggregate demand also feeds back into country 2's aggregate demand, causing a diminution of the original spillover effect. In both countries, the overall effect of a tax financed increase in country 1's government expenditures is an increase in aggregate demand.

An increase in real expenditures by country 1's government, financed through bond issues, directly increases aggregate demand in country 1 and has a positive spillover effect on country 2. As with tax financed expenditures the resultant increase in demand in one country has a negative feedback effect on aggregate demand in the other country. For country 1, the direct effect is stronger than the feedback effect resulting in an increase in aggregate demand. For country 2, the overall effect is indeterminate.

Table 7.6 Effect of changes in policy variables on aggregate demand in country i

	Direct effect	*Feedback effect*	*Overall effect*
Increase in tax financed government expenditures by country i	+	−	+
Increase in bond financed government expenditures by country i	+	−	+
Increase in tax financed government expenditures by country j	+	−	+
Increase in bond financed government expenditures by country j	+	−	±
Increase in real balances	+	−	+

An increase in the real bond holdings of the central bank increases aggregate demand in both countries. This comes directly from the increase in real balances. In both countries, the feedback effect is negative but not strong enough to offset the direct effect.

7.4 EQUILIBRIUM INFLATION AND OUTPUT

The equilibrium inflation and output equations for country 1 are given below and the equations for country 2 are comparable:

$$\begin{aligned}\pi_{1,t-1}=&(A_1\chi_{1,t}+A_4\xi_{1,t})g_{1,t}+(A_2\chi_{1,t}+A_5\xi_{1,t})b_{1,t}\\&+(A_3\chi_{1,t}+A_6\xi_{1,t})\pi^e_{1,t}+(A_4\chi_{1,t}+A_1\xi_{1,t})g_{2,t}\tilde{p}_t\\&+(A_5\chi_{1,t}+A_2\xi_{1,t})b_{2,t}\tilde{p}_t+(A_6\chi_{1,t}+A_3\xi_{1,t})\pi^e_{2,t}\tilde{p}_t\\&+A_7(\chi_{1,t}+\xi_{1,t})b_{m,t}+(\Upsilon_2\tilde{p}\chi_{1,t}+\Upsilon_1\xi_{1,t})i_{t-1}\\&+\omega_{11,t}\pi^e_{1,t-1}+\omega_{12,t}\pi^e_{2,t-1}-(\chi_{1,t}+\xi_{1,t})\bar{y}\end{aligned} \tag{7.41}$$

where:

$$\chi_{1,t}=(\alpha^2\Upsilon_2\tilde{p}_t(\gamma_1\gamma_3-\gamma_2\gamma_4)+\alpha\gamma_1\bar{y})/\Omega_1$$

$$\xi_{1,t}=(\alpha\gamma_2\bar{y})/\Omega_1$$

$$\omega_{11,t}=(\bar{y}\alpha\gamma_3\Upsilon_2\tilde{p}_t+\bar{y}^2)/\Omega_1$$

$$\omega_{12,t}=-(\alpha\bar{y}\gamma_2\Upsilon_2\tilde{p}_t)/\Omega_1$$

$$\Omega_1=\alpha^2\Upsilon_1\Upsilon_2\tilde{p}_t(\gamma_1\gamma_3-\gamma_2\gamma_4)+\alpha\bar{y}(\gamma_1\Upsilon_1+\gamma_3\Upsilon_2\tilde{p}_t)+\bar{y}^2$$

$$\begin{aligned}y_{1,t}=&(A_1\eta_{1,t}-A_4\zeta_{1,t})g_{1,t}+(A_2\eta_{1,t}-A_5\zeta_{1,t})b_{1,t}\\&+(A_3\eta_{1,t}-A_6\zeta_{1,t})\pi^e_{1,t}+(A_4\eta_{1,t}-A_1\xi_{1,t})g_{2,t}\tilde{p}_t\\&+(A_5\eta_{1,t}-A_2\zeta_{1,t})b_{2,t}\tilde{p}_t+(A_6\eta_{1,t}-A_3\zeta_{1,t})\pi^e_{2,t}\tilde{p}_t\\&+(\eta_{1,t}\zeta_{1,t})A_7b_{m,t}+(\Upsilon_1\eta_{1,t}-\Upsilon_2\tilde{p}_t\zeta_{1,t})i_{t-1}\\&-Y_1\eta_{1,t}\pi^e_{1,t-1}-\Upsilon_2\tilde{p}_t\zeta_{1,t}\pi^e_{2,t-1}+\Upsilon_1(\chi_{1,t}+\xi_{1,t})\bar{y}\end{aligned} \tag{7.42}$$

where:

$$\eta_{1,t}=(\alpha\gamma_3\Upsilon_2\tilde{p}_t\bar{y}+\bar{y}^2)/\Omega_1$$

$$\zeta=\alpha\Upsilon_1\gamma_2\bar{y}$$

These were derived using the aggregate demand and supply equations discussed in Section 7.3 (see Pollard (1993) for these derivations). In the standard closed economy model an increase in government spending increases aggregate demand and so has a positive effect on output and prices. An increase in bonds issued by the government causes a contraction in aggregate demand by pushing up interest rates and thereby decreasing investment. Thus output and prices decline. The overall effect of a bond financed increase in government spending on output and prices is generally positive; the crowding out of investment which occurs is not complete. Expansionary monetary policy carried out through open market purchases increases output and inflation in the closed economy, by shifting out the LM curve and thus increasing aggregate demand.

In a model of a large open economy with perfect capital mobility and fixed exchange rates, both the fiscal and monetary policy actions of a country also have an effect on the rest of the world. Expansionary fiscal policy, regardless of how it is financed, has an ambiguous effect on output and prices abroad. The increased spending at home increases aggregate demand abroad through trade effects. At the same time, however, the increase in the world interest rate dampens demand overseas. A bond-financed fiscal expansion will increase the magnitude of the latter effect. In large open economy models it is uncertain as to whether the trade effect or the interest rate effect dominates. Buiter (1988) states that if the countries are of similar size, then a fiscal expansion at home will always have a positive effect on world output and inflation. In the large country case, a monetary expansion at home has a positive effect on output and inflation abroad.

As noted previously, standard open economy models focus on the demand side of the economy. Even where a supply side is modelled these models ignore connections between the demand and supply side of economies. In the model developed in this paper countries are linked on the demand side through the goods market and assets market. Thus, policies which affect aggregate demand in one country lead to spillover effects on demand in the other country. Because of the market linkages, changes in inflation in one country affect the other country. This link comes through the supply side of the economies. Thus, a change in inflation in one country will lead to spillover effects on supply in the other country.

7.4.1 Decomposition of comparative statics

The comparative static results for the model of a monetary union developed in this paper are summarized in Tables 7.7 and 7.8. The first column in each table presents the demand effects, which may be weakened or reversed through the inclusion of supply effects, given in column three. (The analysis for equilibrium output and inflation, in this section, considers only the overall change in demand, and does not look at the component effects.) Determining the conditions under which supply effects weaken or offset demand effects requires an analysis of the spillover demand effects and the magnitude of the supply effects.

For every policy variable in the equilibrium output and inflation equations there are two separate effects that determine the overall result of a change in that variable on output and inflation. A change in fiscal or monetary policy has

Table 7.7 Effect of changes in policy variables on output in country i

	Direct effect	*Feedback effect*	*Total effect*
Increase in tax financed government expenditures by country i	+	−	+
Increase in bond financed government expenditures by country i	+ +	$-(A_4+A_5>0)$ $+(A_4+A_5<0)$	+ +
Increase in tax financed government expenditures by country j	+	−	±
Increase in bond financed government expenditures by country j	$+(A_4+A_5>0)$ $-(A_4+A_5<0)$	− −	± −
Increase in real balances	+	−	+

Table 7.8 Effect of changes in policy variables on inflation in country i

	Direct effect	*Feedback effect*	*Total effect*
Increase in tax financed government expenditures by country i	+	+	+
Increase in bond financed government expenditures by country i	+ +	$+(A_4+A_5>0)$ $-(A_4+A_5<0)$	+ +
Increase in tax financed government expenditures by country j	+	+	+
Increase in bond financed government expenditures by country j	$+(A_4+A_5>0)$ $-(A_4+A_5<0)$	+ +	+ ±
Increase in real balances	+	+	+

a direct effect on aggregate demand, resulting in a change in a country's inflation rate. The feedback effect captures the subsequent impact of this change in inflation on aggregate supply in the other country. (As shown by equations (7.36) and (7.37), an increase in inflation in country i will decrease aggregate supply in country j.) In most cases the aggregate supply changes reinforce the effect on inflation of the change in aggregate demand, but weaken the effect on output.

There are two potential sources for indeterminacy in signing the comparative static effects. First, as noted in Table 7.5, the overall demand effect on country i of a bond financed fiscal policy change by country j (A_4+A_5) is indeterminate, which presents a source of ambiguity in the equilibrium output and inflation effects. Second, as noted above, in many cases the feedback effects work to offset the effect of a change in aggregate demand on output. The result depends on the direction and the magnitudes of the changes in aggregate demand and aggregate supply.

An important determinant of the effects of policies on output and inflation is the steepness of a country's aggregate demand curve. For a given shift in aggregate supply, the flatter the slope of the aggregate demand curve the larger is the effect on output and the smaller is the effect on inflation. The slope of the aggregate demand curve is determined by last period's current account balance of a country. If a country was a net debtor (net creditor) last period its aggregate demand curve will be relatively steep (flat). An increase in inflation reduces the real interest earnings on private holdings of bonds, thereby reducing disposable income (equations 7.9 and 7.22). An increase in inflation also reduces the government's real interest payments on bonds, thereby reducing the government deficit (equations 7.11 and 7.24). A downward sloping aggregate demand curve indicates that an increase in inflation produces a net negative effect on output (the output effect of the inflation benefit to the government can not fully offset the output effect of the inflation cost to the private sector). As expected, a net creditor nation is hurt more by inflation than a net debtor nation, which is reflected in the flatter aggregate demand curve for a net creditor and the steeper aggregate demand curve for a net debtor.

The importance of the slopes of the aggregate demand curves for determining the comparative statics can be illustrated by examining the two types of policy effects which are present in the model: (1) expansionary policies which have positive effects on aggregate demand in both countries; and, (2) expansionary policies which have positive effects on aggregate demand at home, but negative spillover effects on aggregate demand abroad.

Policies which fall into the first category initially increase inflation abroad which causes a decline in aggregate supply at home. The supply effect strengthens the positive own demand effect on inflation but weakens the demand effect on output. If a country is a net creditor the supply effect is more likely to offset the demand effect on output. Whereas, if a country is a net debtor the supply effect is less likely to offset the demand effect on output. This follows from the fact that inflation is less harmful (in output terms) to a net debtor than to a net creditor.

Policies which fall into the second category lead to a reduction in inflation abroad (due to negative demand spillovers) which causes an increase in aggregate supply at home. Since the home demand effect is positive, the supply effect strengthens the demand effect on output but weakens the demand effect on inflation. In this case, a net debtor country is more likely to experience an overall decrease in inflation than a net creditor. However, the output effect is larger for a net creditor than for a net debtor. This result follows from the greater benefit of a reduction in inflation to a net creditor than to a net debtor.

In the foreign country aggregate demand decreases due to the spillover effect, and given the increase in inflation in the home country, foreign aggregate supply will also decrease. This shift in aggregate supply reinforces the demand induced decrease in output but works to counteract the demand induced decrease in inflation. The overall effect on output will be greater if the foreign country is a net creditor. Inflation is more likely to increase if the foreign country is a net debtor.

Policies pursued by one country will have differing effects on the two countries due to differences in the demand effects in the countries and differences in the past behaviour of the two countries. The more similar the past policies of the two countries, the more similar the current account balances of the two and thus the more similar the slopes of their aggregate demand curves. If the countries are symmetric ($b_{12,t-1} = b_{21,t-1}\,\tilde{p}_{t-1}$), the aggregate demand curves have the same slope. In this case an expansionary policy pursued by country 1 has the same effect on country 2 as an expansionary policy pursued by country 2 has on country 1. If the countries are not symmetric this does not hold. For example, if country 1 is a net creditor and country 2 is a net debtor, an expansionary fiscal policy pursued by country 1 may increase output in country 2, but an expansionary fiscal policy pursued by country 2 may decrease output in country 1. In general, policies which increase aggregate demand in both countries are less likely to have an overall positive output spillover if the country pursuing the policies is a net debtor and the other country is a net creditor.

7.4.2 Fiscal policy effects

The analysis in this section concentrates on the effects of changes in policies by country 1 on the two countries. The analysis is the same with respect to changes in country 2's policy variables. See Pollard (1993) for the derivation of the comparative static results given in this section.

Proposition 7.1: *A tax financed fiscal expansion by country 1 increases its inflation and output. If country 1 is a net creditor and country 2 a net debtor, inflation and output also increase in country 2. If country 1 is a net debtor and country 2 a net creditor, inflation in country 2 increases but output may increase or decrease.*

The increase in government spending has a positive effect on aggregate demand in both countries ($A_1 > 0$, $A_4 > 0$). The change in aggregate demand in country 1 increases its inflation rate, thereby reducing aggregate supply in country 2. Likewise, inflation in country 2 increases which reduces aggregate supply in country 1. Therefore, in both countries, the effect on inflation is compounded but the effect on output is reduced.

For country 1, the supply effect does not offset the demand effect regardless of its net debtor/creditor status, so inflation and output increase. Nevertheless, the increase is smaller in the case where country 1 is a net creditor, relative to the case where it is a net debtor, as shown in Figures 7.1 and 7.2. Two factors account for this difference. When country 1 is a net debtor and country 2 is a net creditor, country 1's aggregate demand curve is steeper and the shift in its aggregate supply curve is smaller than in the contrary case. Both of these factors imply that the effect on output of the fiscal expansion will be smaller if country 1 is a net debtor and country 2 is a net creditor. The effect on inflation in country 1 will also be smaller.

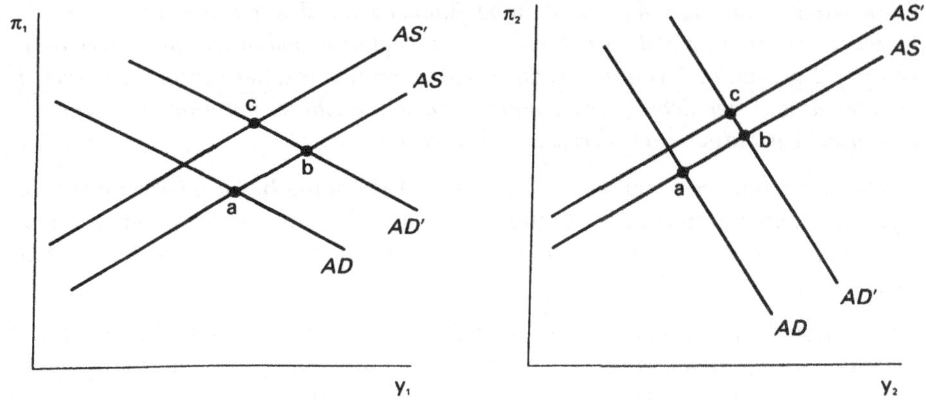

(a) (b)

Figure 7.1 Tax-financed increase in government spending by country 1: (a) country 1 (net creditor); (b) country 2 (net debtor)

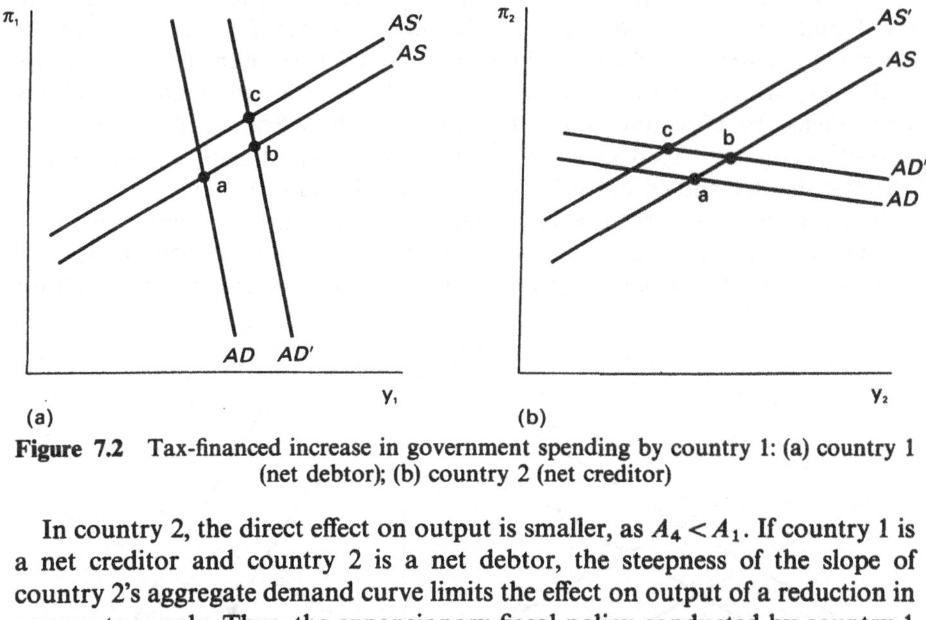

(a) (b)

Figure 7.2 Tax-financed increase in government spending by country 1: (a) country 1 (net debtor); (b) country 2 (net creditor)

In country 2, the direct effect on output is smaller, as $A_4 < A_1$. If country 1 is a net creditor and country 2 is a net debtor, the steepness of the slope of country 2's aggregate demand curve limits the effect on output of a reduction in aggregate supply. Thus, the expansionary fiscal policy conducted by country 1 increases both inflation and output in country 2, as shown in Figure 7.1. If country 1 is a net debtor and country 2 is a net creditor, the slope of country 2's aggregate demand curve is relatively flat, as shown in Figure 7.2.

The decrease in aggregate supply exacerbates inflation and so causes a large (relative to country 1) reduction in output. It is possible that output decreases in country 2. Given that inflation definitely increases, expansionary fiscal policy undertaken by country 1 can lead to stagflation in country 2. The greater the asymmetry between the countries, the greater the differences in the output effects.

Proposition 7.2a: $A_4 + A_5 > 0$. *A bond financed fiscal expansion by country 1 increases its inflation and output. In this case, inflation and output also increase in country 2 if country 1 is a net creditor and country 2 is a net debtor. However, if country 1 is a net debtor and country 2 a net creditor, inflation in country 2 increases, but output may increase or decrease.*

The bond financed increase in government spending has a positive effect on aggregate demand in country 1, and if $A_4 + A_5 > 0$, then aggregate demand also increases in country 2. Thus, the analysis is similar to the tax financed fiscal expansion.

Proposition 7.2b: $A_4 + A_5 < 0$. *A bond financed fiscal expansion by country 1 increases its inflation and output. In country 2, output decreases, but the effect on inflation is indeterminate if country 1 is a net creditor and country 2 is a net debtor. If the balance of payments position of the two countries is reversed, both inflation and output in country 2 decrease.*

The increase in government spending decreases aggregate demand in country 2, and the resultant decline in inflation in country 2 increases aggregate supply in country 1, as shown in Figures 7.3 and 7.4. Since the fiscal expansion had a positive demand effect on country 1, the shift in aggregate supply strengthens the effect on output but weakens the effect on inflation. Thus, output in country 1 increases, and since the supply effect is not strong enough to offset the demand effect on inflation, inflation also increases.

In country 2 the decrease in aggregate demand in conjunction with an increase in aggregate supply, due to the increase in inflation in country 1, work to reduce output, but have opposite effects on inflation. The overall result for

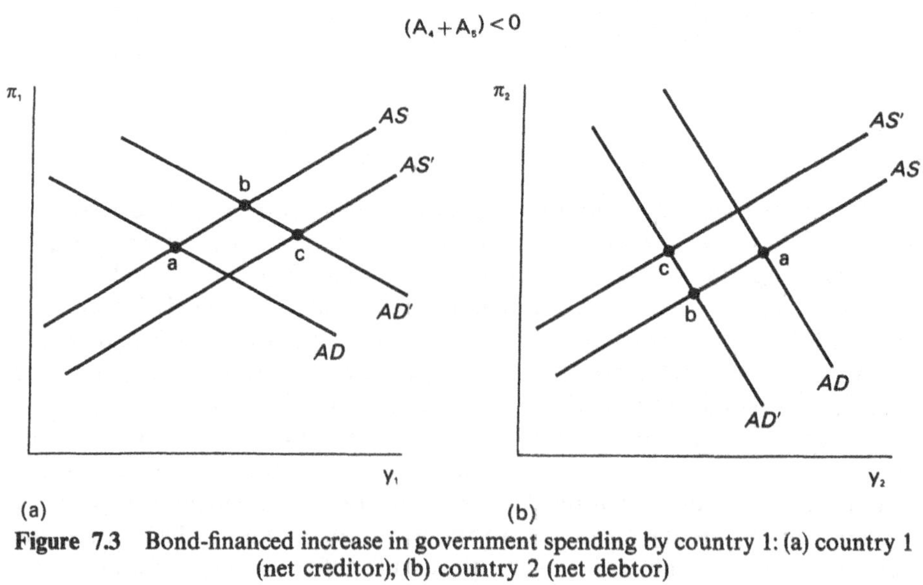

Figure 7.3 Bond-financed increase in government spending by country 1: (a) country 1 (net creditor); (b) country 2 (net debtor)

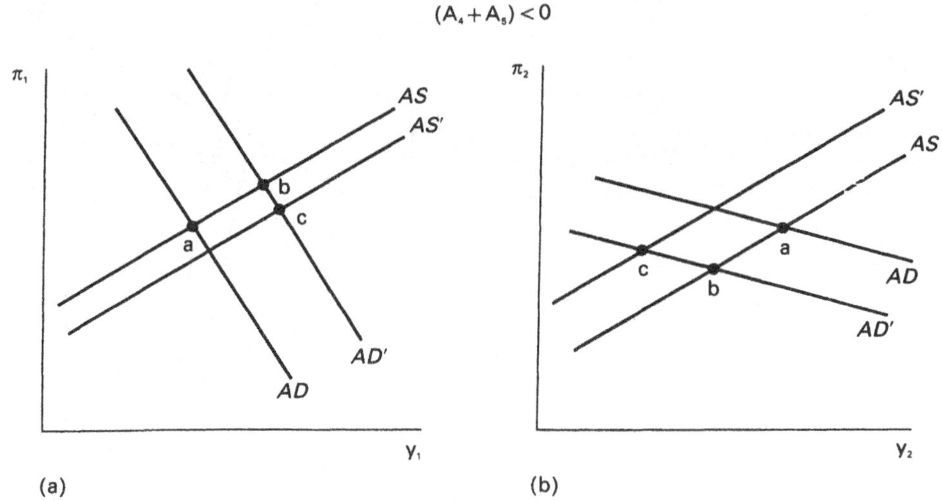

Figure 7.4 Bond-financed increase in government spending by country 1: (a) country 1 (net debtor); (b) country 2 (net creditor)

inflation depends upon the balance of payments status of the two countries. If country 1 is a net creditor and country 2 is a net debtor, the effect on inflation is indeterminate, as shown in Figure 7.3. If the balance of payments positions are reversed, the demand effect is stronger than the supply effect and inflation falls, as shown in Figure 7.4. Consequently, it is possible for a fiscal expansion by country 1 to increase its output and inflation, while decreasing output and inflation in country 2.

7.4.3 Monetary policy effects

Proposition 7.3: *Expansionary monetary policy increases inflation and output in both countries, with the net debtor country experiencing the largest increases.*

The increase in real balances has an identical effect on aggregate demand in the two countries. The increase in aggregate demand in country 1 increases its inflation rate which causes a decrease in aggregate supply in country 2. Likewise, the increase in aggregate demand in country 2 increases its inflation rate which causes a decrease in aggregate supply in country 1. Thus, the aggregate supply effects further increase inflation in both countries, but work to offset the demand induced increases in output in both countries, as shown in Figure 7.5. In both countries the overall effect is an increase in inflation and output. However, the increase in inflation and output is greater in the net debtor country, due to the relative steepness of its aggregate demand curve, compared with the net creditor country.

In summary, if a country is a net debtor any expansionary policies which it enacts or which are undertaken by the central bank have a greater effect on its

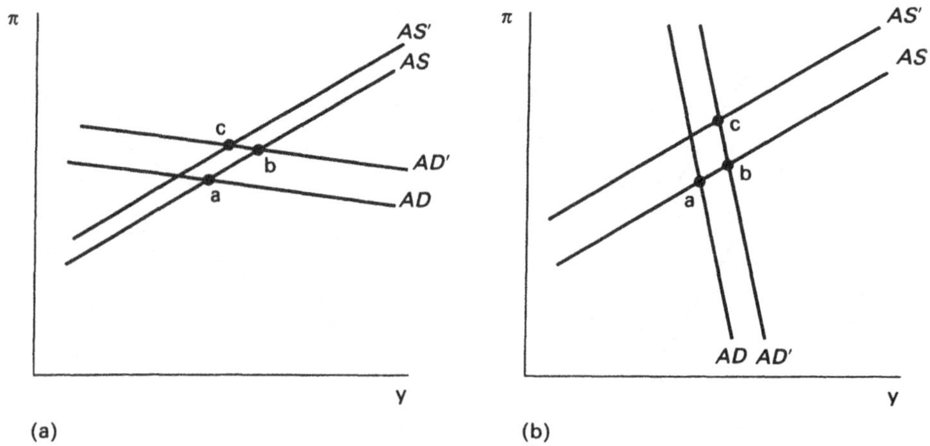

Figure 7.5 Expansionary monetary policy: (a) net creditor; (b) net debtor

inflation rate and level of output than if it is a net creditor. If a country is a net debtor expansionary policies undertaken by the other country are more likely to have positive effects on its output and inflation rate than if it is a net creditor.

These results differ from the standard open economy models due not only to the inclusion of supply effects, but also the addition of interest earnings in the aggregate demand equations for the two countries. The inclusion of supply effects are important because they may work to offset the effects of a change in demand on output and/or inflation. Therefore, the supply effects can change the results one would obtain by solely concentrating on the demand side of economies. The addition of interest earnings in the aggregate demand equations is the means by which the balance of payments status of a country affects the model. As shown above, this status determines the steepness/flatness of the slope of the demand curve which weakens or strengthens the effects of a shift in aggregate supply on output and inflation.

7.5 CONCLUSION

This paper develops a two-country model of a monetary union. In order to depict more fully the nature of the linkages between the countries and the central bank, the model does not begin with reduced form equations, but derives these equations based on a structural model of goods market, bond market and money market interaction. Furthermore, the model developed in this paper does not make the common assumption that output is demand determined, but instead also develops a supply side of the economy to capture both the demand and supply effects on output and inflation. A monetary union introduces linkages between the two countries so that fiscal policy pursued by one country or monetary policy pursued by the central bank affects both aggregate supply and demand in the two countries. The overall effect of a policy on each country's output and inflation rate depends not only on who pursued the policy (a country's own fiscal policy has a greater effect on its aggregate demand than does fiscal policy pursued by the other country) but also on last period's current account balance of each country. In this way present policies affect both countries through aggregate demand and aggregate supply links between the countries, but past policies, through their effect on the current account balances of each country, also determine the overall effect of current policies on output and inflation in each country.

The results of this paper suggest that asymmetries in past policies, reflected in asymmetries in the current account balances of countries, and the continuation of asymmetric fiscal policies can be a source of friction among the countries in a monetary union.

The findings of this paper indicate that fiscal policy convergence and the maintenance of convergence through restrictions on fiscal policies may be necessary to ensure that the monetary union functions smoothly. Restricting fiscal policies, however, may not produce optimal results in a monetary union in which the member countries have dissimilar economies. Given the small degree of labour mobility within the EC and the lack of an automatic redistribution system, constraints on fiscal policies may hinder adjustment to asymmetric shocks. This point has been made by several economists including DeGrauwe (1992) and Feldstein (1992). It is possible that the Maastricht treaty will be interpreted as allowing for deviations in fiscal policies to react to asymmetric shocks. This, however, will depend on the willingness of the Council, and therefore, the member countries, to tolerate such deviations. Bayoumi and Eichengreen (1992) find that asymmetric shocks are more prevalent among the member countries of the EC than the regions in the US. Furthermore they find that the adjustment to such shocks is faster in the US which they conclude is likely due to the higher degree of labour mobility in the US than in Europe.

If fiscal policy restrictions are necessary to ensure the smooth functioning of a monetary union, but restrictions hinder adjustment to economic shocks the solution may be to create a 'two-speed' Europe. A core group of EC countries – France, Germany and the Benelux countries are usually suggested – that experience similar shocks would move forward to form a monetary union, while the other countries would join only when their economies become similar to those of the core. Another solution is to increase the budgetary powers of the European Community government so that it can use taxes and transfer payments to ease the burden of asymmetric shocks. However, given the increasing emphasis on subsidiarity this latter approach is unlikely to be adopted.

More research is needed to examine the macroeconomic costs and benefits of monetary union to the members of the European Community. The analysis is this paper focuses on the impact effects of policies. Two issues which deserve further study are the possibility of strategic behaviour on the part of the policy makers in a monetary union and the long-term policy effects. Further research should explore the long run effects on member countries of allowing independent fiscal policies or of restricting fiscal policies. The advantage of the model developed in this paper is that it can be used to address both of these issues. (For example, Pollard (1992) uses the model developed in this paper to examine effects in a strategic setting.)

ACKNOWLEDGEMENTS

The author is indebted to Rowena Pecchenino, Andrew John and Robert Rasche for helpful comments. The opinions expressed in this paper are those of the author and do not necessarily represent those of the Federal Reserve Bank of St. Louis or of the Federal Reserve System.

REFERENCES

Artis, M. and Bayoumi, T. (1991) Global financial integration and current account imbalances, in *External Constraints on Macroeconomic Policy: The European Experience* (eds G. Alogoskoufis, L. Papademos, and R. Portes). Cambridge University Press, New York, 10–40.

Bayoumi, T. and Eichengreen, B. (1992) Shocking aspects of European monetary unification. *NBER Working Paper # 3949.*

Buiter, W. H. (1988) Macroeconomic policy design in an interdependent world economy: an analysis of three contingencies, in *International Aspects of Fiscal Policies* (ed. J. Frenkel). The University of Chicago Press, Chicago, 121–55.

De Grauwe, P. (1992) *The Economics of Monetary Integration.* Oxford University Press, Oxford.

Feldstein, M. (1992) The case against EMU. *The Economist*, 13 June, 19–22.

Kenen, P. B. (1989) *Exchange Rates and Policy Coordination*, Manchester University Press, Manchester.

Kenen, P. B. (1990) The coordination of macroeconomic policies, in *International Policy Coordination and Exchange Rate Fluctuations* (eds W. Branson, J. Frenkel and M. Goldstein), University of Chicago Press, Chicago, 63–102.

Kole, L. S. (1988) Expansionary fiscal policy and international interdependence, in *International Aspects of Fiscal Policies* (ed. J. Frenkel). The University of Chicago Press, Chicago, 229–65.

Lamfalussy, A. (1989) Macro-coordination of fiscal policies in an economic and monetary union in Europe, in *Collection of Papers Submitted to the Committee for the Study of Economic and Monetary Union*, Luxembourg: Office for Official Publications of the European Communities, 107 and 111.

Oudiz, G. and Sachs, J. (1984) Macroeconomic policy coordination among the industrial economies, *Brookings Papers on Economic Activity*. 1–75.

Pollard, P. (1992) Strategic policymaking in a monetary union. Unpublished paper.

Pollard, P. (1993) Macroeconomic policy effects in a monetary union. *Federal Reserve Bank of St. Louis Working Paper*.

Sachs, J. and Wyplosz, C. (1984) Real exchange rate effects of fiscal policy, *NBER Working Paper # 1255*.

8

Growth and specialization in an enlarged Europe: is a virtuous circle possible?

C.A. Bollino, P.C. Padoan

8.1 INTRODUCTION

All processes of integration are complex and multifaceted, and as such cannot be analysed from any single standpoint but must be approached using a variety of different instruments and points of view. What follows is a series of considerations concerning the problems involved in the integration of the economies of Eastern Europe with the European Community. In other words, in our discussion we consider crucial that integration has to be seen as a strategy to increase the sustainable growth rate of Eastern economies.

First, let us examine the issue from the viewpoint of the Eastern countries. The ultimate goal of the radical economic reforms they are undertaking is to enhance their capacity to grow in a framework of progressive opening to international trade. In other words, they want to maximize the growth rate consistent with current account equilibrium. Failing this condition, in fact, these countries would face an increasing foreign debt that would be unsustainable in the long run, eventually running into the severe problems faced by many developing countries in the recent past.

This issue can be framed in the following terms. In what way should the countries of Central and Eastern Europe modify their specialization pattern so as to raise growth rates without undermining the long-term current account equilibrium? This question immediately raises another one. Given that the relevant area for integration is the European Community, in what way should the community's own specialization pattern be modified to 'accommodate' the request for integration on the part of the former COMECON countries? And

The European Single Market – Monetary and Fiscal Policy Harmonization.
Edited by H.M. Scobie. Published in 1994 by Chapman & Hall,
London. ISBN 0 412 57520 5

what are the institutional as well as the economic implications of such an enlargement of the Community?

In a few pages, it is clearly impossible to touch even superficially on all the complexities and facets of such an integration process. We shall try to sketch a general framework drawing on a recently completed research (Bollino and Padoan, 1992), to offer both theoretical and practical observations. We begin by considering the links between growth, specialization, and institutional arrangements. This is followed by a number of observations on the adjustment mechanisms most appropriate to achieving such a configuration.

8.2 GROWTH AND THE BALANCE OF PAYMENTS

A useful starting point is the relation of identity defining a growth rate consistent with on current account equilibrium, which for convenience we shall call the 'equilibrium' growth rate (Fagerberg, 1988; Padoan, 1992). It is as follows:

$$g^* = qx - qm + (p - pw) + gw \tag{8.1}$$

Equation (8.1) establishes that the equilibrium growth rate of output (g^*) is positively correlated to the change of the export share (qx); negatively correlated to the change of the share of imports over GDP (qm); positively correlated to the difference between the rate of increase of domestic prices (p) and world prices (pw), the term in brackets thus representing the rate of change in the country's terms of trade, assuming a fixed rate. Finally, g^* is positively correlated to the rate of growth of world demand (gw).

The next step is determining what factors affect the changes in the foregoing variables.

The change in export and import shares depends, broadly, on competitiveness. For sake of simplicity, we can restrict our consideration to two determinants: price and technology (see Appendix 8.A for a further development of this point). Without going into detail, it can be shown that as far as effects on the growth rate are concerned, these two factors present a twofold trade-off. First, if domestic prices rise faster than world prices this has a positive effect on growth thanks to an improvement in the terms of trade but a negative one by undermining competitiveness. A country's technological capabilities may be improved either through domestic innovation or by diffusion, i.e. imports of technologies from the rest of the world (for a more extensive treatment of the influence of these effects on the equilibrium growth rate, see Padoan, 1992).

In general, any country will have a number of alternatives at its disposal for raising the equilibrium growth rate. The relevant point here is that the alternatives themselves depend, to a large extent, on the country's pattern of international specialization. This is a complex topic indeed. For our purposes, however, we can consider it by turning directly to the case of integration of the East European economies in the European Community.

8.3 COMPARATIVE ADVANTAGES IN EUROPE

Table 8.1 summarizes the findings of a study by Guerrieri and Mastropasqua (1992) on the economic specialization of the countries of Eastern Europe, comparing them with those of the major EC countries. The specialization patterns are analysed by using an appropriately modified version of Pavitt's taxonomy (1984) which is particularly well-suited to assess the links between technology, changes in relative prices and international competitiveness. Briefly (for a more extensive treatment, see Dosi, *et al.* 1990), a number of sectors are identified, according to the source from which they draw gains in competitiveness. The relevant sectors are the following: the science-based industries, in which competitiveness derives from the ability to generate endogenous innovation; scale-intensive activities, which rely on market size and the consequent ability to exploit static and dynamic returns to scale so as to cut costs, where both technological and price competitiveness play an important role; specialized suppliers, which base competitiveness on price but also on technology, and are heavily dependent on innovations generated elsewhere; traditional sectors, where competitiveness depends chiefly if not exclusively on price. In other sectors of the economy, such as agriculture, resource-intensive industries that exploit their access to raw materials (such as petroleum and coal derivatives), and energy-intensive industries, improvement in the terms of trade plays a fundamental role.

Bearing the foregoing in mind, let us examine Table 8.1, which summarizes the distribution of comparative advantages in the former Soviet Union (now CIS), the countries of Central and Eastern Europe, and the main European Community member states according to Pavitt's classification (Guerrieri and Mastropasqua, 1992). Singling out Eastern Europe, we find that Poland and Hungary present a comparative advantage in agricultural products and traditional manufactures and Czechoslovakia also in scale-intensive industries. All three countries enjoy a comparative advantage in the resource-intensive and energy-intensive sectors, while the former Soviet Union presents comparative advantages only in the two latter sectors.

Combining these observations with those concerning the causal linkage between the determinants of competitiveness and the equilibrium growth rate gives rise to a number of indications.

In all the countries of Eastern Europe the relative importance of agriculture, energy, and resource-intensive sectors suggests that an improvement in the terms of trade would benefit growth. Accordingly, a real devaluation in an effect to make manufacturers more competitive in world markets could have adverse effects on long-term growth. It would be more appropriate, rather, to

Table 8.1 Revealed comparative advantages of European countries

	Science based	*Scale intensive*	*Specialized suppliers*	*Tradi-tional*	*Agricul-ture*	*Resource intensive*	*Energy*
Germany	+	+	+	–	–	–	–
UK	+	+	+	–	–	–	+
France	+	+	+	–	+	–	–
Italy	–	–	+	+	+	–	–
Spain, Portugal, Greece	–	–	–	+	+	–	–
Czechoslovakia	–	+	–	+	–	+	–
Hungary	–	–	–	+	+	+	–
Poland	–	–	–	+	+	+	+
Former USSR	–	–	–	–	–	+	+

Source: adapted from Guerrieri and Mastropasqua, 1992.

seek to improve competitiveness in the manufacturing sector by increasing the pace of technological innovation, which can be achieved by technology imports. From this standpoint, a crucial role could be played by western foreign direct investment, an issue to which we shall return. In some cases, moreover – Czechoslovakia is an example – the possibility of an enlargement of markets will be important insofar as it allows exploiting the comparative advantage associated with economies of scale.

If we turn to the position of the EC economies a number of relevant elements appear. In the first place the comparative advantages of the three largest economies Germany, the UK and France are located in the sectors where the comparative disadvantages of Eastern Europe lie, and vice versa. From this point of view these two groups of countries are in a highly favourable position as far as the process of integration is concerned. The comparative advantage that these three countries enjoy in the science-based sector suggest that these countries are in the position to produce and export the technology Eastern Europe needs to upgrade its competitive position, while they would become importers of the goods for which Eastern Europe enjoys a comparative advantage.

There are of course relevant exceptions to this optimistic scenario. France appears to have a comparative advantage in agriculture, while the UK has one in the energy sector. This could create problems to a 'smooth' integration process in Europe.

Moreover, problems do exist if we turn to the position of Italy and the group of southern members of the European Community, Greece, Portugal and Spain. Their comparative advantage lies in the traditional and agricultural sectors, and also in the specialized suppliers in the case of Italy.

In summary, this overall picture suggests that the integration of Eastern Europe into the European Community is far from being a painless task. Adjustments will have to be made from both 'sides' of Europe. The problem is that as the situation stands today, the distribution of costs and benefits is far from symmetrical.

In the following sections we will take a closer look at this issue.

8.4 INTEGRATION AS A CLUB PROBLEM

In this section we will use a simple model of club formation to consider the problem of the possible enlargement of the EC to include members from Eastern Europe (see De Benedictis and Padoan, 1992 for a more extensive treatment). The model we start from is a version of that introduced by Fratianni and Pattison (1982) to explain the formation of international organizations.

The model assumes that costs and benefits are a function of the size of the club (Q) which can be thought of as the extension of the common 'trade regime', i.e. the rules and institutions which govern trade relations of the club members among themselves.

As is usual in club theory we will assume rising marginal costs and declining marginal benefits with club size. Marginal costs are increasing with the extension of the club good provided because of congestion arising with an increasing number of members. In addition, as Fratianni and Pattison (1982), stress, decision theory suggests that the addition of new members will raise the costs of finding agreements in a more than proportional manner. Costs will also rise more than proportionally for organizational reasons and because of political reasons each new member will have to be given equal opportunity, irrespective of its economic size, to express its viewpoint (Ward, 1991). Institutional arrangements alter the behaviour of costs. For example a shift from a unanimity rule to a majority rule in decision making within the club lowers marginal costs. Marginal benefits are decreasing because of rising congestion determined by the enlarged membership.

We start from the assumption that the actual situation, i.e. European Community with 12 (*EC*12) members is a club equilibrium. This means that $MC=MB$. It is easy to justify this assumption considering otherwise. If $MB<MC$ then the club is too large. In such a case there would be obviously no incentive for the European Community to accept new membership. If $MB>MC$ then the club is too small and, therefore, new members would be seen as beneficial from the Community's point of view. The basic idea is that *EC*12 and *EC*12 plus *EE* are two different clubs and that the latter is not just an extension of the former. (Obviously, by *EC*12 we intend the actual configuration of developed, market economies; the same line of reasoning will still be valid, should the European Community include one more Scandinavian country or Austria.)

The incentives for *EC*12 to launch the Single Market Programme (on the incentives to promote the Single Market Programme see Cameron 1990, and Moravcsik, 1991) were rather different from those that are now being advanced to build a 'Great Integrated Europe'. To use the political scientists' jargon, 'setting the agenda' for Europe 1992 is quite a different matter from 'setting the agenda' for the integration of the former CMEA members into the European Community.

To consider how we move from *EC*12 to *EC*12 plus *EE* recall that the decision of the former members of CMEA to pursue a programme of transition to a market system and integration with the West represents both a great opportunity and a great challenge for the industrialized countries. The opportunity lies in the additional market that *EE* would represent for industrialized countries. The challenge lies in the large costs that *EE* have to face in order to accomplish full market integration.

Both the opportunity and the costs can be represented graphically as follows (Figure 8.1). Point *A* is the intersection of the *MB* and *MC* curves which defines

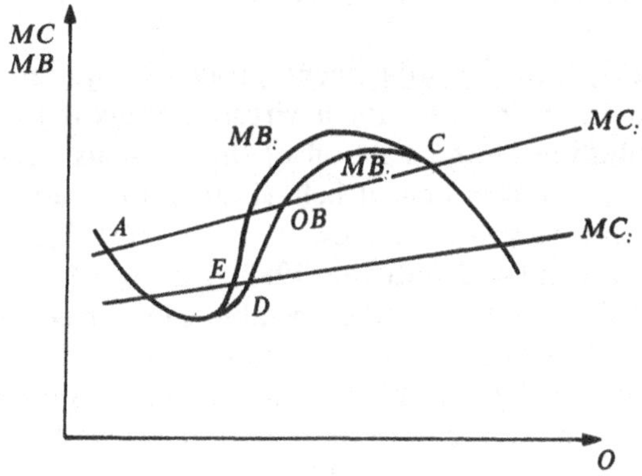

Figure 8.1 Costs and benefits of integration

the initial equilibrium point, *EC*12. A further enlargement would initially produce still decreasing *MB* while marginal costs keep rising. Costs would increase because new membership, even if at partial conditions such as forms of association (Mastropasqua and Rolli, 1992), would increase the amount of negotiation required both with the new members and within the original twelve. At the beginning of the process, therefore, there are no obvious incentives for club enlargement as $MB<MC$. At higher levels of *Q*, however, as a consequence of enlarged membership and hence larger markets, marginal benefits for the club members start to rise and eventually become larger than marginal costs. Benefits would eventually increase – after what can be thought of as a transition phase – if we accept the previous assumption that the inclusion of Eastern Europe within the Community represents a great opportunity in terms of market exploitation and, more generally, because of the benefits of a larger integrated area for all participants.

MB and *MC* equalize at point *B* which, however, is not a stable equilibrium. To the right of point *B* increasing *MB* generate rising incentives to expand the club, i.e. to admit new members and to complete their market liberalization process. After a while congestion becomes important again, *MB* start to decrease until point *C* is reached and the new club 'Greater Europe' is formed.

The crucial region is obviously the one included between *A* and *B*. In this region $MB<MC$ and hence in this region there is no incentive to expand the club while there are incentives to return to point *A*. The region between points *A* and *B* represents the situation of initial adjustment and can be thought of as the present state of things; the economies of the Eastern European countries, much less that of the former Soviet Union, are such that their immediate European Community membership is definitely out of the question.

8.5 CLUB ENLARGEMENT PROBLEMS FOR EAST AND WEST

Figure 8.1 indicates that the adjustment problem requires that club size be pushed beyond point *B* in order for a virtuous process to start and lead to point *C*. A contribution to the start-off of the virtuous circle can come both from a change in cost and in benefit behaviour in the club.

The *MC* curve can be shifted downward (into *MC*2) by, e.g., a loosening of the voting rule (Fratianni and Pattison, 1982), passing e.g. from a unanimity to a majority rule. This would move the unstable equilibrium point from *B* to *D* thus narrowing the dimension of the transition region. The *MB* curve can be shifted upwards (into *MB*2) by an acceleration and/or an improvement of the market liberalization process and of the access to the western market. The shift would further move the unstable equilibrium point to the right, into *E*.

This latter effect can be obtained essentially by two, mutually reinforcing, actions. From the 'east side' effective transition programmes will make the economies of Eastern Europe more like the western ones. From the 'west side' a decisive thrust towards greater liberalization would produce the same effect.

We shall deal with the second aspect in the next paragraph. Here let us consider a simple point about the first aspect. One of the most debated topics in the discussion about the characteristics of the stabilization and adjustment programmes suitable for formerly planned economies is the controversy between shock therapy and gradualism. In this respect Daviddi and Manasse (1992) suggest that the incentive for the (Eastern European) policy maker to implement a credible shock therapy programme increases with the cost of reneging the programme he announces. Such a cost, in turn, has both a fixed and a variable component. While the latter is dependent on the characteristics of the domestic economy, the former can be thought of as the cost of 'international reputation'. Much as in the case of the European Monetary System, 'weak' or 'undisciplined' economies can implement costly adjustment policies thanks to the discipline they import from the outside environment. It can be argued that future Community membership could play such a role in that Eastern Economies will not be granted full access to Western European markets unless their domestic stabilization programmes are carried out. The higher the expected gains of full EC membership the higher are the incentives of the Eastern European policy makers to complete the adjustment programmes.

What is relevant from our point of view is that such a disciplined effect increases the benefits of club membership for all the members, including the present ones, as far as it raises the speed at which eastern economies increase their capacity to absorb western exports.

A substantial obstacle to the enlargement, however, would probably come – as we have already mentioned – from the uneven distribution of costs and benefits for the present members of the European Community. This point is particularly relevant if one considers that the weaker members of the

Community are presently facing two other 'institutional shocks'; the completion of the single market programme and the transition to a fully fixed exchange rate regime (whether in the form of monetary union or 'hard EMS').

The effects of these shocks would produce cumulative pressure on the 'southern' members of the community. To see this in a very simple and impressionistic way consider Figure 8.2.

Assume two countries, both members of the EC: North (*N*) and South (*S*). Given the overall dimension of the EC market – the size of the box – the dotted vertical line separates national markets. In the presence of increasing returns if each country were to exploit only its domestic market for sheer reason of size, country *N* would be able to produce at a lower cost with respect to *S*. The cost differential, *AB*, in the absence of barriers to factor mobility would make production location profitable in *N* for firms operating at the European level. However a barrier of amount *T* (Figure 8.2a) such as to offset the cost differential would maintain a location incentive in *S*. The Single Market can be thought of as the elimination of a barrier needed to offset such a cost differential (Krugman, 1990).

Consider now *S* credibly entering an exchange agreement (Figure 8.2b). As is well known (Branson, 1990; Krugman, 1990), in such a case the currency of the 'weak' country would experience a nominal and, subsequently, real appreciation. This would shift the *S* cost curve upwards, to *S'*, as costs expressed in *N'S* currency increase. The cost differential would rise to *BC*.

Let us now introduce the enlargement effect (Figure 8.2c) and assume that the increase in market size benefits only the North. This is not an unrealistic assumption – even though an extreme one – given the available empirical evidence (Collins and Rodrik, 1991; Guerrieri and Mastropasqua, 1992). The dimension of the market increases and the *N* cost curve shifts to *N'* bringing the cost differential to *DC*.

Clearly the only way in which the South could resist such a combined pressure would be through a massive restructuring process (perhaps also through the support of some form of horizontal industrial policy aimed at improving locational advantages) such as to shift its curve cost down – as in Figure 8.2d – thus narrowing the cost gap. Lacking this, one can easily see that the Southern members of the Community, assuming their loyal commitment to the Single Market programme and to (some form of) monetary integration, would find good reasons for an opposition to a rapid accession of the Eastern European economies to the EC.

Up to now the policy of the European Community in favour of Eastern Europe has apparently followed quite a liberal approach (De Benedictis-Padoan, 1992 and Mastropasqua and Rolli, 1992 for a discussion). An asymmetric opening-up policy in favour of Eastern Europe has been adopted and applied to all sectors, with the relevant exceptions, however, of agriculture, textiles, and, partially, steel; i.e. some of the sectors where Eastern Europe holds its comparative advantage.

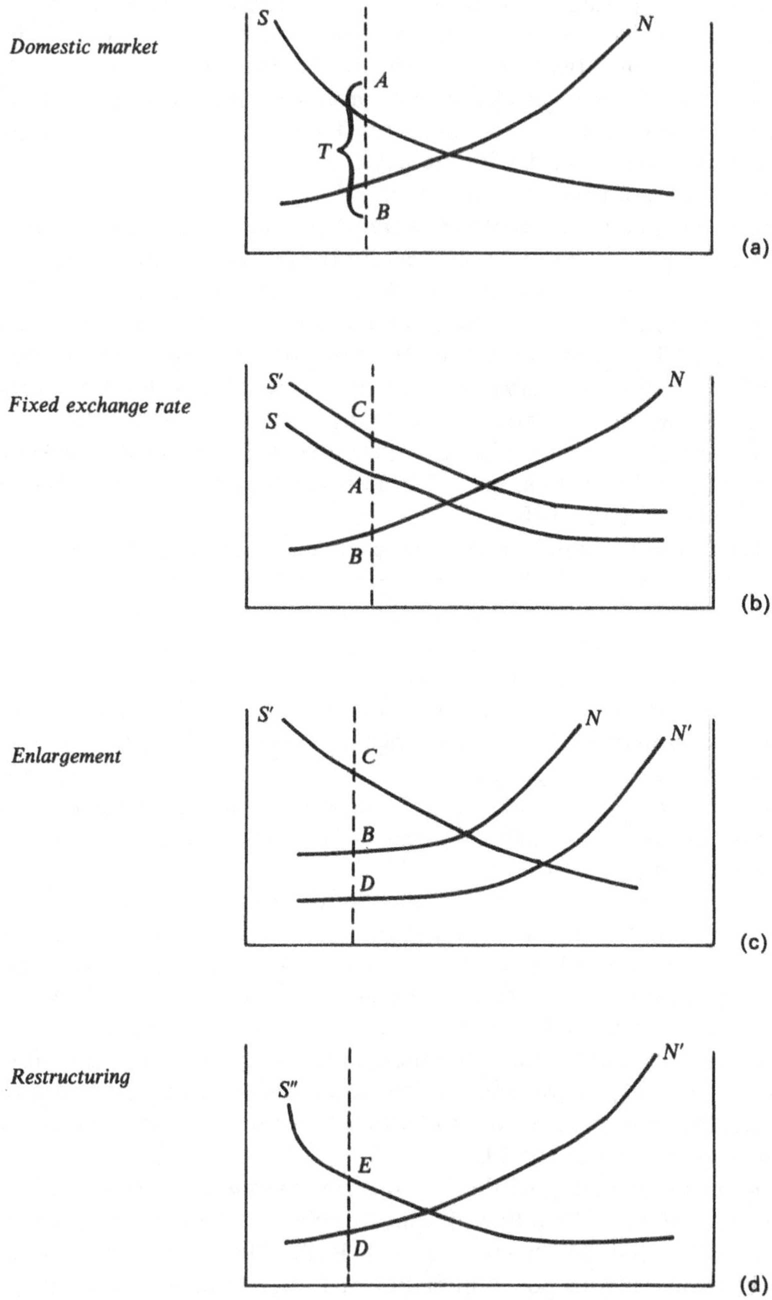

Figure 8.2 Single market and integration: (a) Domestic market; (b) Fixed exchange rate; (c) Enlargement; (d) Restructuring

From this point of view sectoral and national resistance within the Community still stands in the way of a full and smooth enlargement of the club.

8.6 POLICY CONDITIONS FOR A VIRTUOUS CIRCLE

The previous discussion suggests that the elements of a strategy aimed at securing a successful process of integration of Eastern Europe will have to include proper consideration for economic peculiarities and interests of at least four geographical areas: Northern regions in the European Community which are clearly favourable to integration (given their relatively large capital and technological endowment conducive to specialization in scale-intensive activities). Southern regions in the European Community which may resist the required domestic restructuring to compete in the enlarged market, labour-abundant and technology-starving regions in Eastern Europe which are unable to bear the adjustment costs in the short run, and resource-abundant regions in the East which are eager to trade their underground wealth for industrial diversification and economic development in the long run.

Clearly, a thorough assessment of all the implications for a detailed policy design would be beyond the scope of this paper. Here, we attempt to sketch some relevant elements of an integration strategy, drawing also from Bollino and Padoan (1992). Such a strategy should be based on three main building blocks.

1. In order to accelerate the 'widening' process – i.e. the formation of a new 'European club' – strengthening and deepening of the Community must be pursued. Given the asymmetrical distribution of costs and benefits between present European Community members, the Community, directly or through some form of concerted action – a topic we cannot develop further – should secure that resources be devoted to sustain restructuring processes in those countries and regions of the Community which are likely to be hit most severely by the new competitive pressures. In this respect the role of 'structural funds' should be both strengthened and reconsidered within a framework of a Community industrial policy.
2. Eastern European countries should further strengthen their comparative advantages in the sectors (traditional, agricultural, resource intensive, energy intensive) where these lie. To this purpose they should first try to increase the acquisition of technology from the industrialized economies. As far as this point is concerned we support the view, often suggested in the literature, that diffusion of technology in Eastern Europe must be based on a robust flow of western foreign direct investment for which the appropriate incentives must be generated. Evidence already exists (Viesti, 1992) that western direct investment flowing into Eastern Europe is concentrated in those sectors in which the host countries enjoy a comparative advantage.

To strengthen this trend by making investment location more profitable a crucial role will be played by domestic stabilization progrmmes in Eastern Europe (Maugeri and Savarese, 1992), the success of which, in turn, is not marginally influenced by the attitude that the European Community will assume towards enlargement.

3. In addition, Eastern European countries should stabilize their terms of trade with long-term structural policies, clearly much more far-sighted, and therefore wisely complementary, with respect to the existing exchange rate stabilization plans. We envisage that an active policy aimed at exploiting the comparative advantage in the energy sector in Eastern Europe should be started. The remaining section of the paper is devoted to developing this point in more detail.

Although we are aware of the risk of indulging in a pro-energy sector bias, we consider it crucial for the process of economic integration that natural resources, such as energy, and the related resource intensive activities, be developed through an active industrial policy intervention. Of course, an infant-industry argument may be invoked to justify, at least in the short term, the nurturing of the revamping effort of the former Soviet oil and gas industry.

In any case, it seems worthwhile to pursue this line of reasoning, perhaps broadening the view to possible second best intervention, which we may call a trade diversion argument revisited. Therefore, let us consider the problem of policy intervention in favour of energy trade developments between the European Community and Eastern Europe, notably the CIS.

Clearly, at the prevailing international market conditions, the equilibrium level of energy imported by the European Community from the CIS reflects the diversification strategy of the European Community, as a function of price, uncertainty and risk associated with the region, and future expectations of new developments. In turn, new capacity development in the CIS is a function, among others, of future expectations on price and demand potential of the European Community.

A policy which can change such conditions may improve upon existing trade relations.

Consider a cooperation agreement, perhaps in the context of the new *European Energy Charter*, which is centered around the principle of long-term indexation of energy price exported from the CIS to the EC to the export price of manufactures of the EC to the CIS. It is obvious that the partial stabilization of the relative price between energy and manufactures may contribute to halt the negative impact of deteriorating terms of trade on growth rate, as argued in the previous discussion concerning equation (8.1).

There will be four positive consequences. First, the reduction in uncertainty will spur foreign investment in the CIS, both for exploration and production of energy (oil and gas), and for new manufacturing activities.

This view is reflected in the contributions of the theoretical section of our research, dealing with the explanation of strategic motivation of the firm which undertakes foreign investment (Motta, 1992). Firms will not only seek to exploit existing cost advantages, but will attempt to actively modify their market power, through acquisitions, mergers and defensive investments to prevent new entrants. Therefore, a long-term commitment (such as the mechanism of real energy price stabilization sketched above) may reinforce the firms' perception of new strategic opportunities, characterized by a reduction in uncertainty and risk. A follow-the-leader approach (in order to avoid exclusion from the new market), could probably result in a massive investment flow of western firms. The final result will undoubtedly be an increase in productive capacity in the energy sector.

Second, there will be trade creation because stable energy export revenues will allow Eastern countries to increase their level of manufactured imports from the West.

Third, the diversification of European Community energy imports will presumably increase the share of Eastern Europe as a stable and reliable supplier. This means that a new geographical diversification pattern of European Community energy imports may result in significant changes in competition among energy suppliers. On the one hand, an increasing importance of Eastern Europe as an energy exporter could conflict with the Middle Eastern area, generating higher variability and instability. On the other hand, a more balanced market influence of these regions may result in higher competition and lower rental cost for the European Community consumer. Most likely, the final outcome will depend on the relative degree of specialization of each supplying area in different energy sources.

Fourth, the relative mix of European Community imports between oil and gas will probably shift in favour of the latter, given the availability of reserves in Eastern area and future trends in EC energy demand. It is in this sense that we envisage a virtuous scenario of stable market relationship, where European Community additional gas requirements will be satisfied mostly by Eastern supplies, while oil requirements will continue to be predominantly satisfied by the Middle East. This scenario has two implications; first it will improve the environmental situation in Europe and, second it will also leave more oil available worldwide to satisfy the emerging needs of developing countries. In this scenario, a sustainable development of LDC's industrial base will become more and more feasible, because the fierce competition between LDCs and industrialized countries for a scarce resource, the existing oil, will be relaxed. Furthermore, it is rather superfluous to add that higher growth potential for LDCs may feed back into world trade and industrialized countries' output growth.

In this sense, the diverted development of gas resulting from a club-type agreement between the European Community and Eastern Europe may be beneficial for the world market as a whole.

8.7 A FURTHER SUGGESTION: ENERGY AS THE FUEL OF INTEGRATION

We would like to touch upon the implications of a new integration pattern in Europe for the adequacy of financial supply in the short and medium term for Eastern Europe.

We recall that from a microeconomic viewpoint, using the terminology of the life cycle model of consumer behaviour, there may be cases in which a country is faced with liquidity constraints, in the sense that the existence of capital market imperfections induce a higher saving rate with respect to situations without such imperfections, because life cycle consumption-smoothing is limited. Given the relationship of equality between the saving rate and the growth rate times the capital-output ratio which holds for a closed economy with liquidity constraint, at the beginning of the transition process, Eastern Europe may suffer from a reduction in the saving rate.

This is so because Eastern Europe, with the existing obsolete capital stock, may experience a consequent reduction in productivity generated by the incipient opening-up of trade.

Thus, the typical Eastern economy is caught in the trap of insufficient saving to maintain the previous high level of capital-output ratio, which may feed back into a lower growth rate, which generates even lower saving. Therefore, relaxing such liquidity constraint will allow a more efficient intertemporal resource allocation, i.e. larger possibilities to borrow against higher future income streams, providing a positive influence on growth.

Turning to a macroeconomic viewpoint, the discussion of the relationship between liquidity constraint and savings highlights the difficulties of attracting foreign capital when low productivity and low growth potential tend to shift resources to finance import of consumption goods, therefore conflicting with the balance of payment constraint (for a discussion in terms of the balance of payments stages hypothesis see Manzocchi, 1992). Once more, removal of capital market imperfections, within the country, may allow a better resource allocation internationally, paving the way for foreign direct investment.

A policy aimed at reducing market imperfections, such as excessive uncertainty associated with specific commodity export earnings and investment projects, is to reinforce the role of insurance played by international institutions.

There are two related examples, already widely used in the past at the international level: the first is a compensatory fund which can stabilize export earnings of natural resources such as energy resources (oil and gas); the second is a super-insurance fund which provides collateral guarantee for investment in sectors characterized by high risk and long-term profitability.

As far as the compensatory fund is concerned let us recall that the need for a special or complementary facility to assist developing countries with liquidity for shortfalls in their commodity export earnings has been under deliberation in UNCTAD literally since its first session in 1964 and was revamped in 1982, while the International Monetary Fund (IMF) also used such a scheme at the end of the 1970s. The rationale was to alleviate the problem of export shortfall which may impair growth capability of LDCs. Among the justifications set forth in the past of international organizations such as UNCTAD and the IMF, it suffices to indicate that under this scheme drawings from the facility were to be used to finance commodity-related activities intended to stabilize the commodity sector and eradicate the root causes of instability, such as short-term income support in individual commodity sectors and structural adjustment in cases of chronic oversupply or undersupply. Access to the facility was seen as conditional on the elaboration of commodity development programmes in which the intended uses of the resources would be specified and mutually agreed upon between the applicant country and the facility.

Obviously, with such a volatile historical price record, oil is unlikely to be considered a commodity deserving a compensatory financing facility: funds of any amount would be dried up in a short period of time in case of crisis, without real benefits and possibly with the undesired consequence of rewarding speculative behaviour.

A different approach, still aiming at stabilizing terms of trade between the European Community and Eastern Europe, could be based on the idea of long-term indexation of the prices of energy exported from, say, CIS to the European Community to a basket of prices of manufactures exported from the European Community to CIS. Let us stress that according to this project, the players would not be simply an exporting country and a financial fund managed by an international institution (as in the IMF experience), but there shall come into play three actors; an oil exporting country, a manufacturer's exporting country and a financial fund, managed by an international institution.

In this case, it is obvious that in every commercial contract negotiated under this rule, whether we consider a gas supply, whose price is indexed to that of manufactures exported from the European Community to CIS or an industrial good supply, whose price is indexed to the gas price exported from CIS to the European Community, there is a built-in stabilizing mechanism in real terms.

The operational details are not important, here it suffices to establish the principle that even if only a fraction of CIS oil exports could be transacted under this scheme this would represent a sizeable amount. In fact, recall that before the crisis Soviet oil export level was around 2 million barrels/day, and equivalent to $13 billion (at an approximate today's price of $18/barrel), while actual exports have declined by almost 30%, mainly as a consequence of declining productive capacity lacking adequate capital investment.

Thus, consider the possibility of restoring productive capacity to previous levels, arranging, say, 15% of total revenues under this long term indexation scheme: it shall generate approximately an annual flow of $2 billion in real terms, available for development of long-term trade relationships. This is not negligible if it is compared to the total of $6 billion envisaged each year by the plan of the G7 and the international institution whose total amounts to $18 billion in 3 years (Table 8.2).

Table 8.2 Former Soviet Union oil export and revenues

	Annual flows
Oil, exports in million barrels/day (before crisis)	2.0
Oil revenues valued at $18/barrel	$13.0 billion
Long-term contract indexation: (15% of total revenues)	$2.0 billion
memo:	
G-7 plus international institutions' stabilization plan, per year	$6.0 billion

Notice that according to this scheme, the role of a compensatory fund managed by an international institution would be no different from that of an insurance fund, therefore requiring less financial resources than a trade financing facility. In principle, in the best of circumstances, there is no cost to the fund (or to the developed countries' governments which would have to back it), if the indexation of trade flows is full. Otherwise, any financing requirement to cover the residual risks could be met with an escrow account (with the banking sector) or a government contingent fund (set aside in the government budget of financing countries).

As far as the super insurance fund is concerned, the previous discussion is equally valid in this case, if the fund is aimed at fostering investment in capital-intensive industries, say, the energy exploration and production, or refining and distribution. In fact, the amount of financial resources required to cover the burden of high risk and deferred profitability associated with such investment projects could be optimally drawn from a super-insurance fund backed by international institutions or by all governments of involved countries. Obviously, once the fraction of total risk associated with the intrinsic characteristics of energy market uncertainty is covered, financing of investment will flow from private enterprises and banking institutions according to prevailing international financial markets conditions.

In conclusion, we would like to stress that a strategic policy designed to foster market developments in Eastern Europe's energy sector could be beneficial for the whole process of integration, if it is able to stabilize East–West terms of trade. Starting from where there are comparative advantages makes sense: energy endowments in the CIS may very well represent the fuel for the whole integration process.

Backed by a stabilization or an insurance-type scheme, direct investment may start to flow to CIS energy sector. The result will be an optimal allocation of resources to the energy sector, higher productive capacity and higher energy exports revenues. These will, in turn, finance capital investment and, therefore, a positive contribution to the growth rate of the Eastern European economies' output shall be achieved via increased availability of foreign capital and technology for the Eastern countries.

REFERENCES

Bollino, C. A. and Manca, S. (1992) Il settore energetico nella nuova Europa, in *Il circolo virtuoso trilaterale. Commercio e flussi finanziari in un Europa* (eds C. A. Bollino and P. C. Padoan), il Mulino, Bologna, 229–56.

Bollino, C. A. and Padoan, P. C. (eds) (1992) *Il circulo virtuoso trilaterale. Commercio e flussi finanziari in un Europa*, il Mulino, Bologna.

Branson, W. (1990) Financial market integration, macroeconomic policy and the EMS, in *Unity with Diversity in the European Economy* (eds C. Bliss and J. Braga de Macedo), Cambridge University Press, Cambridge.

Cameron, D. (1990) 'Sovereign States in the Single Market: Integration and Intergovernamentalism in the European Community', presented at the Annual Meeting of the American Political Science Association, San Francisco.

Collins, S. and Roderick, D. (1991) 'Eastern Europe and the Soviet Union in the World Economy', Washington, Institute for International Economics, Policy Analyses, Working Paper, no. 32.

Daviddi, R. and Manasse, P. (1992) Esiste una contrapposizione tra 'big bang' e gradualismo? Lezioni dalle esperienze polacca e ungherese, in *Il circolo virtuoso trilaterale. Commercio e flussi finanziari in un Europa* (eds C. A. Bollino and P. C. Padoan), il Mulino, Bologna, 371–96.

De Benedictis, L. and Padoan, P. C. (1992) L'integrazione dei paesi dell'est nella Comunità europea. Un approccio in termini di teoria dei club a di gruppi di interesse, in *Il circolo virtuosa trilaterale. Commercio e flussi finanziari in un Europa* (eds C. A. Bollino and P. C. Padoan), il Mulino, Bologna, 501–32.

Dosi, G., Pavitt, K. and Soete, L. (1990) *The Economics of Technical Change and International Trade*, New York University Press, New York.

Faberberg, J. (1988) 'International Competitiveness.' *Economic Journal*, **98**, 355–74.

Fratianni, M. and Pattison, J. (1982) 'The economics of international organizations'. *Kyklos*, **35**.

Guerrieri, P. and Mastropasqua, C. (1992) Competitività specializzazione e prospettive di integrazione commerciale dei paesi dell'est europeo, in *Il circolo virtuosa trilaterale. Commercio e flussi finanziari in un Europa* (eds C. A. Bollino and P. C. Padoan), il Mulino, Bologna, 257–306.

Krugman, P. (1990) 'Macroeconomic Adjustment and Entry into the EC. A Note', in Bliss, C. (eds) Braga de Macedo, J.: *Unity with Diversity in the European Economy*, Cambridge, Cambridge University Press, 1990.

Krugman, P. (1992) *Integration Specialization and Regional Growth: Notes on 1992, Emu and Stabilization*, mimeo.

Manzocchi, S. (1992) Integrazione economica e fasi della bilancia dei pagamenti. Implicazioni per i paesi dell'est europeo, in *Il circolo virtuoso trilaterale. Commercio e flussi finanziari in un Europa* (eds C. A. Bollino and P. C. Padoan), il Mulino, Bologna, 149–66.

Mastropasqua, C. and Rolli, V. (1992) Il protezionismo dei paesi industrializzati verso l'Europa dell'est. Effetti dell'accordo di associazione della Cee sulle esportazioni di Polonia, Cecoslovacchia e Ungheria, in *Il circolo virtuoso trilaterale. Commercio e flussi finanziari in un Europa* (eds C. A. Bollino and P. C. Padoan), il Mulino, Bologna, 447–78.

Maugeri, M. and Savarese, E. (1992) Aspetti monetari e finanziari della transizione al mercato della Csi, in *Il circolo virtuoso trilaterale. Commercio e flussi finanziari in un Europa* (eds C. A. Bollino and P. C. Padoan), il Mulino, Bologna, 397–445.

Moravcsik, A.: 'Negotiating the Single European Act: National Interests and Conventional Stratecraft in European Community', *International Organization*, vol. 45, Winter 1991.

Motta, M. (1992) Le motivazioni oligopolistiche e strategiche degli investimenti all'estero, in *Il circolo virtuoso trilaterale. Commercio e flussi finanziari in un Europa* (eds C. A. Bollino and P. C. Padoan), il Mulino, Bologna, 83–120.

Nuti, D. M. (1991) Lezioni dei programmi di stabilizzazione dei Paesi dell'Europea centrale e orientale, 1989–91, *Note economiche*, **XXI** (3).

Padoan, P. C. (1992) Competitività crescita e bilancia dei pagamenti. Considerazioni sull'equilibrio di lungo periodo, in *Il circolo virtuoso trilaterale. Commercio e flussi finanziari in un Europa* (eds C. A. Bollino and P. C. Padoan), il Mulino, Bologna, 167–85.

Pavitt, K.: 'Sectoral Patterns of Technical Change. Towards a Taxonomy and a Theory', *Research Policy*, vol. 13, 1984, 343-73.

Schiatterella, R. (1992) Impresa multinazionale e commercio intraziendale nella Nuova teoria del commercio internazionale, in *Il circolo virtuoso trilaterale. Commercio e flussi finanziari in un Europa* (eds C. A. Bollino and P. C. Padoan), il Mulino, Bologna, 121–48.

Viesti, G. (1992) L'internazionalizzazione dell'industria e dei servizi, in *Il circolo virtuoso trilaterale. Commercio e flussi finanziari in un Europa* (eds C. A. Bollino and P. C. Padoan), il Mulino, Bologna, 307–30.

Ward, V.: 'Understanding Cooperative Agreements: the Impact of Differing Objectives on Club Formation Behaviour', presented at the *Annual Meeting of the American Political Science Association*, Washington (DC), August 1991.

APPENDIX A – GROWTH, COMPETITIVENESS AND BALANCE OF PAYMENTS

In this appendix we develop the relationship between the rate of growth of output and the determinants of international competitiveness mentioned in the text. A more articulated discussion can be found in Padoan (1992).

Starting from current account equilibrium

$$PxX = PmZM \tag{8.A.1}$$

where: Px is the price of exports, X their quantity, Pm the price of imports in foreign currency, M the quantity of imports, Z the exchange rate. Calling W foreign demand, and Y domestic output we can write

$$WPxX/W = YPmZM/Y$$

and, calling $SX = X/W$ the export share and $SM = M/Y$ the import share we define the 'equilibrium' level of output

$$Y^* = WPxSX/PmZSM \tag{8.A.2}$$

taking logs (small letters)

$$y^* = px + w + sx - pm - z - sm \tag{8.A.3}$$

Taking the time derivative of (8.A.3) we obtain (eq. 8.1) in the text, assuming a fixed exchange rate. To obtain the relationship between the equilibrium growth rate (i.e. the rate of growth consistent with balance of payments equilibrium) we first consider a model where each of the elements in (8.A.3) is expressed in terms of disequilibrium dynamic equations. We then compute the steady state values of output as a function of the determinants of both the terms of trade and of the trade shares. The equations of the model are as follows. D is the derivative with respect to time.

$$Dy = a_1(y^* - y) \text{ output adjustment (policy reaction function)} \tag{8.A.4}$$

$$Dsx = a_2(sx^* - sx) \text{ export share} \tag{8.A.5}$$

$$sx^* = b_a + b_1(pwz - px) + b_2(t - tw) \tag{8.A.6}$$

$$Dpx = a_3(px^* - px) \text{ export price}$$

$$px^* = b_b + b_3 pw + b_4 z + b_5 v$$

$$Dt = a_4(t^* - t) + b_7 tw \text{ stock of 'technology'} \tag{8.A.7}$$

$$t^* = b_c + b_6 f$$

$$Dsm = a_5(sm^* - sm) \text{ import share} \tag{8.A.8}$$

$$sm^* = b_d + b_8(p - pw - z) - b_9(t - tw)$$

$$Dz = a_6(z^* - z) \text{ exchange rate} \tag{8.A.9}$$

$$z^* = b_e + b_{10} Dy + \cdots$$

$$Df = a_7(f^* - f) \text{ investment in R\&D} \tag{8.A.10}$$

$$f^* = b_f + b_{11}(px - v)$$

Taking derivatives with respect to time of equation (8.A.3) we obtain (8.A.11), which is equivalent to equation (8.1) in the text, assuming that the exchange rate is fixed.

$$r_1 = j_2 + (r_2 - j_1) + (r_2 - r_5) \tag{8.A.11}$$

Substituting for the growth rates of the exogenous variables in equations (A.4)–(A.10) we obtain:

$$r_1 = j_2 + [(b_5 j_3 - j_1)] + (b_1 + b_8)[(j_1 - b_5 j_3)] + (b_2 + b_9)[b_6 b_{11}(b_5 j_3 - j_3) + \\ + (b_7 j_4 / a_4 - j_4)] \tag{8.A.12}$$

Equation (8.A.12) says that, given the rate of growth of foreign demand and the relevant elasticities, the equilibrium rate of growth increases with: an improvement in the terms of trade (first bracket), an improvement in price

Table 8.A.1 Variables and growth rates

Endogenous variables	
$y = y^* + r_1\tau$	output
$sx = sx^* + r_2\tau$	export share
$px = px^* + r_3\tau$	export price
$t = t^* + r_4\tau$	stock of technology
$sm = sm^* + r_5\tau$	import share
$z = z^* + r_6\tau$	exchange rate
$f = f^* + r_7\tau$	expenditure in R&D
Exogenous variables	
$pw = pw^* + j_1\tau$	foreign price
$w = w^* + j_2\tau$	foreign demand
$v = v^* + j_3\tau$	nominal domestic wage
$tw = tw^* + j_4\tau$	stock of foreign technology

*indicates initial values, τ is time.

competitiveness (second bracket), an improvement in technological competitiveness (third bracket) itself determined by domestic innovative activity and/or by international diffusion. The amount of domestically produced 'technology' depends on the amount of R&D expenditure out of profits and on the rate of success of the latter.

9

Exchange rate regime and central bank independence in a small volatile economy: the case of Iceland

M. Gudmundsson

9.1 INTRODUCTION

This paper is concerned with the factors that affect the choice of exchange rate and monetary regimes in Iceland. Iceland is a small open economy with a resource-based export sector. As such it has characteristics that give conflicting indications for the choice of an exchange rate regime. The choice of an exchange rate regime is not only conditioned by the structural characteristics of the economy. The parameters set by structural policies and the legal and political framework for monetary policy is also of importance. Financial liberalization, both internal and external, affects the exchange rate regime and the conduct of exchange rate policy and so does the Central Bank legislation and the relations between the Central Bank and other organs of economic policy making, especially the government. These issues will, therefore, be considered in this paper.

The paper is organized as follows. First, I look at those structural characteristics of the Icelandic economy that are important for the choice of an exchange rate regime, such as the degree of openness of the economy, external mobility of labour and real and nominal wage flexibility. Second, I examine specifically the nature of shocks and fluctuations affecting the Icelandic economy and compare them with those affecting other industrial countries. Third, I consider the issue of economic convergence towards EC and EFTA-countries. Fourth, I discuss financial liberalization, and fifth, I consider the issue of central bank independence. Finally, I put the pieces together and discuss the choice of exchange rate regime for the Icelandic economy.

The European Single Market – Monetary and Fiscal Policy Harmonization.
Edited by H.M. Scobie. Published in 1994 by Chapman & Hall,
London. ISBN 0 412 57520 5

9.2 STRUCTURAL CHARACTERISTICS

It seems to apply among the OECD-countries, that the smaller an economy is the more open it is. Although the Icelandic economy is more open than many OECD-countries, it is not as open as many would think *a priori* given how small it is. Table 9.1 gives exports of goods and services as a percentage of GDP during 1985–9. It shows that there are several OECD-countries more open than Iceland and some considerably more so. The reason for this is probably that Iceland's export industries are not as highly integrated with other economies as many small European economies are. Iceland's exports are based on the use of domestic resources to a high degree in contrast to many small European countries that have a higher share of exports of manufactured goods that are often based on the processing of imported intermediate manufactured goods. That 'throughput' is much lower in Iceland's case. (I owe observations in this paragraph to Krugman (1991). He points out that Iceland is a clear outlier on a plot for OECD-countries of the size of population and the share of exports of goods and services in GDP.)

Table 9.1 Exports of goods and services as a percentage of GDP (average for 1985–1989)

Iceland	37.4
Finland	25.9
Norway	39.8
Sweden	33.1
Netherlands	56.6
Ireland	60.9
West Germany	30.4
EC	28.1
US	8.1
Japan	11.7
OECD	17.7

Source: OECD: Historical Statistics 1960–89.

The predominance of the fishing industry in exports is an important structural feature of the Icelandic economy. Marine products account for nearly 80% of merchandise exports. In this sense Iceland is probably closer than many other OECD-countries to being specialized in production and generalized in consumption. Two factors have to be borne in mind though. First, the fishing industry is very diversified in terms of species, modes of processing and markets. It is also very dynamic in terms of shifting supply between markets on the basis of changes in conditions. Second, the price supply elasticity of the industry as a whole is rather low as changes in relative prices will not increase fish stocks or total allowable catches. (Gudmundsson, M. 1992).

External labour mobility has not been on such a scale that it can be counted on to make the adjustment to external shocks on its own. During the economic recession of 1968–70, which was the deepest in Iceland's post-war history, around 1.7% of the population emigrated, mostly to other Nordic countries. Unemployment increased considerably in spite of this, two large devaluations took place and other adjustment measures were undertaken. External labour mobility seems to be limited by the relatively high standard of living and social and cultural factors. Iceland's participation in the EEA (European Economic Area) might though increase external labour mobility.

Real wage flexibility has been higher in Iceland than in most other OECD-countries (OECD, 1991). (During the period 1970–87 the standard deviation of real wages in Iceland was 2.14 times that of output. Only Portugal had greater variability of real wages and the value for most OECD-countries was around or below 1.) This flexibility is partly the result of the accommodating exchange rate policy that up until few years ago was followed in Iceland, which was to keep the nominal exchange rate fixed during the upturn and devalue on the downturn. Real wages were thereore cut during recessions through devaluations. This cut was always accepted in the end by the population. Real wage resistance did therefore not make inflation explosive. The existence of wage contracts containing indexation of wages did not stop this process from working as wage indexation was either abandoned or weakened by agreements or legislation if recessions made that necessary in order to ensure that nominal devaluations were turned into real devaluations and not dissipated completely in a higher inflation rate.

This policy worked reasonably well in adjusting the real side of the economy to external shocks and in keeping unemployment low. The problem was its inflationary bias. The argument has also been made that it had harmful effects on long-term growth, as the export industries were too strongly insulated from external shocks and did therefore not make necessary internal adjustments. This policy was therefore abandoned and resistance to the use of devaluations grew. The longest period of exchange rate stability of the króna since the early seventies lasted from December 1989 to 23 November 1992, when the króna was devalued by 6% in the wake of the turmoil in European foreign exchange markets. This exchange rate stability played a major role in bringing the inflation rate in Iceland down below the average for OECD countries.

In a low inflation environment the kind of real wage flexibility that has been the case in Iceland in the past, requires flexibility of nominal wages. There is no Icelandic experience to indicate that such a flexibility will be forthcoming and experience from other countries indicates that it will probably not. If Iceland is to live in a low inflation environment in the future, as should be the aim, then real wage flexibility will very probably be much lower than in the past. Real wage flexibility will therefore not play the same role in adjusting the economy to external shocks as in the past.

9.3 SHOCKS AND FLUCTUATIONS

The nature of shocks and fluctuations is one of the more important elements affecting the choice of an exchange rate regime. Economic fluctuations in Iceland are generally more pronounced than in other OECD countries. Iceland is subject to external shocks not faced by other industrial countries, such as falling fish catches, whereas others are common, such as oil price increases. This can cause problems for a fixed exchange rate policy. It seems that external shocks and fluctuations in the economy have become less severe than in the past and the mechanisms to absorb them without recourse to the exchange rate have become stronger. The reasons for this are among others a more efficient fisheries management system, specific stabilization schemes that have until recently been operated for the fishing industry, a more stabilizing tax system, and monetary reforms in recent years.

Tables 9.2–9.6 give various statistics on shocks and fluctuations affecting the Icelandic economy in comparison to other industrial countries. Table 9.2 shows the annual growth and standard deviation of GDP per capita during 1952–89. Iceland has the highest standard deviation among these countries. Table 9.3 gives a measure of the trend in the variability of GDP per capita for the same period and countries. Variability is here measured by the absolute value of the error term from the regression of GDP per capita growth on trend. Variability of GDP per capita growth seems to have been falling significantly

Table 9.2 Average annual growth and standard deviation of GDP per capita (1952–89)

	Growth (%)	*S.D.* (%)
Iceland	2.82	4.93
Austria	3.78	2.31
Denmark	2.58	2.35
France	3.20	1.69
Germany[a]	3.63	3.08
Japan	5.61	3.26
Netherlands	2.97	3.54
Norway	3.23	1.67
Sweden	2.59	1.66
Switzerland	2.23	2.55
UK	2.25	1.98
US	1.73	2.35

[a]Germany in this and following tables refers to West Germany.

Source: Gudmundur Gudmundsson and Magnús Harðarson (1992). Fluctuations in GDP and exports and comparisons with other countries (in Icelandic). *Fjármálatíðindi* **1**, 60–76.

Table 9.3 The trend in variability of GDP per capita (1952–1989)

	Trend	*t-value*	*DW*
Iceland	−0.099	−2.5+	1.9
Austria	−0.019	−1.2	2.2
Denmark	−0.012	−0.7	1.8
France	−0.009	−0.7	1.8
Germany	−0.030	−1.0	2.3
Japan	−0.057	−2.2+	1.7
Netherlands	−0.045	−1.2	2.1
Norway	0.007	0.5	2.5
Sweden	−0.006	−0.5	2.0
Switzerland	−0.009	−0.3	2.1
UK	0.009	0.5	1.7
US	−0.017	−0.8	2.2

Note: The trend value is 100^*b_1, where b_1 is a coefficient from the regression:

$$|e(t)| = bo + b_1{}^*t + u(t),$$

where $|e(t)|$ is the absolute value of the error term from the regression of GDP per capita growth on trend,
t is time,
bo and b_1 are coefficients
and u is an error term
+t-value significant at the 95% level.

Source: Gudmundur G. and Harðarson M. (1992) Fluctuations in GDP and exports and comparisons with other countries (in Icelandic). *Fjármálatíðindi*, 1, 60–76.

in Iceland and Japan during this period whereas the trend is insignificant for other countries.

The fluctuations in GDP are the products of both the external shocks affecting the economy and the domestic adjustment to those shocks. Fluctuations in merchandise exports in terms of import unit values can be considered a rough measure of external shocks, at least for a small open economy as Iceland. It is a product of the terms of trade and the volume of exports, and would in Iceland's case be dominated by changes in fish catches and the terms of trade. Table 9.4 shows the standard deviation from average growth in this series for Iceland and several other industrial countries during the periods 1961–90 and 1976–90. It also shows the simple correlation coefficient with the average for the industrial countries. It demonstrates that Iceland has the highest standard deviation in the first period, and among the highest in the second period. The correlation with industrial countries is significant in both periods but only just so in the second one. Table 9.5 gives a more sophisticated measure of the correlation with the industrial country average using methods of spectral analysis. It shows a significant correlation

Table 9.4 Standard deviation of the growth in merchandise exports in terms of import unit values and correlations with average for industrial countries (annual data)

	1961–90		*1976–90*	
	S.D.	*r*	*S.D.*	*r*
Iceland	0.143	0.528	0.108	0.479
Industrial countries	0.045	1.000	0.040	1.000
Denmark	0.045	0.618	0.032	0.292
Finland	0.057	0.659	0.040	0.472
France	0.053	0.870	0.042	0.870
Germany	0.056	0.838	0.051	0.806
Ireland	0.070	0.541	0.058	0.447
Japan	0.108	0.723	0.119	0.663
Netherlands	0.052	0.801	0.038	0.620
New Zealand	0.120	0.639	0.070	0.468
Norway	0.084	0.067	0.104	−0.392
Portugal	0.101	0.275	0.097	−0.183
Sweden	0.046	0.790	0.044	0.622
UK	0.041	0.253	0.038	−0.033
US	0.061	0.711	0.066	0.703

S.D. = Standard deviation.
r = The simple correlation coefficient.

for Iceland in most frequencies but lower than for many other small industrial countries. Figure 9.1 shows the series for industrial countries on average, Iceland and other Nordic EFTA-countries. It demonstrates clearly the bigger fluctuations in the case of Iceland. Table 9.6 shows the trend in the variability of merchandise exports in terms of import unit values. Variability is measured by the absolute value of the error from the regression of growth in the series on trend. The table shows a fall in the variability in the period for Iceland, although an insignificant one.

9.4 CONVERGENCE

The European currencies will have predominance in any currency peg for the Icelandic króna due to the high share of foreign trade with Europe. In 1992 just over three quarters of merchandise exports went to and nearly three quarters of merchandise imports came from the EC and EFTA-countries. The Icelandic króna is currently pegged to a currency basket composed of 76% of the ECU, 18% of the US-dollar and 6% of the Japanese yen. It was an official policy to consider going over to a full ECU-linking in 1993, but those plans have now been shelved in the aftermath of the currency turmoil in Europe in the autumn of 1992. It is, however, interesting to see how Iceland measures up to the economic convergence criteria that have been widely used recently following the draft Maastricht Treaty.

Table 9.5 The cross coherence between changes in merchandise exports in terms of import unit values in individual countries and industrial countries as a whole 1961–90 (annual data)

	$C(f)$*										
	Frequency = Number of cycles in 30 years										
	3	4	5	6	7	8	9	10	11	12	13
Iceland	0.299	0.368	0.513	0.680	0.563	0.567	0.619	0.530	0.412	0.667	0.438
Denmark	0.668	0.610	0.714	0.848	0.863	0.814	0.835	0.814	0.793	0.696	0.352
France	0.935	0.908	0.861	0.871	0.793	0.755	0.788	0.890	0.845	0.901	0.736
Germany	0.935	0.839	0.852	0.581	0.486	0.442	0.632	0.737	0.829	0.795	0.750
Ireland	0.670	0.627	0.651	0.614	0.486	0.421	0.540	0.310	0.185	0.240	0.145
Japan	0.942	0.825	0.792	0.688	0.573	0.201	0.293	0.294	0.321	0.308	0.671
Netherlands	0.791	0.631	0.530	0.640	0.686	0.686	0.648	0.624	0.690	0.719	0.690
New Zealand	0.362	0.580	0.688	0.806	0.908	0.914	0.808	0.635	0.592	0.531	0.534
Norway	0.059	0.054	0.106	0.119	0.393	0.298	0.455	0.241	0.058	0.047	0.010
Portugal	0.122	0.328	0.739	0.590	0.500	0.418	0.394	0.182	0.554	0.506	0.330
Sweden	0.650	0.437	0.407	0.691	0.710	0.716	0.777	0.840	0.895	0.815	0.786
UK	0.323	0.328	0.339	0.456	0.259	0.141	0.081	0.071	0.056	0.040	0.167
US	0.546	0.635	0.592	0.583	0.525	0.614	0.681	0.804	0.779	0.902	0.866

*$C(f)$ bigger than around 0.52 is significant at the 90% level.

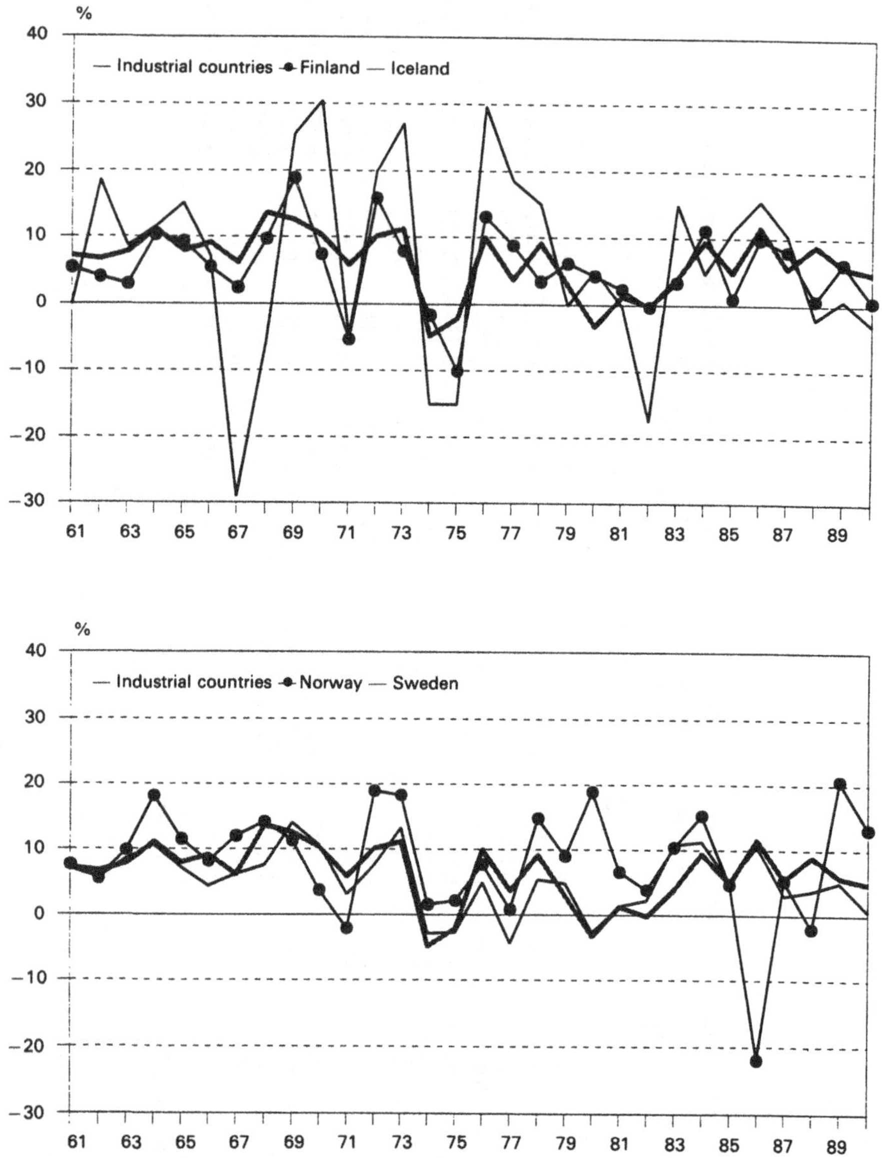

Figure 9.1 Merchandise exports in terms of import unit values (percentage change)

Figure 9.2 gives some of the measures of economic convergence in the Maastricht Treaty for Iceland and the EC and the Nordic-EFTA excluding Iceland. In 1992 Iceland fulfilled the Maastricht criteria on the general government deficit, public debt, inflation and the long-term nominal interest rate. Iceland is not a member of the EMS, but the criteria on exchange rate stability would not be fulfilled anyway as Iceland devalued by 6% on 23

Table 9.6 The trend in variability of merchandise exports in terms of import unit values (1961–90)

	Trend	*t-value*	*D.W.*
Iceland	−0.202	−1.07	1.66
Industrial countries	0.036	0.62	1.55
Denmark	−0.040	−0.65	2.02
Finland	−0.022	−0.28	1.57
France	−0.040	−0.57	1.52
Germany	0.064	0.89	1.51
Ireland	−0.094	−1.02	1.86
Japan	0.075	0.54	2.08
Netherlands	−0.039	−0.70	1.53
New Zealand	−0.222	−1.26	0.89[b]
Norway	0.218	1.83[a]	2.68
Portugal	0.040	0.28	1.48
Sweden	0.040	0.63	2.02
UK	0.039	0.80	2.02
US	0.122	1.41	2.14

Note: The trendvalue is 100*bl, where bl is a coefficient from the regression:

$$|e(t)| = b0 + b1 * t + u(t),$$

where $|e(t)|$ is the absolute value of the error term from the regression of the growth of merchandise exports in terms of import unit values on time trend.

t is time,
$b0$ and $b1$ are coefficients,
and u is an error term.

[a] t-value significant at the 90% level.
[b] Significant autocorrelation at the 5% level.

November 1992 and again by 7.5% on 28 June 1993. The fact that Iceland fulfils the other Maastricht criteria for economic convergence can say as much about these criteria as Iceland. The public debt figures exclude government guarantees and other contingent liabilities, which are widespread in Iceland. The government is also involved in the credit market through government owned financial institutions. Real interest rates have been high in Iceland, partly as a result of the strong expansion of borrowing by firms and households with government guarantees. These high real interest rates indicate imbalances that can have consequences for a stable exchange rate policy if not addressed in time.

9.5 FINANCIAL LIBERALIZATION

Financial liberalization began later in Iceland than in many industrial countries. The process of financial liberalization has followed the theory that correct sequencing and gradualism is important in order to avoid instability. The liberalization of the domestic credit market started well before the gradual

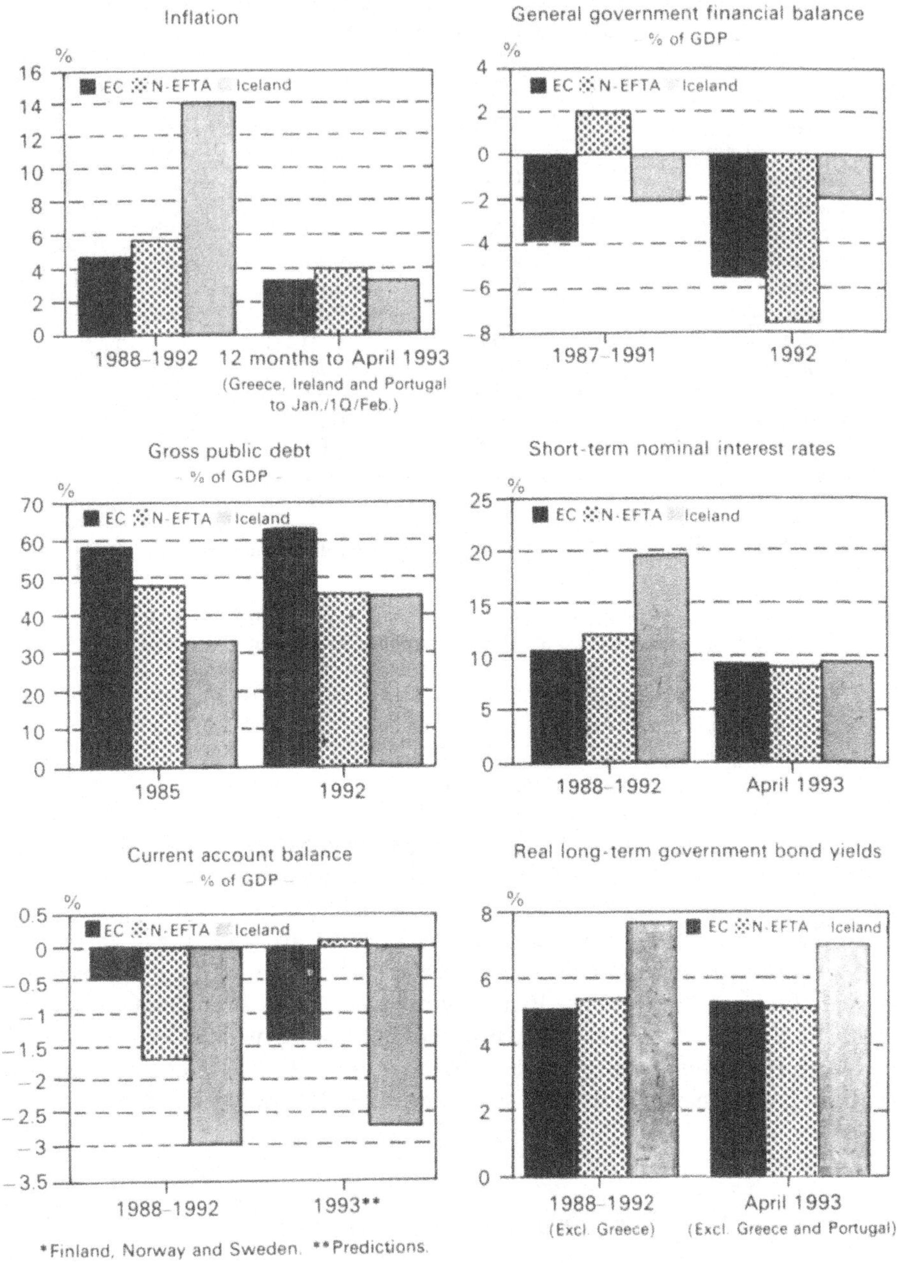

Figure 9.2 Economic convergence EC, N-EFTA* and Iceland (weighted by 1900 purchasing power parity GDP)

liberalization of capital movements. The banks were allowed to set their own interest rates late in 1986 but the Central Bank had for two years before surrendered part of its power to set interest rates to the banks. The liberalization of capital movements did not begin in earnest until the summer of 1990 when it was decided to lift gradually most restrictions on long-term capital movements until the beginning of 1993. Direct investment abroad by Icelandic residents and long-term portfolio investment abroad by residents has been subject to ceilings in the adjustment process, but the final step in lifting the restrictions was postponed from the beginning of 1993 until such time as the EEA-agreement enters into force, or until the end of 1993 at the latest.

A new foreign exchange legislation was adopted by parliament (Althing) in November 1992. It codifies the main rule that all foreign exchange transactions and all capital movements shall be free. Both permanent and temporary exceptions to this rule are then defined in law. These include a general safety clause concerning speculative short-term capital movements, which is a standardized EC-version and conforms with the draft EEA-agreement. Foreign exchange transactions and capital movements linked to foreign direct investment and the acquisition of real estate, that are limited by specific legislation on these matters (investment in fisheries for example), are controlled. The Minister of Commerce can limit short-term capital movements and foreign exchange transactions such as futures, swaps and options that involve the króna, until the end of 1994. The foreign exchange regulation that is based on the new legislation implies that short-term capital movements will be liberalized gradually until the end of 1994. The surrender requirement for foreign currency that existed in Iceland when the law was passed is softened in the regulation and will be finally abolished at the end of 1994. Forward transactions, options and swaps involving the króna are allowed if there is an underlying business risk to hedge against and will become fully liberalized from the beginning of 1995.

There have been no problems so far with the liberalization of capital movements. But domestic financial liberalization was much more abrupt. Real interest rates increased considerably in a short period and a better access by individuals to credit resulted in a considerable increase in their borrowing.

The process of financial liberalization has affected the conduct of exchange rate policy and will do even more so in the future. The price of foreign currencies was until the end of May 1993 quoted by the Central Bank in the morning. The quotations were based on foreign cross-rates in international markets and the desired value of the official currency index. The Bank quoted both buying and selling rates. These rates were then used by the banks in all their transactions with their customers during that day. The banks could place orders with the Central Bank to buy and sell currencies in any amounts at the quoted rates for two hours after the morning quotation. The current balance between supply and demand for foreign exchange had therefore no immediate effect on the exchange rate. This system would have become impossible to manage once all capital movements had been fully liberalized. For that reason and due to the perceived necessity to let market forces have a bigger role to play in the determination of the exchange rate, an organized inter-bank market for foreign currency began to operate in Iceland at the end of May 1993.

The introduction of the inter-bank market for foreign currency did as such not imply a basic change in the exchange rate policy. The implementation of the policy did though change, as the króna will be allowed to fluctuate within a band of ±2.25%. It will be the role of the Central Bank to keep the exchange rate within the band with interventions in the foreign exchange market and the use of its monetary policy instruments. The króna was devalued by 7.5% at the end of June 1993, but the band width was kept unchanged.

9.6 CENTRAL BANK INDEPENDENCE

The Icelandic central bank is on many criteria rather dependent. It has many and contradictory goals. The use of some of its monetary policy instruments needs consent from a minister or the government. The Treasury has had access to central bank financing within the year, but a new agreement between the Bank and the Treasury limited that access in the middle of 1992 and closed it from the beginning of 1993. It is rather more independent concerning its own finances and it does not have the same duty to report to parliament or the government as in many other countries. It has on occasions had a strong influence on the formulation of economic policy in general and its directors tend to sit for long periods.

Given the methodology used by Starck (1992), which is adopted from Swinburne and Castello-Branco (1991), the Central Bank of Iceland is between the Bank of Japan and the Bank of England in its degree of independence, as can be seen from Figure 9.3. The method is based on ranking certain attributes of central banks on the scale of 1–5, where a higher value indicates more independence. These attributes relate to the mandate of the central bank to formulate and implement monetary policy, its goals, the terms of appointments of its directors and governors, its independence in deciding its own budget and its obligations to report to government and the public. These attributes are then weighted into a single measure using the weights of 0.45 for mandate, 0.05 for goals, 0.2 for the terms of appointments, 0.2 for lending to government, 0.05 for own finances and 0.05 for reporting. This measure is of course very rough and can only be interpreted to give broad indications.

A new draft legislation on the Central Bank has been put before parliament. The draft implies a considerable increase in the degree of independence. The Bank will have a clear goal to keep the value of the currency stable. Its independence in formulating and implementing monetary policy will increase considerably. A consent from the minister or the government will no longer be needed in applying the instruments of monetary policy. The government will,

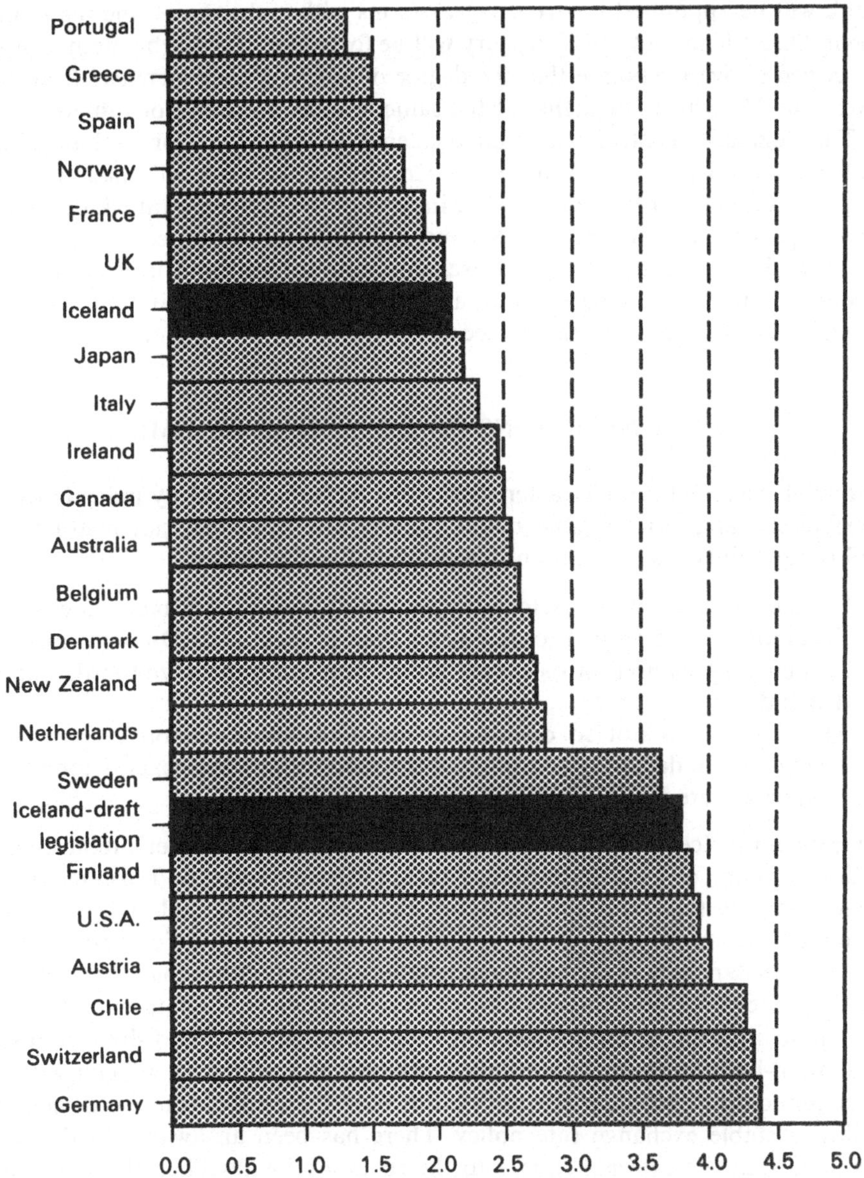

Source: Starck (1992). Own calculations for Iceland.

Figure 9.3 The degree of central bank independence

though, have the final word on the exchange rate regime. The directors of the bank will be appointed for fixed 7-year terms with a change of one reappointment. Direct lending to the Treasury will be forbidden. Using the methodology described above I estimate that the degree of independence increases from just over 2 to 3.8, which is roughly at the same level as the Bank of Finland.

The degree of central bank independence is important for exchange rate policy in two ways. First, a more independent central bank will make it easier to provide a credible nominal anchor instead of the exchange rate if a policy of an independent float is adopted. Second, a more independent central bank will increase the credibility of a fixed exchange rate or the band in a target zone system. It can therefore be said that a more independent central bank increases the degrees of freedom in the choice of an exchange rate regime.

9.7 CONSLUSIONS ON EXCHANGE REGIME

Many of the structural characteristics of the Icelandic economy indicate that a flexible exchange rate regime might be optimal. Here one can mention the following points that have been demonstrated in this paper:

- Iceland is faced with asymmetric external shocks and real shocks and fluctuations have tended to be greater than in most OECD-countries.
- Iceland is specialized in its export production and generalized in its import demand.
- The economy is not so open as to make the microeconomic costs from exchange rate flexibility too big and the macroeconomic benefits too small.
- Real wages are flexible in the face of external shocks.

In spite of this Icelandic governments have for several years been attempting to follow a policy of a stable exchange rate. There are very good arguments for that policy. Without a stable exchange rate the economy will lack a credible nominal anchor in the present circumstances. It is very difficult to define a stable monetary rule in a small open volatile economy other than the exchange rate. The devaluation strategy followed in the past had an inflationary bias and had possibly also harmful effects on long-term growth. The fishing industry had an in-built tendency to overinvest, which was made more difficult with an accommodating exchange rate policy. For both these reasons it was decided to follow a stable exchange rate policy. There has been an awareness that this required that the external shocks to the economy be absorbed through other channels than the exchange rate. It was also hoped that the external shocks themselves had been reduced in size in recent years. There is some evidence to corroborate that view.

Although Icelandic governments have been attempting to follow a stable exchange rate policy, they have not always been successful. Fixed-exchange rate policies have periodically collapsed due to the combination of external shocks and internal demand pressures. The clearest episode of that nature in recent years took place in 1988. But the turmoil on European foreign exchange markets in the autumn of 1992 and external shocks to the economy have recently thrown the fixed exchange rate policy off course as the króna was devalued in November 1992 and then again in June 1993. This experience indicates that the Icelandic authorities have *de facto* resolved the contradiction between the need for a flexible rate due to the characteristics of the real side of the economy and the need for a stable exchange rate to provide a nominal anchor and an intermediary goal for monetary policy, by following an adjustable peg regime for the Icelandic króna. The challenge is how to prevent an adjustable peg from developing into an accommodating exchange rate policy.

A target zone system, where short-term flexibility of the exchange rate can be combined with long-term stability, could also help in solving the above mentioned contradiction. This alternative has though until recently been closed to Iceland due to the lack of an organized inter-bank market for foreign exchange. It is now opening up as a real alternative with the ongoing process of financial liberalization. The plans for a more independent central bank will, if realized, make the operation of such a target zone system more credible than was possible in the past.

REFERENCES

Gudmundsson, G. and Hardarson, M. (1992) Fluctuations in GDP and exports and comparisons with other countries. (in Icelandic). *Fjármálatidindi* (Economic journal published by the Central Bank of Iceland) **1**, 60–76.

Gudmundsson, M. (1992) Export supply and the exchange rate: The case of a small open economy with a natural resource based export sector, in *Economic Policy Co-ordination in an Integrating Europe*, (eds H. Motamen-Scobie and C. C. Starck), Bank of Finland, Helsinki, 203–17.

Krugman, P. (1991) Iceland's exchange rate regime: policy options. (Published in Icelandic), *Fjámálatíðindi*, **3**, 175–85.

OECD (1991) *Economic Surveys: Iceland 1990/1991.*

Starck, C. (1992) The independence of central banks (in Swedish). *Ekonomiska samfundets tidskrift* **2**, 83–95.

Swinburne, Mand Castello-Branco, M. (1991) Central bank independence: issues and experience. *International Monetary Fund Working Paper WP/91/58*, Washington, DC.

10

The twin-debt problem in an interdependent world

R. de Groof and M. van Tuijl

10.1 INTRODUCTION

The reduced supply of and an increasing demand for world savings suggest continuously high interest rates in the years to come. The IMF, OECD and BIS recently expressed their concern about the sustainability of the external deficits in view of the persistent large US external deficit, the substantial German external deficit caused by the unification, the increased demand for savings to finance the restructuring of the Eastern European economies and the environmental policies. This question seems relevant, especially to the US. For, total claims to the limited US savings as represented by the combined financing needs of private domestic investment and the federal budget deficit, points to an awkward situation. The persistence of this 'savings gap' (Corrigan, 1990), accompanied with a growing budget deficit creates a serious twin-deficit-twin-debt problem (Kremers, 1990).

In this paper we examine two rather obvious ways to deal with this problem in a world consisting of two interdependent economies. For that purpose, a two-country perfect foresight model, allowing for intertemporal budget constraints, current account dynamics, wealth effects, capital accumulation, imperfect asset and commodity substitution, floating exchange rates and international factor immobility is formulated. In his study of a related problem within the context of a symmetrical two-country general equilibrium model, Van de Klundert (1991) suggests that international institutional differences concerning wage formation between the two economic regions, might be highly relevant. Therefore, in the search for a more realistic version of the global problem posed by the US savings gap, we take account of various hypotheses with respect to wage formation.

The European Single Market – Monetary and Fiscal Policy Harmonization.
Edited by H.M. Scobie. Published in 1994 by Chapman & Hall,
London. ISBN 0 412 57520 5

There are three ways of dealing with the problem of the savings gap: using the printing press; wait and see or tackle the causes underlying the gap. The awkward situation can produce pressures on the monetary authorities to crank up the printing press. However, money creation does not create savings. The fundamental cause of the external debt, which is the savings gap, cannot be eliminated definitely by inflationary finance. For these reasons we will not explore this alternative. That leaves only two options: either to do nothing or to eliminate the savings gap.

In the case of an unchanged US position, foreign debt would tend to grow infinitely. Eventually the market-place might prove to be quite harsh as it goes about financing the US persistent external deficits. Following Van de Klundert, we will investigate the case in which the share of US assets in foreign portfolios exceeds a critical value. This is supposed to result in a 'financial crisis', which is modelled as an exogenous shift in European asset preferences away from US bonds. This 'policy' of wait and see will result in a reduction of the US external debt. However, the price tag reads: a higher goverment debt and lower consumption for a long time to come. It will be shown, that in the long run this passive attitude would be profitable in terms of external debt as well as consumption and employment. However, it is questionable whether, from the policy makers' point of view, the long run is a relevant time horizon.

There seems to be only one acceptable active way to eliminate the savings gap. A reduction in the rate of investment would be disastrous and one can not expect a rise in the savings ratio to do the job quickly and safely enough. So, nothing seems left but to reduce the budget deficit, which can be achieved by either increasing taxes or by cutting government spending. An increase in taxes does not seem to be an attractive alternative in times of a low growth rate and increasing worldwide competition (Chimerine and Young, 1986 and Knoester and Kolodziejak, 1992). Therefore, we will confine ourselves to the case of a reduction in US government spending. A fiscal contraction in the US, causing a real depreciation of the dollar, turns out to be an efficacious remedy for the twin-deficit, twin-debt-problem. This finding upholds Van de Klundert's (1991) and Branson's (1988) proposition concerning the possibility to restore international equilibrium by means of fiscal policy.

This conclusion is proof against all kinds of variations in the wage equations. The latter is not true with respect to the effects and spillover effects of the shocks mentioned above, measured in terms of real output or consumption. Here, wage formation proves to play a rather dominant role.

The chapter is organized as follows. In section 10.2 the basic model is presented. Its complexity makes an analytical solution intractable. Instead, a comprehensive set of simulations is carried out. Appendix A gives the numerical assumptions with respect to the initial steady state situation. Analytical models sacrifice reality by ruling out several sources of dynamics, in order to keep the analysis manageable. On the other hand, the results of the simulations approach are coefficient specific. To overcome this dilemma, the system has been submitted to extensive sensitivity analysis. Therefore, Appendix B contains the intervals of robustness for all behavioural parameters (Karakitsos, 1989). This sensitivity analysis not only gives insight in the generality of the numerical example, but also in how dispensible or indispensible the various variables are, in connection with the present problem. In section 10.3 we consider the effects and spillover effects of the shocks, brought about by the two alternatives mentioned above. This will be done for the basic case, in which nominal wage rigidity is assumed to prevail in one country and real wage rigidity in the other. In the text, a number of figures is presented which may be of some help to understand the dynamics of the system. In section 10.4, we report on the consequences of variations in the wage equations. These variations concern the type (nominal or real) of wage rigidity, as well as the Phillips mechanism. The latter relates to the traditional versus the so-called 'weak' version of the Phillips mechanism. Section 5 concludes the paper.

10.2 A TWO-COUNTRY MODEL WITH REAL AND NOMINAL WAGE RIGIDITY AND IMPERFECT GOODS AND FINANCIAL ASSETS SUBSTITUTION

In this section we present a symmetric two-country model by focusing on the equations of country j ($j=1,2$); the variables concerning the foreign country contain the subscript k ($k=1,2,\ j\neq k$). Country 1 stands for Europe and country 2 for the US. Except for nominal wage formation, the two countries are identical.

All variables are expressed as percentage deviations from their initial steady-state values. Exceptions are f and t, which are percentage deviations from steady-state output measured in terms of consumption goods, and r and r_n, which are absolute deviations (*100%).

Greek letters denote parameters, which are all defined positively. The parameters ε and φ refer to partial demand elasticities and elasticities of substitution, respectively. For instance, ε_{mr} is the nominal interest rate (r_n) elasticity of the demand for real cash balances (m), and φ_{kl} is the elasticity of substitution between capital (k) and labour (l). The parameter γ refers to a ratio applying to the initial steady state. For instance, γ_{k_b} is the initial steady-state ratio of bonds issued by firms (k) to the total supply of bonds (b). All parameters are defined in Appendix A.

Exogenous variables are barred. The superscript 'e' refers to expectational variables. In order to save space, we present nominal and real exchange rates as country-specific variables. All initial steady state prices are assumed to equal unity.

The portfolio sub-system of the model draws on Van de Klundert (1991). Agents divide their real non-human wealth (we) into real cash balances (m), domestic bonds (b_{jj}) and foreign bonds (b_{jk}). Asset demand decisions depend on the rates of return on bonds, which are determined by the nominal interest rates (r_n) and the expected change in the nominal exchange rate (Δe^e). The real interest rate (r) equals the difference between the nominal interest rate (r_n) and the expected rate of inflation (Δp_c^e)

$$r_j \equiv r_{n_j} - \Delta p_{c_j}^e \qquad (10.1)\text{–}(10.2)$$

The real value of bonds is assumed to be fixed within a period (Haas and Masson, 1986). Bonds are indexed to the consumers' price index (CPI), thus constituting sure claims on given amounts of future consumption goods (baskets). Expectations are assumed to be rational. Furthermore, stochastic components are absent. Therefore, agents have perfect foresight.

Transactions demand for (domestic) real cash balances is supposed to increase with real output in terms of consumption goods ($y+p_y-p_c$), exclusively at the expense of domestic bonds. Moreover, we ignore currency substitution (McKinnon, 1990). Under these assumptions, the demand for the pertinent assets as fractions of real non-human wealth can be written as

$$m_j - we_j = \varepsilon_{m_y}(y_j + p_{y_j} - p_{c_j}) - \varepsilon_{m_j r_j}\left(\frac{r_{n_j}}{\tilde{r}}\right) \qquad (10.3)\text{–}(10.4)$$

$$b_{jj} - we_j = -\varepsilon_{b_{jj}y}(y_j + p_{y_j} - p_{c_j}) + \varepsilon_{b_{jj}r_j}\left(\frac{r_{n_j}}{\tilde{r}}\right)$$

$$-\varepsilon_{b_{jj}r_k}\left(\frac{r_{n_k} + \Delta e_j^e}{\tilde{r}}\right) + \underline{b}_{h_j} \qquad (10.5)\text{–}(10.6)$$

$$b_{jk} + q_{c_j} - we_j = -\varepsilon_{b_{jk}r_j}\left(\frac{r_{n_j}}{\tilde{r}}\right) + \varepsilon_{b_{jk}r_k}\left(\frac{r_{n_j} + \Delta e_j^e}{\tilde{r}}\right)$$

$$-\frac{\gamma_{b_{jj_b}}}{(1-\gamma_{b_{jj_b}})}\underline{b}_{h_j} \qquad (10.7)\text{–}(10.8)$$

where q_{c_j} and $\tilde{r}$ are the real consumption exchange rate (the real consumption exchange rate, $q_{c_j} = p_{c_k} + e_j - p_{c_j}$, will henceforth be indicated by 'real exchange rate' as distinguished from the 'real production exchange rate', which is $q_{y_j} = p_{y_k} + e_j - p_{y_j}$. The nominal exchange rate, e_j, is expressed in currency of country j per unit of currency of country k) applying to country j, and the initial world interest rate, respectively. Since symmetry is assumed in the initial steady state, interest rates are equal across regions. The numerical assumptions with respect to the asset demand functions satisfy the familiar 'adding-up' constraints (Turnovsky, 1977).

The supply of real cash balances equals the difference between exogenous money supply ($\underline{M}$) and the CPI (p_c).

$$m_j = \underline{M}_j - p_{c_j} \qquad (10.9)\text{–}(10.10)$$

Net investment of firms is completely financed by bond issues. It is assumed that all transactions are paid for at the beginning of the period. So, investment goods are bought against today's prices. As a result, the amount of bonds supplied by firms is determined by the real value, in terms of consumption goods, of capital equipment at the beginning of the next period, thus including net investment of that present period. The supply of government bonds equals outstanding government debt (*d*), comprising this period's budget deficit as well. For simplicity, it is assumed that bonds issued by firms and the government are perfect substitutes. Therefore, the supply of domestic bonds (*b*) reads

$$b_{j}=\gamma_{k_b}(k_{+1_j}+p_{y_j}-p_{c_j})+(1-\gamma_{k_b})d_{j} \qquad (10.11)\text{–}(10.12)$$

where p_y denotes the price of home-produced goods.

Equilibrium in the international bond-markets is stated by

$$b_{j}=\gamma_{b_{jj_b}}b_{jj}+(1-\gamma_{b_{jj_b}})b_{kj} \qquad (10.13)\text{–}(10.14)$$

Finally, real wealth of domestic households consists of real domestic and net foreign assets (*f*)

$$we_{j}=\gamma_{m_{we}}m_{j}+(1-\gamma_{m_{we}})b_{j}+\gamma_{we_y}^{-1}f_{j} \qquad (10.15)\text{–}(10.16)$$

where

$$\gamma_{we_y}\equiv\kappa+\gamma_{d_y}+\gamma_{m_y},$$

in which κ is the initial steady-state capital-output ratio. The microunderpinnings of the equations above concerning the portfolio subsystem are no more than rudimentary. In this respect, the commodity expenditure equations show close resemblance, as they lack explicit microfoundations in the form of intertemporal choices made by households and firms as well (as, for example, in Van der Ploeg, 1991). As Van de Klundert (1991) observes, a thorough microeconomic foundation of macroeconomics requires an integration of saving, investment and portfolio decisions. Research in this field is still in its infancy (e.g. Rankin, 1991). Moreover, we agree with Allen (1991), who argues that optimizing models cannot avoid *ad hoc* qualities either, be they of a different nature than non-optimizing models.

Total private consumption (*c*) is split up between consumption of home (c_h) and foreign produced (c_m) goods. First, consumers decide upon total consumption expenditure according to

$$c_{j}=\varepsilon_{cy}(y_{j}+p_{y_j}-p_{c_j}-t_{j})+\varepsilon_{cw}we_{j}-\varepsilon_{cr}\left(\frac{r_{n_j}-\Delta p_{c_j}^{e}}{\tilde{r}}\right) \qquad (10.17)\text{–}(10.18)$$

Thus, total consumption is positively related to purchasing power of nominal output and real non-human wealth of the private sector, whereas it depends negatively on lump-sum taxes (*t*) and the real interest rate (*r*).

Having decided upon total consumption, consumers choose between home (c_d) and foreign (c_m) produced goods and services, by maximizing a CES utility function

$$c_{d_j} = c_j - \varphi_{hm}(p_{yj} - p_{c_j}) \qquad (10.19)–(10.20)$$

$$c_{m_j} = c_j - \varphi_{hm}(p_{y_K} + e - p_{c_j}) \qquad (10.21)–(10.22)$$

The accumulation of capital (k) is described by

$$\Delta k_j = \delta(i_j - k_j) \qquad (10.23)–(10.24)$$

where δ and i denote the rate of depreciation and gross investment, respectively. Firms produce under perfect foresight and maximize the present value of the cash flow. Account is taken of installation costs of newly installed capital. These are assumed to be such, that the costate variable associated with the state variable k, coincides with the average 'Q' or Tobin's Q (Hayashi, 1982). The rate of investment then, is a function of the latter. Under these conditions, the functions with respect to gross investment, the behaviour of Q and the demand for labour (l) are given by the first order conditions, resulting from the application of the maximum principle

$$i_j = k_j + \frac{\alpha}{\delta} Q_j \qquad (10.25)–(10.26)$$

$$Q_{+1_j} = (1 + \tilde{r} + \delta)Q_j + r_{n_j} - \Delta p^e_{y_j} + \frac{\tilde{r} + \delta}{\varphi_{kl}}(k - y) \qquad (10.27)–(10.28)$$

$$l_j = y_j - \varphi_{kl}(w_j - p_{y_j}) \qquad (10.29)–(10.30)$$

where w is the money wage. (Equations (10.27)–(10.28) can easily be checked, by taking the discrete-time form of the Tobin's Q relation derived by Van de Klundert (1993).) Equations (10.27)–(10.28) reflect the above assumption, that firms finance their investment outlays on the domestic market for loans. The term $r_n - \Delta p^e_y$ represent the discount rates, which are relevant for investment, since we assume investment outlays to fall entirely on the domestic sector. The last terms on the right-hand side of equations (10.27)–(10.28) reflect the assumption of linear homogeneous CES production functions, with φ_{kl} representing the elasticity of substitution between capital and labour (l).

Under the assumptions above, the equations for output read

$$y_j = \lambda l_j + (1 - \lambda)k_j \qquad (10.31)–(10.32)$$

Equilibrium in the goods markets is represented by

$$y_j = \gamma_{d_h} c_{h_j} + \gamma_i i_j + \gamma_{g_h} \underline{g}_{h_j} + \gamma_{b_h} c_{m_K} + \gamma_{mg_h} \underline{g}_{m_K} \qquad (10.33)–(10.34)$$

Here $\underline{g}_h$ and $\underline{g}_m$ denote exogenous government expenditure on home and foreign produced goods, respectively.

The labour markets are assumed to be segmented internationally. Furthermore, they do not clear in the short run, due to rigidity of either nominal wages or real consumers' wages. Empirical evidence points, at least for the short and medium term, to a high degree of nominal wage rigidity in the US and real wage rigidity in Europe (Branson and Rotemberg, 1980; Attenasio *et al.*, 1987; Van der Ploeg, 1988). For expositional purposes we assume inertia on the labour market causing (almost) perfect short-run nominal and real wage rigidity in the US and Europe, respectively. According to Attenasio *et al.* (1987), empirical evidence does not reject the existence of an error-correction mechanism in the wage relation, ensuring consumers' wages to return to their long-run equilibrium value. We assume a stylized version of this mechanism to apply, so that nominal wages adapt gradually to the labour market situation (Phillips mechanism), as well as to the development of CPI. So, in the long run unemployment is at its natural rate. As mentioned previously, we investigate the role of wage formation, by modifying the wage equations in a number of ways. Assuming country-specific labour supply to be exogenous, these conditions imply

$$\Delta w_j = (1-\zeta_j)\Delta w_{j_{-1}} + \zeta_j \Delta p_{c_j} + \eta l_j - \eta(1-\zeta_j) l_{j_{-1}} \qquad (10.35)-(10.36)$$

in which ζ and η denote the real wage inertia coefficient and the Phillips coefficient, respectively.

Government outlays, total real government expenditure plus interest payments on outstanding debt, are financed by lump-sum taxes (t), the issue of bonds, or by means of the 'printing press' ($\Delta\underline{M}_j$). The selling of bonds raises government debt, which immediately becomes clear from writing the government budget identity (Buiter, 1986) as

$$d_j = (1+\tilde{r}_j) d_{j_{-1}} + r_j + \gamma_{d_y}^{-1}(g_j - t_j) - \gamma_{m_y}\gamma_{d_y}^{-1}\Delta\underline{M} \qquad (10.37)-(10.38)$$

where g indicates total real government expenditure. Equations (10.37)–(10.38) reflect the above assumption of government bonds being indexed to the CPI. In order to prevent government debt from escalation, we specify a feedback rule for taxes. We choose not to use a feedback rule for government expenditure, because this variable is intended to serve as a policy instrument. A sensible tax rule was introduced by Buiter (1987). Here, it takes the form

$$t_j = \gamma_{d_y}\beta d_j, \quad \beta > \tilde{r} \qquad (10.39)-(10.40)$$

where β denotes the tax rule feedback coefficient.

The real current account surplus of a country (Δf_j), by definition equals the sum of its balance of trade surplus and its capital income account surplus. Under flexible exchange rates, this sum equals the capital account deficit, and, consequently, the increase in country j's net real foreign asset position.

$$\begin{aligned}\Delta f_j = {} & \Phi(r_k - r_j + \Delta q_{c_j}) + \tilde{r}\Phi(q_{c_j} + b_{jk_{-1}} - b_{kj_{-1}}) \\ & + \gamma_{b_h}(c_{m_k} - c_{m_j} - q_{y_j}) + \gamma_{mg_h}(\underline{g}_{m_k} - \underline{g}_{m_j} - q_{y_j}) \\ & + (1-\gamma_{b_{jj_b}})\kappa(\Delta Q^* - \Delta Q) \qquad (10.41)-(10.42)\end{aligned}$$

in which

$$\Phi \equiv (1-\gamma_{b_{jjb}})(\kappa+\gamma_{d_y})$$

and q_{y_j} represents the real production exchange rate.

Evidently, the exchange rates are related as follows

$$e_k = -e_j \tag{10.43}$$

$$q_{c_k} = -q_{c_j} \tag{10.44}$$

The macroeconomic real exchange rate by definition equals

$$q_{c_j} = p_{c_k} + e_j - p_{c_j} \tag{10.45}$$

The presence of both home and foreign produced goods causes the real consumption exchange rate, q_c, to be different from the real production exchange rate, q_y:

$$q_{y_j} = p_{y_k} + e_j - p_{y_j}$$

however, it can be verified that

$$q_{c_j} = (2\gamma_{h_c} - 1)q_{y_j}$$

assuming 'local good preference' ($\gamma_{h_c} > 0.5$), q_{c_j} and q_{y_j} are positively related, so that there is no need to distinguish carefully between these two types of real exchange rates.

The consumers' price index is defined as

$$p_{c_j} \equiv \gamma_{h_c} p_{y_j} + (1-\gamma_{h_c})(p_{y_k} + e_j) = p_{y_j} + (1-\gamma_{h_c})q_{y_j} \tag{10.46)–(10.47}$$

The system is completed by a definitional equation for real government expenditure (in terms of consumption goods)

$$g_j \equiv \gamma_{g_h}(\underline{g}_{h_j} + p_{y_j}) + \gamma_{b_{gh}}(\underline{g}_{m_j} + p_{y_k} + e_j) - (\gamma_{g_h} + \gamma_{b_{gh}})p_{c_j} \tag{10.48)–(10.49}$$

There are 49 equations in 48 endogenous variables; r_n, r, m, b_{jj}, b_{jk}, b, we, c, c_d, c_m, i, Q, y, w, l, k, d, g, t, f, p_c, p_y, e, q_c. Invoking Walras' law, one of the equilibrium equations is redundant. As a result, equation (10.14), which is the condition for equilibrium in the market for foreign bonds, can be eliminated.

The model contains eight backward-looking state variables: k, w, d and f, since these are constrained by their history. The five remaining state variables, p_y, Q and $e_j = e_k^{-1}$ are unconstrained by their past values and are forward-looking. For saddlepoint stability to hold, one should therefore have eight stable roots and five unstable roots.

10.3 TWO ALTERNATIVE ATTITUDES TOWARDS THE US DEFICITS-DEBTS PROBLEM

As mentioned before, two ways of dealing with the twin-deficit-twin-debt problem are studied: to let things take their course, which by assumption leads to a financial crisis, or to cut US government spending. In this section, the international transmission effects of the unanticipated once-and-for-all shocks, connected with these alternatives, will be analysed. This will be done by passing in review the results of numerical exercises. The simulations have been carried out with the PSREM package for policy simulation of linear dynamic models with constant coefficients and rational expectations of future events, developed by Van der Ploeg and Markink (1991). The simulation of similar nonlinear models generally takes a lot of computing time. We have experimented with the full nonlinear model, using the SIMPC package developed by Don Econometrics (1990). It was found to have the same properties as the linear version of the model. To avoid potential computing constraints, we chose to use the linear version. The numerical assumptions, along with the results of the sensitivity analyses, are presented in Appendix A. The consequences of the shocks mentioned above, are shown in Table 10.1.

The first column summarizes the effects and spill-over effects of a preference shift towards European bonds ($\underline{b}_{h_1} = 10$) as a consequence of a financial crisis. So, on impact the demand for European bonds increases at the expense of the demand for US bonds, leading to a fall in the European and a rise in the US real interest rate. As a consequence, US real interest payments and government debt increase (see Figure 10.1a). On the contrary, the US external debt position improves (Figure 10.1b), owing to a real depreciation of the dollar (Figure 10.1c). The latter implies a strengthening of the US competitiveness and, therefore, a significant trade balance surplus. Increased net exports cause an upward pressure on the US producers' price and, because of nominal wage rigidity, a downward pressure on the real producers' wage. So, in the short run, US real output and employment increase. In Europe the fall in the real interest rate boosts private expenditure and, therefore, real output and employment. The required supply-side adjustment comes from a decreased real producers' wage. A real appreciation of the ECU causes European CPI and, hence, the nominal as well as the real producers' wage to fall, while European producers' prices increase.

When describing effects and spillover effects of shocks in the medium run ($t = 4$), one should distinguish carefully between the level and the movement of a variable. The level is represented by the relative deviation of a variable from its initial steady-state value, while the movement is the period-to-period change of this level.

In the present case, the medium-term picture for the US can be sketched as follows. There is a further improvement of the external debt position (Figure 10.1b), notwithstanding a real appreciation of the dollar, as compared with the

Table 10.1 Effects and spillover effects of a financial crisis ($b_{h_1} = 10$) and reductions in US government spending ($g_{d_2} = -10$)

Type of shock		$b_{h_1} = 10$			$g_{d_2} = -10$	
Period	1	4	∞	1	4	∞
Europe						
Real output (y_1)	1.51	1.53	−2.06	0.08	0.04	−0.13
Inflation (Δp_{c_1})	−3.15	1.20	0	0.05	0.04	0
Employment (l_1)	2.16	1.63	0	0.12	0.06	0
consumption domestic goods (c_{d_1})	4.24	4.21	−7.48	0.15	−0.08	−0.65
consumption foreign goods (c_{m_1})	21.69	15.89	−23.04	1.11	0.71	0.18
Real interest rate (r_1)	−0.99	−0.84	0.87	−0.04	−0.00	0.06
Nominal interest rate (r_{n_1})	0.28	0.33	0.87	0.04	0.03	0.06
Government debt (d_1)	−0.62	−1.41	1.80	−0.02	−0.02	0.13
U.S.						
Real output (y_2)	2.01	0.09	2.06	−0.66	−0.34	0.47
Inflation (Δp_{c_2})	3.25	−0.69	0	−0.54	−0.03	0
Employment (l_2)	2.86	0.54	0	−0.95	−0.55	0
consumption domestic goods (c_{d_2})	0.09	−1.73	7.47	0.83	1.52	2.97
consumption foreign goods (c_{m_2})	−17.37	−13.40	23.04	−0.12	0.73	2.15
Real interest rate (r_2)	0.73	0.62	−0.87	−0.16	−0.13	−0.20
Nominal interest rate (r_{n_2})	0.46	0.32	−0.87	−0.18	−0.17	−0.20
Government debt (d_2)	0.44	1.02	−1.80	−1.35	−3.38	−4.54
World						
Real exchange rate ($q_{c_1} = -q_{c_2}$)	−4.19	−2.80	3.73	−0.23	−0.19	−0.20
US foreign debt ($f_1 = -f_2$)	−10.08	−16.46	−86.30	−0.17	−0.39	−2.80

first period (Figure 10.1c). However, a lower, but still high real interest rate causes government debt to rise even further. Production and employment have decreased. The reasons are: a decumulation of capital brought about by crowding out of investment in the past, and an increased real producer's wage,

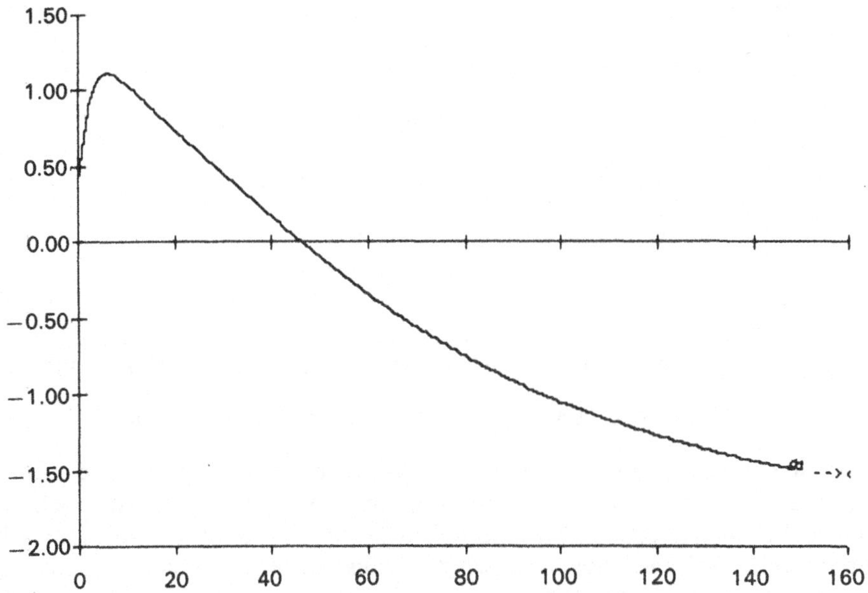

Figure 10.1a Effects of $b_{h_1}=10$ on US government debt

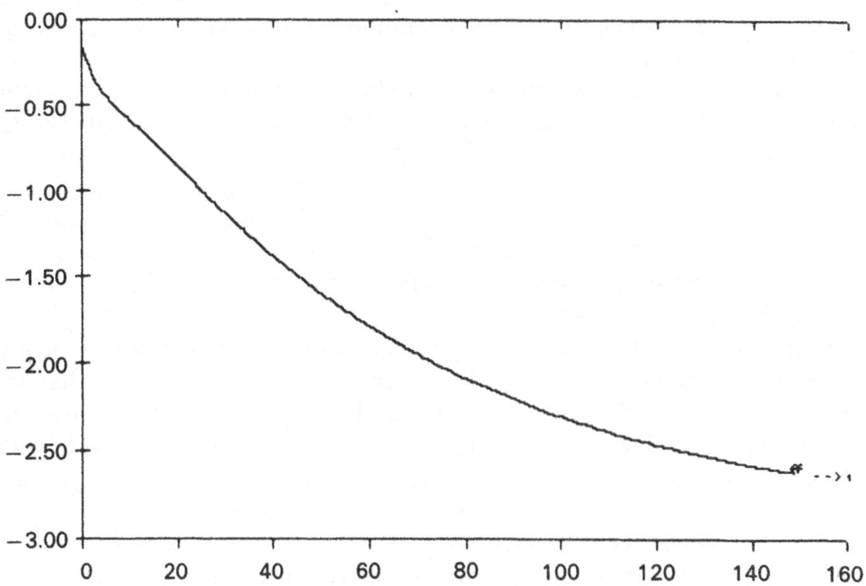

Figure 10.1b Effects of $b_{h_1}=10$ on US external debt

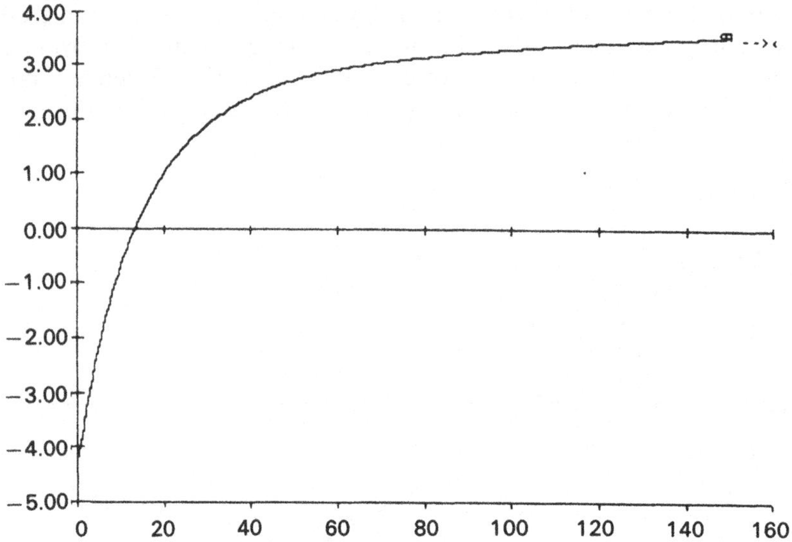

Figure 10.1c Effects of $b_{h_1}=10$ on the real exchange rate

due to a deflationary pressure on the producers' price. The latter comes from a low level of investment and consumption, due to a high real interest rate and a high real exchange rate of the dollar. In Europe, real output is still above its initial level. It has even risen somewhat, because the effect of capital accumulation dominates the effect of the rise in the European real producers' wage. The latter follows from the real depreciation of the ECU (Figure 10.1c), exerting an upward pressure on the CPI and, thus, on money wages, which exceeds the rise in the producers' price.

In the long run, the twin-debt will be reduced at last; both US government and external debt get below their initial values (Figures 10.1a and b). The US acquire a considerable surplus on their capital income account. The reason is, that the real interest rate in Europe has risen fast, choking off excess demand in the goods market. The opposite is true for the US. Europe has to service its long-term external debt by maintaining a trade balance surplus. A real depreciation of the ECU (Figure 10.1c), takes care of the required strengthening of Europe's competitiveness.

The second column of Table 10.1, summarizes the consequences of a cut in US government spending ($\underline{g}_{d_2}=-10$). It can be seen, at a glance, that this policy measure can do the job: it instantly and continually reduces the twin-debt problem (Figures 10.2a and b). The price to be paid for that is lower real output and employment in the short and medium term. On the contrary, US private consumption benefits from this measure continually.

In the short term, the decreased issue of government bonds lowers the real interest rate in the US, boosting domestic private expenditure. Meanwhile, a real depreciation of the dollar (Figure 10.2c) induces an increase in US net exports, leading to a decline in external debt. Nevertheless, on impact, the negative effect of the fiscal contraction on total expenditure dominates. This is accompanied by a rise in the real producers' wage, due to a fall in the producers' price. In Europe, the producers' wage falls because of a real appreciation of the ECU, choking off the increase in CPI and thus in money wages. The budget cut and the connected fall in the interest rate decreases the US government debt.

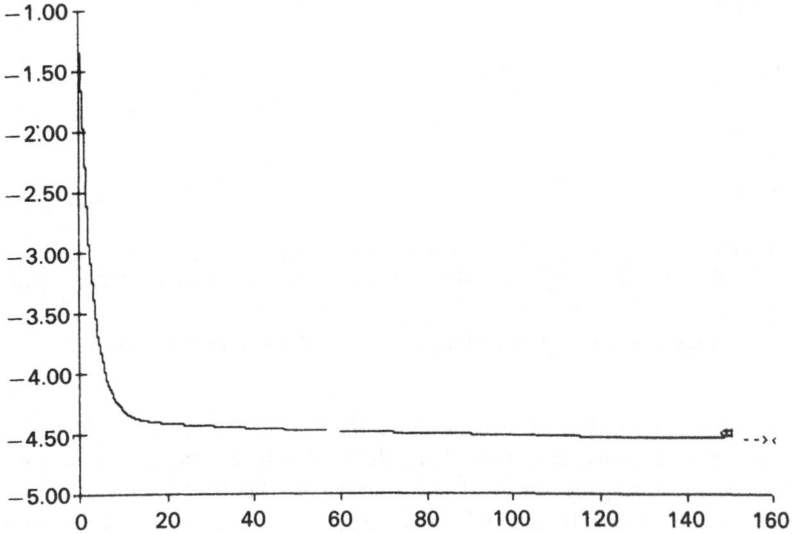

Figure 10.2a Effects of $g_{d_2} = -10$ on US government debt

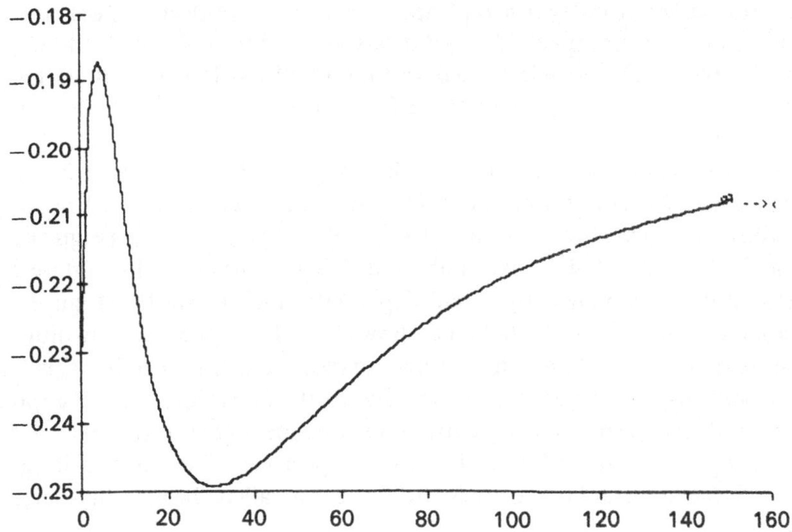

Figure 10.2b Effects of $g_{d_2} = -10$ on US external debt

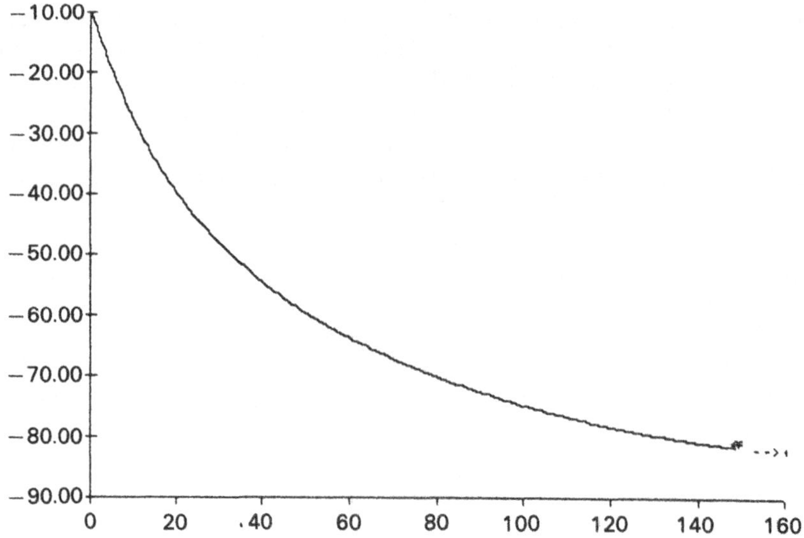

Figure 10.2c Effects of $g_{d_2} = -10$ on the real exchange rate

The US government debt continues to decline in the medium term (Figure 10.2a), in spite of a rise (movement) in the real interest rate. The reasons are, a still low level of the interest rate and the lasting effect of the fiscal contraction. The US external debt also keeps falling (Figure 10.2c), owing to a surplus on the capital income account. To be sure, the surplus on the capital income account has fallen, due to a somewhat less favourable real interest rate differential and a real appreciation of the dollar. Real output in the US increases because of capital accumulation and a decline in the producers' wage. Nevertheless, real output is still below its initial level. In Europe the real depreciation of the ECU causes the CPI and, thus, money wage to rise.

These tendencies are reinforced in the long run by a decrease in the real interest rate in the US and an increase in the real interest rate in Europe. The US government debt falls gradually to a new steady-state level (Figure 10.2a). The same is true for US external debt (Figure 10.2b). This interest rate differential is accompanied by a real depreciation of the dollar (Figure 10.2c). Nevertheless, the US trade balance shows a deficit, due to crowding in of private expenditure. On the other hand, Europe needs this trade balance surplus, in order to service its debt. Crowding in of capital in the US and crowding out of capital in Europe explain the rise and fall in real output in the US and Europe, respectively. So, in the long term the US fiscal contraction proves to be a so-called beggar-thy-neighbour policy.

10.4 THE ROLE OF WAGE FORMATION

The assumption of nominal and real wage rigidity holding for the US and Europe respectively, only partly investigates the role of wage formation in the two regions distinguished.

In this section we give a more complete picture of this role, by summarizing the most important qualitative deviations from the reference situation, caused by alternative assumptions with respect to wage formation. These assumptions not only concern the type of wage rigidity, but the Phillips mechanism as well. As for the latter, apart from the standard specification used in section 10.3, we also take a 'weak' version into consideration. In this weak Phillips mechanism, only a change in the level of unemployment induces *ceteris paribus* changes in the nominal wage rate. (As changes in the labour supply are not taken into consideration here, the two options with respect to the weak Phillips mechanism in literature, i.e. the change in the unemployment rate and the rate of change in employment, do coincide.)

It is found, that the conclusions with respect to the elimination of the twin-debt are untouched by the use of alternative specifications of the wage equations. The same is true with respect to the long-term spillover effects, with the exception of employment. This is because the weak Phillips mechanism permits long-term effects on employment, due to hysteresis.

However, in the short term the spillover effects are effected by the alternative assumptions. Table 10.2 depicts them for the regions' real output. For all

Table 10.2 Short-term deviations from the reference situation (Table 13.1), due to alternative assumptions with respect to wage formation

		b_{h_1}		g_{d_2}	
Europe	*US*	y_1	y_2	y_1	y_2
R/ST	R/ST		—		
R/ST	R/W		—		
R/W	R/ST		—		
R/W	R/W		—		
R/ST	N/W		—		
R/W	N/ST				
R/W	R/W				
N/ST	N/ST	—			
N/ST	N/W	—			
N/W	N/ST	—			
N/W	N/W	—			

Note:
R = Real wage rigidity.
N = Nominal wage rigidity.
ST = Standard version of Phillips mechanism.
W = Weak version of Phillips mechanism.

possible combinations of wage rigidities and Phillips mechanisms, the *qualitative* (signs) deviations from the reference situation (Table 10.1) are presented. The indications R, N, ST and W stand for Real wage rigidity, Nominal wage rigidity, Standard and Weak version of the Phillips mechanism respectively.

Inspection of Table 10.2 shows that the type of wage rigidity is predominant; the type of the Phillips mechanism does not matter. In case of a financial crisis, the US real output shows a fall instead of a rise, if real instead of nominal wage rigidity prevails in the US. The reason is that the real depreciation of the dollar increases CPI causing the US producers' wage to rise. A cut in US government spending decreases instead of increases European real output, if nominal instead of real wage rigidity prevails in Europe. For, the choking off of the increase in CPI, due to the real appreciation of the ECU, will then not be passed through in the money wage.

10.5 CONCLUSION

It has been shown that the US twin-debt can immediately and continually be reduced by a fiscal contraction. In terms of real output, consumption and employment, this measure proves to be a beggar-thyself policy in the short term. In the long term the model does not permit any effect on employment, while in terms of real output as well as real consumption, the cut in government expenditure is a beggar-thy-neighbour policy.

A passive 'policy', resulting in a financial crisis in the form of a preference shift against US bonds, will not bring about a simultaneous reduction of both debt positions in the short or medium term. The best that can be accomplished is a reduction in the external debt at the cost of an increasing government debt. Furthermore, the price of this irresolution is less real consumption for a long time. Only in the long run a simultaneous reduction of the twin-debt will be attained.

Our conclusions with respect to the elimination of the twin-debt are in line with those reached by Van de Klundert (1991). This suggests that the type of wage rigidity is not of overriding importance, at least as far as the twin-debt problem is concerned. Gordon (1988), Garretsen and Lensink (1989) and Van der Ploeg (1992) cast some doubt on whether from 1982, European wage formation can be characterized by real rather than nominal wage rigidity. This raises the question of whether the above conclusion of wage formation being of minor importance, stretches to the situation of nominal wage rigidity in both regions. We showed that such is the case. The same is true for a two-sided real wage rigidity and a one- or two-sided weak Phillips mechanism for that matter. This means that the financial markets dynamics are predominant.

The above results apply within the boundaries, given by the sensitivity analysis of Appendix B. This analysis proves the above conclusions to be fairly robust. The system shows a relative sensitivity to the elasticity of substitution between home and foreign produced consumption goods. In case of a cut in US government expenditure, the long-run zone between the lower boundary and the reference value of this parameter is relatively narrow. A value of this elasticity below its critical value, creates a situation, in which for a large number of years the effect of the real dollar depreciation dominates the effect of the trade flows. The US, therefore, runs a current account deficit, raising its external debt.

An interesting extension of the analysis would be a disaggregation of the model, by allowing for a tradables and a non-tradables sector. There are reasons to presume, that such a disaggregation would make a difference (De Groof and Schaling, 1991; and De Groof and Van Tuijl, 1991). One obvious but probably not the only reason is that in a meso model, the notion 'fiscal contraction' requires further specification. For, a fiscal contraction may fall on tradables or non-tradables, triggering different transmission mechanisms, which may lead to different macroeconomic (spillover) effects. Another point for further research is the extension of the asset menu of the portfolio by allowing for (partial) financing capital investment by the issue of equities.

ACKNOWLEDGEMENTS

This paper has benefited from comments made at the Workshop on Policy Formulation in Interdependent Markets, March 1993, Vienna. We are also indebted to Theo van de Klundert, Jacques Sijben and Sjak Smulders for helpful comments on an earlier draft of the paper.

REFERENCES

Allen, P. R. (1991) Open economy macroeconomics, a review essay. *Journal of Monetary Economics*, **27**, 151–6.

Attenasio, O., Manasse, P. and van der Ploeg, F. (1987) Interdependence in the OECD Economies: An Econometric model of the Group of Seven, *London School of Economics Working Paper*, no. 914.

Branson, W. (1988) International adjustment and the dollar: policy illusions and economic constraints, in *Economic Policy Coordination*, (ed. W. Guth), IMF, Washington D.C., 44–84.

Branson, W. and Rotemberg, J. (1980) International adjustment with wage rigidity. *European Economic Review*, **13**, 309–32.

Buiter, W. (1986) Fiscal prerequisites for a viable managed exchange rate regime: A non-technical eclectic introduction, *Praeadviezen voor de Vereniging voor de Staathuishoudkunde*, (Stenfert Kroese, Leiden), 99–117.

Buiter, W. (1987) Fiscal policy in open interdependent economies, in *Economic policy in theory and practice*, (eds A. Razin and E. Sadka), Macmillan, London, 101–4.

Corrigan, E. G. (1990) The US savings gap and global imbalances. *De Economist*, **138**, no. 4, 464–71.

Chimerine, L. and Young, R. M. (1986), Economic surprises and messages of the 1980s. *The American Economic Review*, **76**, no. 2, 31–6.
Don Econometrics (1990) Manual SIMPC 3.0, The Hague, September.
Gordon, R. J. (1988) Wage gaps versus output gaps: Is there a common story for all of Europe?, in *Macro and micro policies for more growth and employment* (ed. H. Giersch), J. C. B. Mohr, Tübingen, 97–151.
Garretsen, H. and Lensink, R. (1989) International policy coordination and European wage rigidity. *De Economist*, **137**, 76–90.
De Groof, R. J. and Schaling, E. (1991) Monetary and fiscal policy in interdependent two-sector economies. *De Economist* **139**, 427–44.
De Groof, R. J. and van Tuijl, M. A. (1993) Financial integration and fiscal policy in interdependent two-sector economies with real and nominal wage rigidity. *European Journal of Political Economy*, **9**, 209–232.
Haas, R. D. and Masson, P. R. (1986) MINIMOD: specification, simulation and results, *IMF Staff papers*, **33**, no. 4, 722–67.
Hayashi, F. (1982) Tobin's marginal *q* and average *q*: a neoclassical interpretation. *Econometrica*, **50**, 213–24.
Karakitsos, E. (1989) Monetary policy, exchange rate dynamics and the labour market. *Oxford Economic Papers*, **41**, 410–33.
Knoester, A. and Kolodziejak, A. M. M. (1992) Effects of taxation in economic models, a survey. *Economic Modelling*, **9**, 352–64.
Kremers, J. J. M. (1990) External imbalances and fiscal policy in the United States, Japan and Germany: the role of stock-flow dynamics, in *Public Finance and Steady Economic Growth*, (ed. G. Kraus), Proceedings of the 45th Congress of the IIPF, 53–69.
McKinnon, R. I. (1990) Why floating exchange rates fail: A reconsideration of the liquidity trap. *Open Economies Review*, **1**, 229–50.
Van de Klundert, Th. (1991) Reducing external debt in a world with imperfect asset and commodity substitution. *European Journal of Political Economy*, **7**, 17–40.
Van de Klundert, Th. (1993) Crowding out of private and public capital accumulation in an international context. *Economic Modelling*, **10**, 273–84.
Van der Ploeg, F. (1988) International interdependence and policy coordination in the OECD economies. *Greek Economic Review*, **10**, 1–48.
Van der Ploeg, F. (1991) Money and capital in interdependent economies with overlapping generations. *Economica*, **58**, 233–56.
Van der Ploeg, F. and A. J. Markink (1991) Dynamic policy in linear models with rational expectations of future events, A computer package. *Computer Science in Economics and Management*, **4**, 175–99.
Van der Ploeg, F. (1992) Fiscal stabilisation and monetary integration in Europe: a short-run analysis. *De Economist*, **140**, 16–45.
Rankin, N. (1991) Exchange rate risk and imperfect capital mobility in an optimizing model. *Discussion Paper* no. 9116, Center for Economic Research, Tilburg University.
Turnovsky, S. (1977) *Macroeconomic Analysis and Stabilization Policy*, Cambridge University Press, Cambridge, 36–69.

APPENDIX A – NUMERICAL ASSUMPTIONS

Parameter values for the reference situation

Partial demand elasticities

$\varepsilon_{m_j r_j} = 0.3$ interest-elasticity of real cash balances

$\varepsilon_{b_{jj}y}$	= 0.0833	income elasticity of domestic bonds
$\varepsilon_{b_{jj}r_j}$	= 0.05	elasticity of domestic bonds held by residents with respect to the domestic nominal interest rate
$\varepsilon_{b_{jj}r_k}$	= 0.05	elasticity of domestic bonds held by residents with respect to the expected yield on foreign bonds
$\varepsilon_{b_{jk}r_j}$	= 0.10	elasticity of foreign bonds held by residents with respect to the domestic nominal interest rate
$\varepsilon_{b_{jk}r_k}$	= 0.2	elasticity of foreign bonds held by residents with respect to the expected yield on foreign bonds
ε_{cy}	= 0.8	elasticity of private consumption with respect to the purchasing power of nominal output
ε_{cr}	= 0.225	interest-elasticity of private consumption
ε_{cw}	= 0.1	(real) wealth-elasticity of private consumption

Elasticities of substitution

φ_{hm}	= 2.5	between home- and foreign-produced consumption goods
φ_{kl}	= 0.55	between capital and labour

Other behavioural parameters

α	= 0.125	acceleration coefficient
β	= 0.5	tax rule feedback coefficient
ζ_1	= 0.999	real wage inertia coefficient for Europe
ζ_2	= 0.001	real wage inertia coefficient for the US
η	= 0.1	Phillips coefficient

Initial steady-state ratio of

γ_{k_b}	= 0.8	bonds issued by firms to total supply of bonds
γ_{m_y}	= 0.25	real cash balances to real output in terms of consumption goods
$\gamma_{b_{jj}b}$	= 0.8	holdings of domestic bonds to total bonds holdings of residents
γ_{b_h}	= 0.1333	private sector imports to output
γ_{mg_h}	= 0.0267	government imports to output
γ_{c_h}	= 0.5333	private consumption of home produced goods by residents to output
γ_{g_h}	= 0.14	government expenditure on home produced goods to government output
γ_i	= 0.1667	gross capital investment to output
γ_{h_c}	= 0.8	consumption of home produced goods to total consumption
γ_{d_y}	= 0.75	government debt to real output in terms of consumption goods
γ_{mw_e}	= 0.0625	real cash balances to real wealth
γ_{we_y}	= 4	real wealth to real output in terms of consumption goods

Other non-behavioural parameters

δ	= 0.0556	rate of technical obsolescence
κ	= 3	capital-output ratio
λ	= 0.7	wage share
$\tilde{r}$	= 0.0444	real interest rate in the initial steady state

APPENDIX B – SENSITIVITY ANALYSIS

Table B.1 summarizes the results of the sensitivity analysis, by presenting the intervals of robustness of the behavioural parameters with respect to the signs of the US external and government debt.

Table 10.B.1 Intervals of robustness with respect to the US twin-debt

Parameter	*Value in the reference situation*	$t=1$	$t\rightarrow\infty$
φ_{kl}	0.55	0.01–1	0.01–1
φ_{hm}	2.5	1–1000	2–1000
ε_{cy}	0.8	0.6–1	0.6–1
ε_{cw}	0.1	0–0.4	0–0.225
ε_{cr}	0.225	0.12–0.5	0.12–0.4
α	0.125	0.01–0.2	0.01–0.2
β	0.5	0.1–1.33	0.1–1.33
η	0.1	0.02–∞	0.02–∞
ζ_1	0.999	0–1	0–1
ζ_2	0.001	0–1	0–1
ε_{my}	1	0.6–1.2	0.6–1.2
ε_{mr}	0.3	0.05–0.6	0.05–0.6
$\varepsilon_{b_{jj}r_j}$*	0.05	0.03–0.25	0.03–0.25
$\varepsilon_{b_{jk}r_k}$*	0.2	0.04–0.8	0.04–0.8

*With corresponding changes in $\varepsilon_{b_{jk}r_j}$ or $\varepsilon_{b_{jj}r_k}$, obeying the adding-up constraints

The sensitivity analysis with respect to the signs of the spillover effects in terms of real output, gives almost the same intervals of robustness as those in Table 10.B.1. One exception worth mentioning is the nominal inertia coefficient for the US, ζ_2. The upper boundary of this parameter is 0.65, in the case of the financial crisis.

11

Implied versus historical volatility: an empirical test of the efficiency of the currency options market

C. Dunis

11.1 METHODOLOGY AND SUMMARY OF RESULTS

Dealing in currency options has probably been one of the fastest growth areas in the foreign exchange market over the last decade. However, whereas economic research in the field of foreign exchange (forex) markets largely focused on devising structural models of exchange rate determination and the issue of efficiency, most of the literature on options has concentrated on improving the basic Black–Scholes formula and only a few articles have so far addressed the issue of the efficiency of the currency options market.

Still, these articles generally tried to demonstrate market efficiency through an empirical verification of the Put–Call Parity Theorem as, for instance, Klemkosky and Resnick (1979)[1]. Furthermore, they used data from listed options on exchanges rather than over-the-counter (OTC) data.

In this note however, bearing in mind that the options market is basically a market for volatility, we attempt to test directly the efficiency of the currency options market, using Chemical Bank's data bank on implied volatilities for the following exchange rates: USD/DEM, GBP/USD, USD/CHF, USD/JPY, GBP/DEM and DEM/JPY. These volatilities were obtained from brokers via Reuters on a daily basis, at the close of business in London.

Historical volatilities were computed as the annualized root mean square variation (RMSV) of the former exchange rates, which were downloaded from Reuters via a data feed on a daily basis at 4.50 pm London time.

We carried out usual efficiency tests drawn from the economic literature on the efficiency of the foreign exchange market: in such circumstances, if one assumes economic agents to be risk neutral, the efficient markets hypothesis

The European Single Market – Monetary and Fiscal Policy Harmonization.
Edited by H.M. Scobie. Published in 1994 by Chapman & Hall,
London. ISBN 0 412 57520 5

implies that the forward rate should be an unbiased predictor of the future spot rate (see, for instance, MacDonald and Taylor (1992), particularly pp. 28–34).

Conversely, for the currency options market, the efficient markets hypothesis should entail that the volatility quoted today for, say, the next three-month period is an unbiased predictor of the empirical exchange rate volatility that will occur over that three-month period (i.e. the ex post three-month historical volatility as recorded in $t+3$ for the three-month period from t to $t+3$).

Let $VI_{3,t}$ and $VH_{3,t}$ be respectively the three-month implied volatility quoted in t for the next three-month period, and the historical three-month volatility recorded in t for the previous three-month period.

Then, the condition for $VI_{3,t}$ to be an unbiased predictor of the future historical volatility $VH_{3,t+3}$ is given by equation (11.1):

$$VH_{3,t+3} = a + b\,VI_{3,t} + e_t \qquad (11.1)$$

which will be tested against the null hypothesis where the expectation is that the constant term should be equal to zero, the slope coefficient should not differ significantly from unity and, last but not least, the error term is not serially correlated. The satisfaction of these conditions implies the acceptance of what is known as the 'weak efficiency hypothesis'.

Furthermore, if the currency options market is efficient, then the information contained in $VI_{3,t}$ should summarize all the information at time t that is relevant to the determination in t of $VH_{3,t+3}$. In particular, the addition of part of the information stock available at time $t-1$, namely $VI_{3,t-1}$, should not add anything new to the information content already in $VI_{3,t}$. Specifically, the inclusion of $VI_{3,t-1}$ as a further explanatory variable to the right hand-side of the equation (11.1) should change nothing: it should not significantly affect the coefficient of determination $\bar{R}^2$ and $VI_{3,t-1}$ should have a coefficient not statistically different from zero.

Thus, a further and even more demanding test of market efficiency, i.e. the 'strong efficiency hypothesis', will be given by equation (11.2)

$$VH_{3,t+3} = a + b\,VI_{3,t} + c\,VI_{3,t-1} + e_t \qquad (11.2)$$

where the same constraints apply to a, b and e_t as in equation (11.1) and where the null hypothesis further requires that $c=0$.

Equations (11.1) and (11.2) were tested on daily data for the six exchange rate volatilities mentioned above, both for one-month and three-month time horizons, over the period 11 September 1989 to 14 July 1992 (the starting date was in fact 9 November 1989 for both GBP/DEM and DEM/JPY).

The empirical results are shown in Tables 11.1–11.6. Table 11.7 gives an overall summary of our efficiency tests. Figure 11.1 gives a pictorial representation.

In the case of the one-month USD/DEM volatility, the slope coefficient for equation (11.1) is only marginally above unity and the constant term does not differ from zero significantly. A Fisher test was separately conducted on coefficients a and b: as can be seen from Table 11.1, the null hypothesis where

Table 11.1 Empirical results of efficiency tests for USD/DEM (1 and 3-month horizons) 11 September 1989–14 July 1992

Dependent variable VH:	*Independent variables:*				*Statistics:*					*F-test:*		
1-month	Constant	VI(1,t)	VI(1,t−1)	$\hat{p}$	$\bar{R}2$	SSR	DW	Q(df)	N	a	b	c
USD/DEM	−1.40	1.04			0.23	6479.7	0.09	4433.3	672	2.47	0.34	—
	(−1.6)	(14.6)						(75)		(**)	(**)	
USD/DEM	11.51	−0.08		0.98	0.95	359.5	1.87	106.4	636			
	(7.6)	(−1.2)		(115.1)				(75)				
USD/DEM	0.38	1.10	−0.21		0.22	5893.4	0.09	3940.7	630	0.14	1.22	5.44
	(0.4)	(12.2)	(−2.3)					(75)		(**)	(**)	(*)
USD/DEM	12.15	−0.05	−0.06	0.98	0.95	340.1	1.88	91.2	579			
	(6.0)	(−0.7)	(−0.8)	(106.1)				(72)				
3-month	Constant	VI(3, t)	VI(3, t−1)	$\hat{p}$	$\bar{R}2$	SSR	DW	Q(df)	N	a	b	c
USD/DEM	−0.58	0.99			0.17	3684.9	0.03	11093.0	635	0.31	0.03	—
	(−0.6)	(11.3)						(75)		(**)	(**)	
USD/DEM	11.57	−0.10		0.99	0.98	69.5	1.84	40.7	604			
	(6.5)	(−1.9)		(192.4)				(72)				
USD/DEM	−0.95	0.92	0.10		0.17	3484.7	0.03	10067.2	598	0.66	0.44	0.70
	(−0.8)	(7.5)	(0.8)					(72)		(**)	(**)	(**)
USD/DEM	13.34	−0.11	−0.07	0.99	0.99	40.6	1.92	118.6	555			
	(4.0)	(−2.6)	(−1.7)	(235.2)				(69)				

T—statistics are shown in parenthesis below each variable's coefficient
$\hat{p}$ is the final value of the autocorrelation coefficient
(a Hildreth–Lu transformation was used to account for first-order serial correlation)
$\bar{R}_2$ is the coefficient of multiple correlation adjusted for degrees of freedom
SSR: Sum of Squared Residuals
DW: Durbin–Watson statistics
Q: Box–Pierce test for white noise
df: degrees of freedom
N: Number of events
F-Test: Fisher Test against null hypothesis where $a=0$, $b=1$ and $c=0$
(Critical values are 3.84 at 5% significance level (**) and 6.64 at 1% significance level (*)).

Table 11.2 Empirical results of efficiency tests for GBP/USD (1 and 3-month horizons) 11 September 1989–14 July 1992

Dependent variable VH:	*Independent variables:*				*Statistics:*					*F-test:*		
1-month	Constant	VI(1,t)	VI(1,t−1)	p̂	R̄2	SSR	DW	Q(df)	N	a	b	c
GBP/USD	0.05	0.87			0.18	6112.5	0.08	4807.9	672	0.004	3.10	—
	(0.1)	(12.2)						(75)		(**)	(**)	
GBP/USD	11.31	−0.13		0.98	0.95	321.9	1.89	122.5	636			
	(7.6)	(−2.1)		(115.7)				(75)				
GBP/USD	3.61	1.02	−0.45		0.19	5316.9	0.10	3620.4	630	13.44	0.04	29.00
	(3.7)	(12.1)	(−5.4)					(75)		—	(**)	—
GBP/USD	11.62	−0.09	−0.04	0.98	0.95	288.2	1.91	117.4	579			
	(5.9)	(−1.5)	(−0.6)	(107.7)				(72)				
3-month	Constant	VI(3,t)	VI(3,t−1)	p̂	R̄2	SSR	DW	Q(df)	N	a	b	c
GBP/USD	6.83	0.32			0.02	3153.4	0.02	12297.6	635	45.97	65.96	—
	(6.8)	(3.8)						(75)		—	—	
GBP/USD	9.98	−0.03		0.99	0.99	42.7	1.75	139.5	604			
	(5.6)	(−0.7)		(207.2)				(72)				
GBP/USD	9.05	0.64	−0.51		0.05	2945.4	0.02	10271.0	598	63.27	9.69	21.37
	(8.0)	(5.6)	(−4.6)					(72)		—	—	—
GBP/USD	11.56	−0.05	−0.05	0.99	0.99	37.4	1.81	140.7	555			
	(4.5)	(−1.1)	(−1.2)	(205.4)				(69)				

T—statistics are shown in parenthesis below each variable's coefficient
$\hat{p}$ is the final value of the autocorrelation coefficient
(a Hildreth–Lu transformation was used to account for first-order serial correlation)
$\bar{R}^2$ is the coefficient of multiple correlation adjusted for degrees of freedom
SSR: Sum of Squared Residuals
DW: Durbin–Watson statistics
Q: Box–Pierce test for white noise
df: degrees of freedom
N: Number of events
F-Test: Fisher Test against null hypothesis where $a=0$, $b=1$ and $c=0$
(Critical values are 3.84 at 5% significance level (**) and 6.64 at 1% significance level (*)).

Table 11.3 Empirical results of efficiency tests for USD/CHF (1 and 3-month horizons) 11 September 1989–14 July 1992

Dependent variable VH:	*Independent variables:*				*Statistics:*					*F-test:*		
1-month	Constant	VI(1,t)	VI(1,t−1)	$\hat{p}$	$\bar{R}2$	SSR	DW	Q(df)	N	a	b	c
USD/CHF	6.11	0.47			0.07	4818.9	0.08	5209.8	672	59.13	70.23	—
	(7.7)	(7.4)						(75)		—	—	
USD/CHF	12.42	−0.07		0.97	0.93	325.4	2.01	99.0	636			
	(10.8)	(−1.1)		(93.8)				(75)				
USD/CHF	9.42	0.64	−0.44		0.10	4042.2	0.10	3745.7	630	114.44	24.07	34.73
	(10.7)	(8.6)	(−6.9)					(75)		—	—	—
USD/CHF	13.25	−0.05	−0.06	0.98	0.92	311.8	2.00	92.4	579			
	(8.6)	(−0.9)	(−1.0)	(84.2)				(72)				
3-month	Constant	VI(3,t)	VI(3,t−1)	$\hat{p}$	$\bar{R}2$	SSR	DW	Q(df)	N	a	b	c
USD/CHF	9.46	0.21			0.02	1828.9	0.04	9948.5	635	160.83	170.57	—
	(12.7)	(3.6)						(75)		—	—	
USD/CHF	11.80	−0.0001		0.99	0.97	57.5	1.89	43.8	604			
	(12.8)	(−0.004)		(133.1)				(72)				
USD/CHF	9.99	0.31	−0.14		0.02	1635.4	0.03	9172.1	598	146.44	79.89	3.40
	(12.1)	(4.0)	(−1.8)					(72)		—	—	(**)
USD/CHF	12.70	−0.01	−0.02	0.99	0.98	32.8	1.91	90.4	555			
	(9.0)	(−0.4)	(−0.6)	(158.9)				(69)				

T—statistics are shown in parenthesis below each variable's coefficient
$\hat{p}$ is the final value of the autocorrelation coefficient
(a Hildreth–Lu transformation was used to account for first-order serial correlation)
$\bar{R}^2$ is the coefficient of multiple correlation adjusted for degrees of freedom
SSR: Sum of Squared Residuals
DW: Durbin–Watson statistics
Q: Box–Pierce test for white noise
df: degrees of freedom
N: Number of events
F-Test: Fisher Test against null hypothesis where $a=0$, $b=1$ and $c=0$
(Critical values are 3.84 at 5% significance level (**) and 6.64 at 1% significance level (*)).

Table 11.4 Empirical results of efficiency tests for USD/JPY (1 and 3-month horizons) 11 September 1989–14 July 1992

Dependent variable VH:	*Independent variables:*				*Statistics:*					*F-test:*		
1-month	Constant	VI(1,t)	VI(1,t−1)	$\hat{\rho}$	$\bar{R}2$	SSR	DW	Q(df)	N	a	b	c
USD/JPY	2.97	0.65			0.21	3968.4	0.11	3354.0	672	36.38	52.88	—
	(6.0)	(13.6)						(75)		—	—	
USD/JPY	9.31	−0.03		0.97	0.94	294.4	1.85	86.4	636			
	(9.5)	(−0.6)		(97.3)				(75)				
USD/JPY	3.31	0.59	0.02		0.20	3523.4	0.11	3255.5	630	37.68	41.24	0.13
	(6.1)	(9.3)	(−0.4)					(75)		—	—	(**)
USD/JPY	9.76	−0.02	−0.03	0.98	0.93	282.3	1.88	75.3	579			
	(7.0)	(−0.4)	(−0.5)	(98.5)				(72)				
3-month	Constant	VI(3,t)	VI(3,t−1)	$\hat{\rho}$	$\bar{R}2$	SSR	DW	Q(df)	N	a	b	c
USD/JPY	4.75	0.50			0.13	2121.9	0.04	14558.7	635	82.53	94.46	—
	(9.1)	(9.6)						(75)		—	—	
USD/JPY	9.10	−0.01		0.99	0.98	41.3	1.88	57.9	604			
	(6.3)	(−0.6)		(183.8)				(72)				
USD/JPY	5.43	0.84	−0.40		0.20	1841.1	0.09	10043.5	598	93.06	4.90	31.23
	(9.6)	(11.7)	(−5.6)					(72)		—	(*)	—
USD/JPY	9.68	−0.02	0.03	0.99	0.99	30.6	1.89	79.9	555			
	(6.0)	(−0.8)	(1.0)	(196.2)				(69)				

T—statistics are shown in parenthesis below each variable's coefficient
$\hat{\rho}$ is the final value of the autocorrelation coefficient
(a Hildreth–Lu transformation was used to account for first-order serial correlation)
$\bar{R}^2$ is the coefficient of multiple correlation adjusted for degrees of freedom
SSR: Sum of Squared Residuals
DW: Durbin–Watson statistics
Q: Box–Pierce test for white noise
df: degrees of freedom
N: Number of events
F-Test: Fisher Test against null hypothesis where $a=0$, $b=1$ and $c=0$
(Critical values are 3.84 at 5% significance level (**) and 6.64 at 1% significance level (*)).

Table 11.5 Empirical results of efficiency tests for GBP/DEM (1 and 3-month horizons) 9 November 1989–14 July 1992

Dependent variable VH:	*Independent variables:*				*Statistics:*					*F-test:*		
1-month	Constant	VI(1,t)	VI(1,t−1)	$\hat{\rho}$	$\bar{R}2$	SSR	DW	Q(df)	N	a	b	c
GBP/DEM	−0.32 (−1.3)	1.01 (24.1)			0.47	2488.9	0.10	3788.5 (75)	650	1.68 (**)	0.05 (**)	—
GBP/DEM	6.71 (5.2)	−0.42 (−5.6)		0.98 (159.8)	0.97	153.2	1.88	100.0 (72)	614			
GBP/DEM	0.05 (0.2)	1.00 (14.8)	−0.08 (−1.2)		0.55	1423.6	0.14	3068.3 (72)	608	0.05 (**)	0.001 (**)	1.47 (**)
GBP/DEM	5.37 (4.6)	−0.21 (−2.6)	0.07 (0.8)	0.98 (117.2)	0.95	132.0	1.81	90.2 (69)	557			
3-month	Constant	VI(3,t)	VI(3,t−1)	$\hat{\rho}$	$\bar{R}2$	SSR	DW	Q(df)	N	a	b	c
GBP/DEM	0.08 (0.6)	0.96 (41.0)			0.73	563.5	0.08	4740.3 (72)	617	0.34 (**)	2.94 (**)	—
GBP/DEM	4.51 (4.4)	−0.07 (−1.8)		0.99 (260.6)	0.99	18.9	1.96	71.2 (72)	588			
GBP/DEM	0.08 (0.7)	0.69 (13.5)	0.25 (5.1)		0.79	360.0	0.08	5501.6 (72)	576	0.45 (**)	38.28 —	25.56 —
GBP/DEM	4.19 (2.9)	−0.09 (−2.3)	0.05 (1.2)	0.99 (242.1)	0.99	15.5	1.94	70.8 (69)	533			

T—statistics are shown in parenthesis below each variable's coefficient
$\hat{p}$ is the final value of the autocorrelation coefficient
(a Hildreth–Lu transformation was used to account for first-order serial correlation)
$\bar{R}^2$ is the coefficient of multiple correlation adjusted for degrees of freedom
SSR: Sum of Squared Residuals
DW: Durbin–Watson statistics
Q: Box–Pierce test for white noise
df: degrees of freedom
N: Number of events
F-Test: Fisher Test against null hypothesis where $a=0$, $b=1$ and $c=0$
(Critical values are 3.84 at 5% significance level (**) and 6.64 at 1% significance level (*)).

Table 11.6 Empirical results of efficiency tests for DEM/JPY (1 and 3-month horizons) 9 November 1989–14 July 1992

Dependent variable VH:	*Independent variables:*				*Statistics:*					*F-test:*		
1-month	Constant	VI(1,t)	VI(1,t−1)	p̂	R̄2	SSR	DW	Q(df)	N	a	b	c
DEM/JPY	2.64	0.67			0.21	3148.0	0.08	4258.2	650	22.71	39.92	—
	(4.8)	(13.1)						(75)		—	—	
DEM/JPY	11.28	−0.11		0.98	0.95	195.8	1.87	121.5	614			
	(9.5)	(−1.8)		(107.6)				(72)				
DEM/JPY	4.95	0.80	−0.33		0.18	2919.2	0.10	3181.7	608	51.58	8.50	24.77
	(7.2)	(11.5)	(−5.0)					(72)		—	—	—
DEM/JPY	11.78	−0.12	−0.02	0.98	0.94	199.0	1.87	116.4	557			
	(8.3)	(−1.8)	(−0.3)	(93.8)				(69)				
3-month	Constant	VI(3,t)	VI(3,t−1)	p̂	R̄2	SSR	DW	Q(df)	N	a	b	c
DEM/JPY	0.03	0.11			0.01	1486.9	0.02	10080.4	617	341.35	364.48	—
	(18.5)	(2.4)						(72)		—	—	
DEM/JPY	10.88	−0.06		0.99	0.98	24.0	1.85	140.2	588			
	(9.1)	(−1.9)		(186.1)				(72)				
DEM/JPY	11.22	0.09	−0.18		0.01	1357.4	0.02	8888.9	576	351.30	151.27	7.65
	(18.7)	(1.2)	(−2.8)					(72)		—	—	—
DEM/JPY	10.46	−0.06	0.003	0.99	0.98	23.7	1.89	126.1	533			
	(6.0)	(−1.7)	(0.1)	(168.5)				(69)				

T—statistics are shown in parenthesis below each variable's coefficient
$\hat{p}$ is the final value of the autocorrelation coefficient
(a Hildreth–Lu transformation was used to account for first-order serial correlation)
$\bar{R}^2$ is the coefficient of multiple correlation adjusted for degrees of freedom
SSR: Sum of Squared Residuals
DW: Durbin–Watson statistics
Q: Box–Pierce test for white noise
df: degrees of freedom
N: Number of events
F-Test: Fisher Test against null hypothesis where $a=0$, $b=1$ and $c=0$
(Critical values are 3.84 at 5% significance level (**) and 6.64 at 1% significance level (*)).

Table 11.7 Summary of results of efficiency tests

		a=0	*b=1*	*c=0*	*white noise*	*conclusion*
USD/DEM	equation (1)	yes	yes	n.a.	no	semi-efficiency
(1-month)	equation (2)	yes	yes	yes	no	semi-efficiency
USD/DEM	equation (1)	yes	yes	n.a.	no	semi-efficiency
(3-month)	equation (2)	yes	yes	yes	no	semi-efficiency
GBP/USD	equation (1)	yes	yes	n.a.	no	semi-efficiency
(1-month)	equation (2)	no	yes	no	no	efficiency rejected
GBP/USD	equation (1)	no	no	n.a.	no	efficiency rejected
(3-month)	equation (2)	no	no	no	no	efficiency rejected
USD/CHF	equation (1)	no	no	n.a.	no	efficiency rejected
(1-month)	equation (2)	no	no	no	no	efficiency rejected
USD/CHF	equation (1)	no	no	n.a.	no	efficiency rejected
(3-month)	equation (2)	no	no	yes	no	efficiency rejected
USD/JPY	equation (1)	no	no	n.a.	no	efficiency rejected
(1-month)	equation (2)	no	no	yes	no	efficiency rejected
USD/JPY	equation (1)	no	no	n.a.	no	efficiency rejected
(3-month)	equation (2)	no	yes	no	no	efficiency rejected
GBP/DEM	equation (1)	yes	yes	n.a.	no	semi-efficiency
(1-month)	equation (2)	yes	yes	yes	no	semi-efficiency
GBP/DEM	equation (1)	yes	yes	n.a.	no	semi-efficiency
(3-month	equation (2)	yes	no	no	no	efficiency rejected
DEM/JPY	equation (1)	no	no	n.a.	no	efficiency rejected
(1-month)	equation (2)	no	no	no	no	efficiency rejected
DEN/JPY	equation (1)	no	no	n.a.	no	efficiency rejected
(3-month)	equation (2)	no	no	no	no	efficiency rejected

Note: Semi-efficiency is defined in this table as resulting from the satisfaction of two out of three, or three out of four, of our efficiency criteria.

$a=0$ and $b=1$ is accepted at the 5% significance level.[2] However, the Durbin–Watson statistics indicate that the residuals are serially correlated, which is further corroborated by the high value of the Box–Pierce test for white noise (note that when a Hildreth–Lu transformation is used to account for first-order serial correlation, the coefficients will be modified, so that checking their value against the null hypothesis is not relevant anymore). For equation (11.2), the same remarks apply, but the coefficient for the second explanatory variable $VI_{1,t-1}$ is not significantly different from zero, in line with the efficient market hypothesis.

Table 11.1 also shows that we get comparable results for the three-month time horizon. Still, strictly speaking, our tests led to a rejection of the assumption of a full market efficiency for the USD/DEM volatility.

For the GBP/USD volatility, as evidenced in Table 11.2, the efficient market hypothesis has to be rejected for the three-month horizon. Nevertheless, for the one-month time horizon, equation (11.1) shows, in line with the null hypothesis, a slope coefficient that is both significant and close to unity and a constant

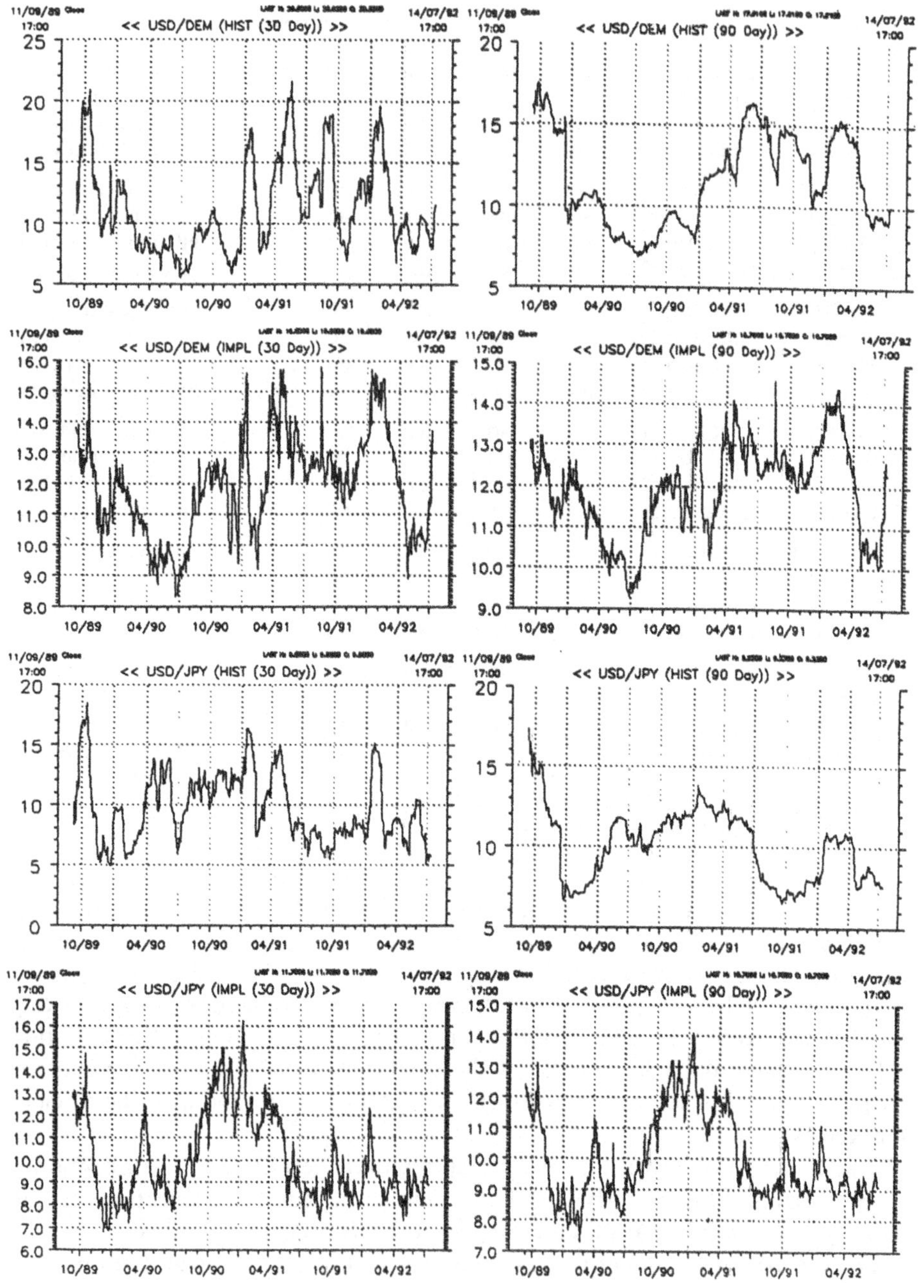

Figure 11.1 Pictorial representation of the results

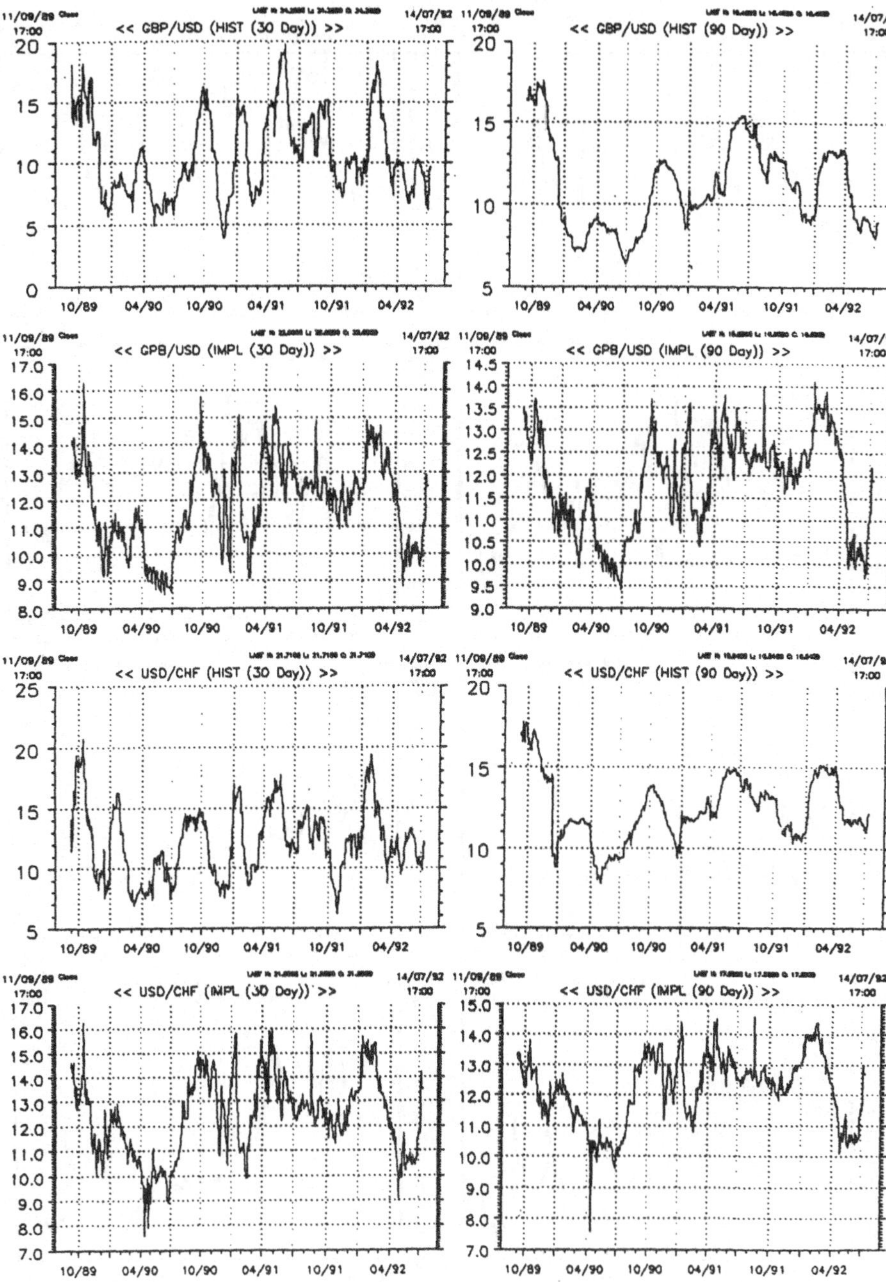

Figure 11.1 *contd.*

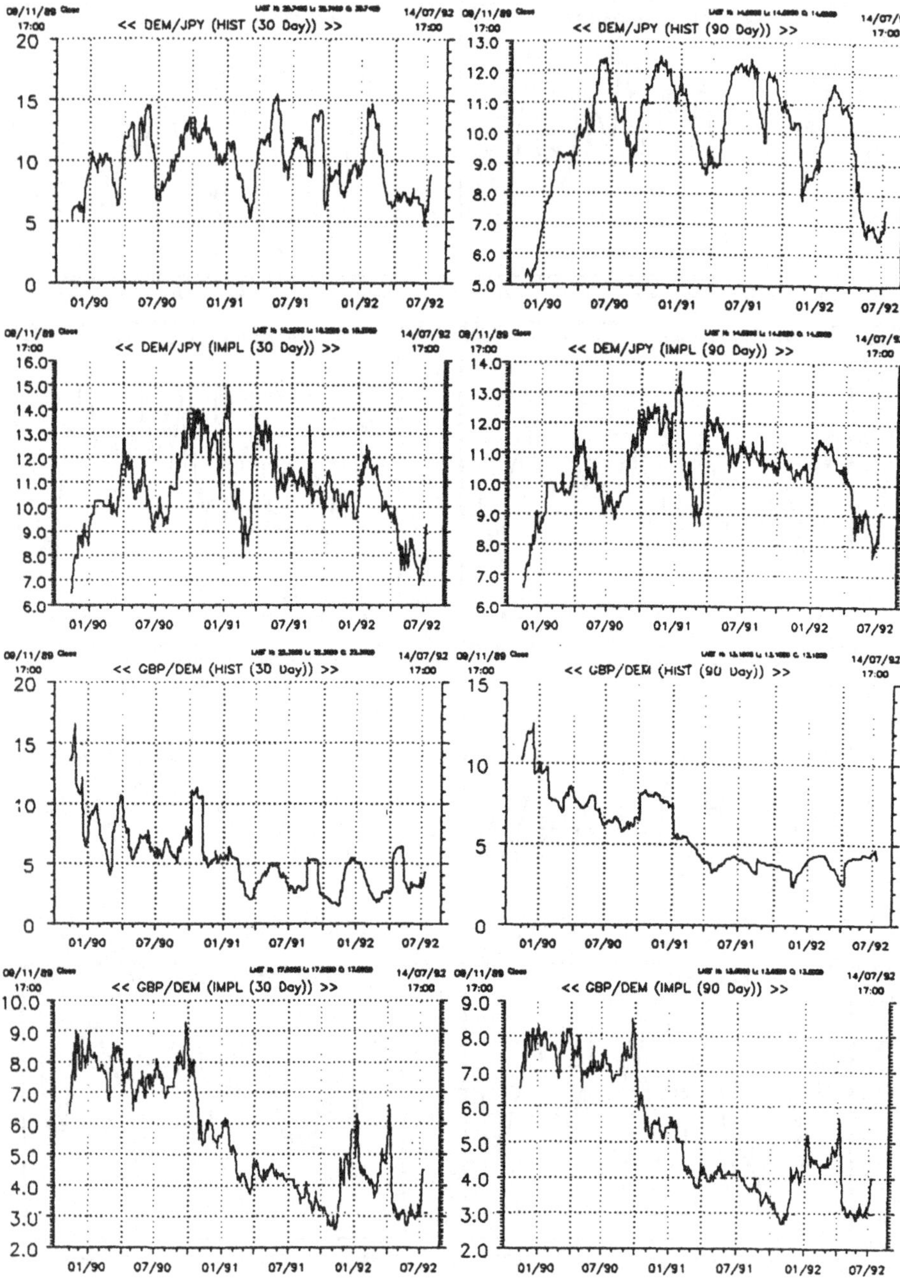

Figure 11.1 *contd.*

term that does not significantly differ from zero. Still, even in that case, the Durbin–Watson statistics show remaining residuals autocorrelation whose very existence goes against the efficient market hypothesis. With equation (11.2), if the coefficient for $VI_{1,t-1}$ does differ from zero somewhat, contrary to expectations, the slope coefficient is only marginally above unity, albeit significantly. Unfortunately, the constant term is statistically different from zero and, here too, the Durbin–Watson statistics and the Box–Pierce test lead us to reject the null hypothesis.

For the USD/CHF and DEM/JPY volatilities, the null hypothesis is clearly violated for both time horizons and equations, as shown in Tables 11.3 and 11.6.

This is also true for the USD/JPY volatility as only one efficiency criterion is satisfied in equation (11.2) at both time horizons and none in equation (11.1), as can be seen from Table 11.4.

Finally, we find slightly more encouraging results with the GBP/DEM volatility. Admittedly, at the three-month horizon, Table 11.5 shows that the strong market efficiency hypothesis must be rejected on the basis of the results for equation (11.2). For equation (11.1), however, the slope coefficient is only marginally different from unity and the constant term is not significantly different from zero: still, here again, the Durbin–Watson statistics and the Box–Pierce test indicate that the residuals are serially correlated, thus leading to a rejection of the null hypothesis.

At the one-month time horizon, the slope coefficient for equation (11.1) is very close to unity while the constant term is not significantly different from zero. For equation (11.2) the slope coefficient is exactly equal to unity and the constant term does not differ significantly from zero while, in line with expectations, the coefficient for $VI_{1,t-1}$ is not statistically different from zero. Unfortunately, once again, the values for the Durbin–Watson statistics show the existence of first-order serial correlation of the residuals for both equations (11.1) and (11.2), a conclusion that is reinforced by the Box–Pierce test for white noise. In other words, despite the fact that some criteria are satisfied, the joint hypothesis that the slope coefficient does not differ significantly from unity, the constant term is equal to zero and the error term is not serially correlated must be rejected, i.e. on that basis, implied volatility should not be considered as an unbiased predictor of future exchange rate volatility.

11.2 DISCUSSION

On the whole, the empirical results of the efficiency tests we carried out on the USD/DEM, GBP/USD, USD/CHF, USD/JPY, GBP/DEM and DEM/JPY volatilities do not support the view of an efficient market for currency options. As a matter of fact, we were not able to find a single case where efficiency could be safely assumed. At best, an assumption of 'semi-efficiency' can be made for those cases where, out of our three 'efficiency criteria' in equation (11.1) two were satisfied, e.g. for the GBP/DEM volatility at the one-month time horizon (but remember the case for efficiency rests on the *joint* satisfaction of all three criteria).

The same would apply to equation (11.2), when three out of four of our 'efficiency criteria' were met. Even then, as summarized in Table 11.7 the 'semi-efficiency' we have just defined is still rejected in two thirds of the cases examined: true, we can only accept it for the USD/DEM and GBP/DEM volatilities (but, for the latter, not for equation (11.2) at the three-month time horizon).

In practical terms, our findings imply that at least part of the information stock available at time t remains unexploited, which means that the implied volatility forecast of future exchange rate volatility may be beaten for a profit by those operators who are capable of spotting and using successfully that extra information neglected by the rest of the market.

True, a more comprehensive study should include alternative efficiency tests, namely orthogonality tests of forecast errors.[3] More importantly, our tests were conducted on overlapping data. They should therefore be supplemented by a similar study with non-overlapping time series observations as recent econometric research has shown the incidence of overlapping data on the serial correlation of the error term e_t[4]: this technical consideration could well explain, at least partly, the low values we experienced in our optimality tests for the Durbin–Watson statistics and the high ones for the Box–Pierce test and, in some cases, even lead to the acceptance of the efficient market hypothesis.

11.3 CONCLUSIONS

Still, and despite this last remark, our results appear significant and they should go a long way towards rejecting the efficient market hypothesis for currency options: if the case for using implied volatility as the optimal predictor of future exchange rate volatility has a strong intuitive appeal, the empirical evidence we have produced for the period end-1989 to mid-1992 does not tend to support this view. This leaves the issue of how to improve on this predictor's performance open for future research.

In the meantime, options traders will continue to use historical volatility to price currency options for those exchange rates for which there is no implied volatility market, thus attesting in practice of the links that exist between historical and implied volatility.

NOTES

1. The Put–Call Forward Parity (PCFP) states that, for any exercise price E, the difference between a put and a call, $P_{(E)} - C_{(E)}$, equals the difference

between E and the forward rate F, discounted to the present at the interest rate r:

$$C_{(E)} - P_{(E)} = (F - E)/(1 + r)^t \tag{11.3}$$

Buying the call and selling the put at the given exercise price E is equivalent to a 'long' forward contract at price E. The total cost of this 'synthetic' forward contract must include the difference between the cost of the call and the proceeds from the put. Since this difference is paid (or received) in advance, it must be discounted at the interest rate r:

$$F = E + ((C_{(E)} - P_{(E)}) \cdot (1 + r)^t) \tag{11.4}$$

In an efficient market, buying the currency forward 'synthetically' at price E and then selling it at the prevailing forward price F should produce a zero profit, since this is a risk-free arbitrage.

It also follows from equation (11.1) that, in the case where the exercise price is equal to the forward rate, i.e. $E = F$, then $C_{(F)} = P_{(F)}$, i.e. the price of the call and that of the put are equal. For more details on foreign exchange options relationships, see Giddy (1983).

2. As the Fisher test is used here to check for specific values of the coefficients and not to reject the null hypothesis as usual, the readings for the test are inverted, i.e. the 5% significance level is more restrictive than the 1% level.
3. Orthogonality tests can be implemented by estimating an equation of the form:

$$\mathrm{VH}_{3,t+3} - \mathrm{VI}_{3,t} = \mathrm{GX}_t + e_t \tag{11.5}$$

where X_t is a vector of variables part of the stock of information available at time t, G is a vector of parameters and e_t is the error term. The null hypothesis requires that G should be the null vector so that the 'forecasting errors' are orthogonal to the set of information available at time t. For more details on such tests, see for instance Hansen and Hodrick (1980) and MacDonald and Taylor (1991).
4. See Cumby, Huizinga and Obstfeld (1983), Hansen (1982), Hansen and Hodrick (1980), Levich (1989) and MacDonald and Taylor (1989) on the advantages of using non-overlapping time series observations.

REFERENCES

Cumby, R. E., Huizinga, J. and Obstfeld, M. (1983) Two-step two-stage least squares estimation in models with rational expectations. *Journal of Econometrics*, **21**, April, 333–55.

Dunis, C. and Feeny, M. (eds) (1989) *Exchange Rate Forecasting*, Woodhead-Faulkner, Cambridge.

Giddy, I. H. (1983) Foreign exchange options. *Journal of Futures Markets*, **3**, No. 2, 143–66.

Hansen, L. P. (1982) Large sample properties of generalized method of moments estimators. *Econometrica*, **50**, July, 1029–54.

Hansen, L. P. and Hodrick, R. J. (1980) Forward exchange rates as optimal predictors of future spot exchange rate: an econometric analysis. *Journal of Political Economy*, **88**, October, 829–53.

Klemkosky, R. C. and Resnick, B. G. (1979) Put-call parity and market efficiency. *Journal of Finance*, **34**, December, 1141–55.

Levich, R. M. (1989) Forward rates as the optimal future spot rate forecast, in Exchange Rate Forecasting, (eds C. Dunis and M. Feeny), Woodhead-Faulkner, Cambridge, 95–98.

MacDonald, R. and Taylor, M. P. (1989) Foreign exchange market efficiency and cointegration: some evidence from the recent float. *Economics Letters*, **29**, (1), 63–8.

MacDonald, R. and Taylor, M. P. (1991) Risk, efficiency and speculation in the 1920s foreign exchange market: an overlapping data analysis. *Weltwitschaftliches Archiv*, **127**, (3), 500–23.

MacDonald, R. and Taylor, M. P. (1992) Exchange rate economics: a survey. *IMF Staff Papers*, **39**, March, 1–57.

12

The past as prologue: a retrospective on the EC negotiations

D.P. Hanson, C. Lackman and T. Petinaux

12.1 INTRODUCTION

The European Community (EC) is currently poised between the paradise of Maastricht and the purgatory of rejection. This is a familiar condition for the EC; the European negotiations over the EC have a history of lurching from crisis to crisis. Despite repeated setbacks though, neither the negotiations nor the institutions have collapsed.

How serious are present circumstances? What are the impediments to unity and can they be overcome? For an answer, we will look at the history of the four-power EC negotiations between 1972 and 1991 to see what progress has been made, where progress is lagging and why.

We can account for the pattern of successes and failures in the EC negotiations in terms of the persistence of national institutions and expectations. The negotiating positions of each EC member is strongly influenced by internal arrangements regarding national security, sovereignty and self-concept, domestic prosperity and the patterns of elite recruitment, function and interest.

Since the relevant internal arrangements are well entrenched in national institutions, they are not changed easily. Thus, the emphasis placed by each country on protecting established national practices can be expected to persist.

We begin by looking at the requirements for governance. Governments are unlikely to make decisions that in turn will make governing more difficult. There are three broad types of constraints on governmental decision-making.

1. National security and prosperity. What measures are the government expected to take in the face of serious economic reversals?

The European Single Market – Monetary and Fiscal Policy Harmonization.
Edited by H.M. Scobie. Published in 1994 by Chapman & Hall,
London. ISBN 0 412 57520 5

2. Political legitimacy. The government must maintain a public commitment to the values that most voters feel should be embodied by the government.
3. Elite security. Governments tend to protect the roles and legitimacy of the groups that are making the high-level decisions in government.

The factors summarized under national prosperity, political legitimacy and elite security jointly define the implicit 'social contract' between government and citizens in key positions of the society. These responses reflect enduring patterns in social and political organization.

12.2 POLITICS AND POLICY IN THE FOUR POWERS

If this analysis is correct, then we should be able to account for national positions on the EC negotiations in terms of these three factors and these negotiating priorities should be consistent over time.

12.2.1 France

One pattern has persisted in French national history; political change has generally involved civil war or the threat of war. The resolution of these conflicts have often contributed to the strengthening of the central government and to a deepening of the divisions within the society.

For example, the monarchy was weak during most of the Hundred Years War (Seward, 1978). Eventual success in the war strengthened the monarchy to the point where the government had control of a standing army and was able to outlaw private armies. The concern for protecting royal power eventually led to persecution and expulsion of both the Huguenots and Jesuits. The Ancien Regime also monopolized access to high commerce and government perquisites (Braudel, 1990). This led to major splits between the old aristocracy and the newer commercial interests (Bitton, 1969).

The absolutist but ineffectual regime of Louis XIV led to the equally absolutist but far more effective regime of Napoleon I. The intervening civil war created tensions along the lines of class, historical affiliations and political sympathy that persist to the present. In more recent times, the conflict over empire during the feeble Third (Shirer, 1969) and Fourth Republics was resolved by De Gaulle after a civil war in Algeria and France (Horne, 1984). The successor state, The Fifth Republic, is far more centralized and energetic.

In general, the losers in the great political battles retired to the insularity of private institutions or the countryside to nurse their grievances (Shirer, 1969). The resulting potential for provoking a latent opposition generally inhibits the Central Government from extending control too aggressively (Horne, 1984; Traugott, 1985).

Since the 1600s, the most prevalent strategy for governance has been to recruit the best people, strengthen the control of the central government and build support on the basis of a chauvinistic nationalism (Zeldin, 1980). In the Ancien Regime, recruitment was handled via a system of selective patronage (Behrens, 1985). Since 1814, recruitment has generally been through a system of very select 'Great Schools' (Suleiman, 1978; Millot, 1981). Institutionalized nationalism has been combined in the Great Schools with an emphasis on leadership and class superiority (Weiss, 1982).

The modern French system therefore includes the following elements:

1. Legitimacy. The government has consistently emphasized the *mision civilitrice*, a strong sense of the unique and highly advanced nature of French culture and the destiny of France to lead the world (de Gramont, 1969; Zeldin, 1980).

   In the EC, this is reflected in the French insistence on assertive EC foreign policy to contest American hegomony (Barnes, 1971; *New York Times* 6 April 1972, p. 5; 24 January 1973, p. 4; 13 February 1974, p. 28; 25 July 1974, p. 43; 9 January 1984, p. 1; 15 November 1989, I14; 23 December 1990, I1; 1 December 1991, 16), and on the importance of France as the spokesperson for Europe through the EC (*New York Times* 8 February 1972, p.1; 2 June 1973, p. 1; 15 February 1974, p. 15; 4 November 1979, III1; 7 July 1976, p. 8; 18 March 1979, IV3; 8 March 1982, IV7; 11 July 1989, I1; 17 March 1991, p. 8).
2. National prosperity. In keeping with the overall strategy for governance, the French government has traditionally followed a highly interventionist economic policy. Economic policy is loosely coordinated through a Five Year Plan which is the basis for allocating government controlled credit, subsidies and market restrictions. Capital allocation is influenced through state ownership of the major banking and insurance companies. Protection has been strongest in agriculture, high technology and energy areas that are important for modernizing the French economy and in agriculture (Price Waterhouse, 1989). Private firms often recruit retiring senior bureaucrats in order to gain better access to government decision makers. In turn, this also enhances the ability of government officials to influence the private sector.

   In the EC negotiations, France has pushed strongly for French access to EC markets. However, the government has also been willing to protect French economic interests over EC collegiality by unilaterally devaluing the franc (*New York Times* 21 January 1974, p. 1; 21 March 1976, III2) and by restricting the free movement of Arab oil from France to the Netherlands during the 1973 crisis (*New York Times* 20 November 1973, p. 9; 16 January 1974, III2; 15 February 1974, p. 3; 11 March 1974, p. 5; 19 March 1974, p. 20; 16 September 1975, p. 1). France has also been a strong advocate of restricting Japanese trade and investment in the EC as a means of defending uncompetitive industries and promoting EC investments in new technologies (*New York Times* 28 May 1985, V2; 7 November 1988, D4; 22 March 1989, p. 6; 21 September 1990, A11; 20 July 1991, A43).

3. Elite security. One consequence of France's revolutionary history has been the informal division of the country into a progressive, modern and authoritarian centre and a traditional, backward and relatively isolated periphery. Rural France has a tradition of erupting into disorder whenever any serious economic stresses occur. As a result, the Centre government has generally tolerated an inefficient agricultural sector and has been willing to subsidize rural incomes through market price supports (Ardagh, 1990).

   In the EC, the French have insisted on a strong Common Agricultural Policy (CAP) a component of this regime security strategy (*New York Times* 22 March 1972, p. 73; 9 March 1973, p. 51; 31 March 1982; IV1; 19 January 1984, p. 1; 28 June 1984, IV2; 1 July 1987, I9).

12.2.2 Germany

Germany can be understood as a bureaucratic-military state without a strong military. The roots of present Germany can be traced back to the growth of Prussia in the eighteenth century. The Thirty Years War made it clear that a strong military was essential for national survival. A strong economy was essential to support the development of a strong army. The new Prussian state was organized through the forced cooptation of agricultural, military and commercial elites. Willing participants were rewarded with honour, wealth and carefully circumscribed delegations of authority (Barker, 1916; Maehl, 1979; Fischer-Fabian, 1981).

This pattern of economic development pushed by political elites through authoritarian methods to support a strong military has persisted through several cycles of German history. The power of the North German Confederation was broken during the Napoleonic wars. Prussian fortunes were revived under Bismarck's leadership through internal reform, an external customs union and a policy of cautious international expansion (Munro, 1938; Clapham, 1961; Hamerow, 1969; Snyder, 1978). Under Hitler, Germany arose for a third time as the major military power in Europe. This was followed again by war and catastrophe.

1. Legitimacy. German culture stresses the idea of a disciplined, well-organized society with a place for everyone. Elites have an obligation to safeguard the development of the community. Subordinates have an obligation to obey the rules and to carry out their assigned responsibilities to the best of their abilities. 'All is in good order,' is still a proud claim in Germany.

   In the EC, the Germans want it to be efficient and orderly (*New York Times* 22 February 1972, p. 2; 18 February 1974, p. 3; 6 July 1975, p. 10; 14 February p. 33; 1 July 1984, IV3; 6 December 1987, I3; 2 December 1991, p. 3).
2. Elite security. The administration of post-war Germany reflects many of the earlier traditions. An establishment of elite political leaders and the senior

civil service, is very influential in German political decision-making (Edinger, 1968). Like Frederick the Great, they are the 'first servants of the state'. Policy is made through endless rounds of organized consultations among commercial, political, scientific and cultural groups. Thus, pride of position rests as much on the role of manager and intermediary as on any power of ultimate decision making.

In the EC, the German Government has been willing to discuss devolving sovereign authority to the EC as long as German interests are safeguarded through a system of orderly, high-level participation (*New York Times* 23 September 1973, p. 13; 21 February 1974, p. 2; 11 July 1975, p. 2; 23 March 1982, p. 8; 26 March 1984, p. 18; 16 June 1991, IV2; Habermas, 1992; see also Lowell, 1914).

3. Peace. The magnitude of the last war has discredited a militaristic strategy. The horrors of the last regime has given the German government a strong motive for stressing a peaceful integration into a larger Europe. The partition of Germany and the redefinition of the Polish borders has given the regime a special interest in Eastern Europe.

   In European affairs, Germany has followed a two-pronged approach. On one hand, Germany has enthusiastically embraced NATO and the American alliance. On the other, their eastern interests led first to trade with the German Democratic Republic and later to unification.

4. Prosperity. German prosperity has been promoted through the policy of a 'social free market'. The government assists in developing export markets through a strong Deutschmark and support for free trade agreements. The economy has been modernized by orderly planning and selected subsidies for emerging industries. The German Government has generally been reluctant to protect declining industries from foreign competition.

   In the EC, Germany has emphasized the importance of internal free trade, low external tariffs and rapprochement with East Germany and Poland (*New York Times* 16 March 1973, p. 14; 21 February 1974, p. 2; 27 May 1976, p. 14; 5 December 1982, p. 3; 8 July 1983, p. 19; 18 December 1988, A45; 3 August 1990, D17; 20 July 1991, A43; *Wall Street Journal* 29 October 1990, B4D).

12.2.3 United Kingdom

Historical background. A cohesive aristocracy was consistently able to triumph over the monarchy and lead an imperialist/capitalist revolution. Aristocratic cohesion was based in part on the traditions of primogeniture. The effect was twofold; it tended to preserve the economic basis of aristocratic power and it created a steady stream of younger brothers who needed to make their own way in the world (Winchester, 1982). These non-titled but privileged younger relations often sought their fortunes through careers in the military or commerce (Seward, 1978). The existence of an untitled aristocracy helped legitimate the role of the senior gentry (Namier, 1961; Trevelyan, 1987).

Between 1215 and 1688, English politics reflected the reality that the great lords in England often controlled armies that were larger than those commanded by the king (Trevelyan, 1987). As long as the English king was waging war in France, his control at home was weakened. Many military leaders during the Hundred Years War raised private armies and became quite wealthy through plunder and ransom provided by their forces in France. These factors were reflected in the *laissez faire* strategy of the English government, a policy which generally reflected the weaknesses of the crown as much as any deliberate policy choice.

Capitalism developed as the non-titled aristocracy formed commercial alliances with the rising bourgeoisie (Melada, 1970; Sampson, 1982) through select recruitment to elite education and occupations (Giddens, 1979; Winchester, 1982; Cunningham, 1986; Rubenstein, 1986; Castronovo, 1987). Power and culture were eventually controlled by the 'establishment', an upper class with strong ties to the aristocratic strata. Economic prosperity and political liberalization legitimated the leadership of this quasi-aristocratic upper class (Alderman, 1986; Smith, 1990; Pinto-Deuschinsky, 1973).

1. National legitimacy. There is a strong sense that England is 'different', that these differences are rooted in a unique and honoured English history, and that leadership should naturally be assumed by a benign English upper class (Cunningham, 1986).

   In the EC, British political leaders have generally emphasized the need for limits to EC control and their opposition to EC policies, especially when out of office. The British government has consistently resisted proposals to devolve sovereign authority to the EC (*New York Times* 11 April 1972, p. 5; 3 January 1973, p. 1; 24 January 1975, p. 1; 6 October 1977, p. 8; 26 November 1978, p. 55; 29 November 1979, p. 7; 13 February, IV3; 20 May 1982, I2; 6 June 1989, IV7; 18 April 1989, IV2; 1 May 1990, A23; 30 June 1991, I3).
2. Peace. British policies in both areas tend to reflect an inconsistent mixture of isolationism and internationalism. National security issues have historically been handled through a strong fleet, a strong army and a willingness to use them. Thus, the UK has developed an almost invisible independent nuclear strategic force and will still go to the defence of the Falklands, Northern Ireland, and Kuwait. In reality, Britain has dropped to the level of a smaller regional power.

   In the EC, Britain is a strong supporter of NATO and the American alliance (*New York Times* 27 May 1976, p. 14; 28 September 1988, I1; 27 April 1989, I13; 17 March 1991, p. 8).
3. Prosperity. Economic policy has become equally inconsistent. The combination of an neo-aristocratic elite culture, well-entrenched working class

sub-cultures, and a sense of traditional entitlement seems to pose major difficulties in the development of a strong manufacturing sector (Caves, 1980).

The traditional response has been strongly protectionist. The initial policy was to reserve trade with the Empire for British companies. With the ending of the Empire, this became a policy of protecting British manufacturers from foreign competition through devaluations, high tariffs and import restrictions. British standards of living were maintained through cheap agricultural imports. At present though, British exporters have become quite dependent on access to European markets through the EC.

In the EC, British support for the free market has depended on the specific effects on British industries (*New York Times* 11 July 1988, D4; *Washington Post* 11 April 1990, H1; *Wall Street Journal* 2 July 1992, A10). British support for the 1992 project reflects the export potential of Japanese investment in the UK and the expected benefits of liberalizing financial markets, an area in which the UK remains strong. Britain has bitterly opposed the direct and indirect costs of the CAP and has pushed vigorously for a liberalization of the Community agricultural policies (*New York Times* 3 January 1975, p. 9; 6 November 1978, p. 15; 29 November 1979, p. 7; 23 March 1980, p. 3; 12 July 1983, IV6; 1 July 1989, I9; 30 January 1988, I3; Burkitt and Bambridge, 1990).

12.2.4 Italy

The historical factors shaping the development of Italy have promoted cultural fragmentation and the loss of political legitimacy. Cultural unity was lost first with successive invasions by the Lombards, Byzantine Greeks, Arabs and Franks. In more recent times, the Spanish, French, and Austrians invaded the Italian Peninsula. By 1500 virtually all of Italy was under foreign domination.

Successive wave of invasion and colonial annexation also destroyed the legitimacy of government in Italy. All too often, government was exploitive and corrupt. The political response was predictable; it became a patriotic duty to cheat the authorities. Political repression and the frequent reliance on a colonial policy of divide and rule impeded the development of a shared sense of civic responsibility (Putnam, 1993). Cultural and political fragmentation also slowed the development of Italian nationalism (Barzini, 1964).

Independence and unification were achieved in the nineteenth century through the armed invasion of Southern Italy by Savoy in Northern Italy (Holt, 1971). The new government was faced with the same pattern of parochialism, mistrust and corruption that had developed under colonialism. As a result, Italy was almost ungovernable. The Italian government lurched from crisis to catastrophe between 1870 and 1944. The political divisions between Left and Right, North and South and Catholic and laity became almost unmanageable.

Italy has achieved a degree of political stability in the post-war era through machine politics. Power is in the hands of the party faction leaders. Political fragmentation and paralysis in parliament has led to a shift of power to the cabinet. Cabinets are put together on the basis of factional coalitions. The office of prime minister is relatively weak, giving control over political decision-making to subordinate cabinet ministers. In turn, the cabinet ministers use their authority to place supporters throughout the bureaucracy. Faction leaders then use their power over patronage and political favours to build support from voters and businesses (Shinn, 1985; Santoro *et al.*, 1987).

These factors have resulted in the development of a unique set of political expectations.

1. Elite security. Support from the major political party and faction leaders is critical for any Italian regime. In turn, the political leaders must be able to maintain control over business permits, contracts, jobs, pensions, taxes, and subsidies. They do not need to control the overall direction of policy as long as they can create exceptions for their supporters through selective policy implementation.

   In the context of the debates over the EC, the *de facto* Italian policy has been to respond to EC rules in a manner that does not interfere with the ability of Italian politicians to reward their friends (*New York Times* 24 June 1972, p. 11; 15 February 1973, p. 26; 17 April 1977, p. 1; 21 June 1980, p. 1; 26 March 1984, p. 18; 14 December 1990, A11).
2. Political legitimacy. The Italian government has little legitimacy. Support for government is based in large part on the expectation that private political contacts can be used for personal advantage.

   With regard to the EC, the Italian government has consistently argued for higher subsidies for regional development efforts. In exchange for these subsidies, the government has generally been willing to go along with the dominant EC coalition of the time (*New York Times* 16 September 1973, 4; 12 April 1990, A11).
3. Peace and prosperity. After the historic debacles of an assertive Italian foreign policy, the government has come to rely strongly on the EC, NATO and US alliances for national security.

   When the government has taken a position in EC negotiations, Italy has favored unity with the EC, NATO and the US (*New York Times* 15 July 1972, p. 3; 13 December 1973, p. 4; 30 May 1980, p. 7; 22 October 1982, p. 5).

   The *de facto* Italian economic policy has been to make sure that Italian companies have access to EC and other export markets, and to limit foreign competition for Italian companies as much as possible (Shinn, 1985).

12.3 SUCCESSES AND FAILURES IN THE NEGOTIATIONS

A major success of the EC has simply been to maintain the present membership. The fight between France and the UK over budget contributions and the

CAP involved both threats and invitations for the UK to withdraw from the EC. (*New York Times* 1 February 1975, p. 27; 23 March 1980, p. 3; 13 May 1980, p. 2; 25 April 1984, p. 9.) Italy was also invited to reconsider EC membership in light of the persistent failure of the government to either meet budgetary obligations or to implement EC directives (*New York Times* 24 June 1972, p. 1; 10 July 1973, p. 1). The repeated collapse of the European Monetary System (EMS) has not lead to a collapse of either the EC or to efforts to integrate the EC currencies (*New York Times* 22 July 1985, IV1; 7 March 1986, I1). The role of the EC bureaucracies in international negotiations has gradually been growing over time (Lavant, 1978).

A related triumph has been the expansion of the EC membership from seven countries to the present twelve members. These negotiations have not been painless; British membership was delayed in part because De Gaulle vetoed the original application. There was widespread debate over the wisdom of bringing Greece, Spain and Portugal into the Community. The common thread to these disputes has been the effect of new members on the trade interests and political influence of the existing members (Runge and Witzke, 1990; *New York Times* 2 February 1974, p. 8; 24 January 1976, p. 6; 27 February 1977, IV6; 8 June 1980, IV2; 22 December 1983, p. 3; 3 December 1984, p. 3).

A third area of success has been the dampening of conflicts that threaten EC unity. The principal example has been the resolution of the demands of the UK related to the CAP and UK budget contribution. The UK dropped the demand for wholesale changes in the CAP. In turn, the contribution made by the UK to the EC (in large part to finance the CAP) was substantially reduced (*New York Times* 20 June 1983; 21 April 1984; 28 April 1984; 27 June 1984). Community questions about German trade with Eastern Europe and the German unification process have also been contained (*New York Times* 23 January 1973, p. 13; 21 March 1982, p. 16; 8 December 1989, IV5).

The success of the EC in containing these issues has been primarily based on two factors. One is the shared reliance on access to the Community for domestic prosperity. Threats to withdraw from the EC can only be made for major issues involving clear national interests. There is little reason to press disputes on less important issues to the point of disruption (*New York Times* 19 December 1980, p. 19; 7 December 1986, p. I25).

The second factor is the eventual willingness of Germany to increase national contributions to the EC in order to resolve the dispute over the level of UK contributions (*New York Times* 23 March 1982, p. 8; 19 June 1983, p. 3; 27 June 1984, p. 1). German support was probably based on the political and economic importance of the EC for Germany, the importance of continued UK membership as a counterweight to France, and the relatively flush state of the German budget. Given the slow-down in the German economy and the unexpected costs of unification, the willingness of the German government to increase future EC payments is probably quite limited.

Despite the general rigidity of national positions and the persistence of old arguments, substantial progress has been made in strengthening other aspects of EC unity. Change has generally been prompted by two factors. One is the changing external circumstances, in particular the end of the Cold War. The second factor reflects the 'tar baby' phenomenon. Once a country is committed to participation in the EC, problems are likely to arise that can only be solved through even higher levels of international cooperation.

The changing position of France on European integration illustrates the effects of changing circumstances despite the persistence of established political preferences. Twenty years ago, France was the undisputed leader of the Western European alliance. The UK was not yet a member of the EC. The role of Germany was still limited by the lingering memories of war and the need to rebuild their internal economy. As a result, France could afford to push for an anti-US foreign policy, claim leadership for the EC and resist any delegation of authority to the Community.

By 1992, France was faced with the growing reality of German domination (*New York Times* 9 November 1989, I13; 26 December 1989, I27; 2 March 1990, A1). Germany had the strongest economy and currency in the EC. When the Bundesbank raised interest rates to control inflation in the early 1990s, the other EC countries were forced to either raise interest rates or to devalue. In effect, France had to either accept the leadership of the German central bank or to push for the creation of an EC central bank in which France would have some administrative participation. Thus, France became a strong advocate of Maastricht and a common monetary system while Germany suddenly became reluctant to give up financial independence (*New York Times* 22 June 1989, IV19; 17 March 1991, 8; 2 December 1991, p. 3).

The debates over a possible unified European army also highlight the effects of changing circumstances on national positions. France had traditionally been strongly opposed to sharing military authority. The French government rejected the proposed European Defence Community in 1954. De Gaulle developed an independent nuclear *force ce frappe* and pulled France out of NATO. This did not endanger French security because the American nuclear defence of Europe necessarily included France as well.

By 1992, French–German military cooperation had been strengthened greatly (*New York Times* 2 March 1986, p. 13; 2 September 1987, I6; 23 January 1988, I3). France had become a strong advocate of an EC-based military alliance (*New York Times* 17 March 1991, p. 8). This shift in policy again reflected changes in circumstances. The end of the Cold War and the collapse of the USSR made the American defense far less credible. Turmoil in Russia and Yugoslavia threatened the stability of the eastern flank of Europe. Germany's eastern interests raised the possibility of German neutrality (*New York Times* 23 January 1973, p. 13; 21 February 1982, p. 16; 8 December 1989, IV5). A close Franco-German military alliance became one way to guarantee

German participation in European defence. An 'EC army' would be a way to wean the Europeans away from NATO and the American Alliance.

The failures in the EC negotiations fall into three categories: (1) an inability to reach agreement; (2) a failure to implement agreements; and (3) a breach of obligations under existing agreements. The failures of the EC members generally occur on issues that touch more closely to the core domestic interests of the member states.

One example is the conflict between France and Great Britain over the CAP. Most recently, France has apparently stood alone against her allies in rejecting a compromise over agricultural subsidies that could resolve the impasse at the GATT negotiations (*New York Times* 31 March 1982).

The allies have also been in persistent disagreement over the devolution of more authority to the EC. Italy and Germany have generally supported strengthening the EC (*New York Times* 21 February 1974 and 16 June 1991, IV2), Britain has consistent opposed it, and France has strongly argued both sides of the issue (*New York Times* 27 November 1973, p. 33; 30 November 1973, p. 7; 10 May 1975, p. 3; 19 January 1984, p. 1). Given the differences in the national historical experiences and the impact of institutionalized political culture on this issue, these debates will probably persist indefinitely.

The Single Europe Act of EC 1987 and the 1992 completion of the free market were responses to the partial non-implementation of national obligations under the Treaty of Rome. The 300 directives became necessary because of the creativity of national governments in erecting non-tariff trade barriers (nttbs) to protect domestic interests. In most cases, governments created nttbs on a selected basis while remaining in technical compliance with EC directives. The failure of Italy and Greece to comply with EC requirements has been relatively overt (*New York Times* 24 March 1972, p. 11; 26 June 1973, p. 8; 17 March 1977, p. 1; 20 June 1980, p. 1; 26 March 1984, p. 18; 21 March 1991, D21).

The most spectacular example of a breach of international obligation under the Treaty of Rome was the inability of the EC members to maintain free trade in oil in the face of a selective Arab oil boycott during the 1973 crisis (*New York Times* 24 May 1973, p. 75; 20 November 1973, p. 9; 31 January 1974, p. 11; Dolan and Caporaso, 1978; Kohn, 1978).

Another example was the periodic collapse of the EMS. The oil dollar crises (Brenner, 1978) of the early 1970s led first to the 'basket', an agreement among the central banks to maintain exchange rate stability through a joint float against the dollar. The failure of the joint float led to a more ambitious experiment, the EMS and the creation of an EC central bank. Unfortunately, the member states only transferred paper reserves to the EC central bank, retaining control over real reserves in national hands (*New York Times* 12 September 1972, p. 59; 13 September 1972, p. 61). The EMS arrangements have collapsed several times as a result of the unilateral devaluations by the member states (*New York Times* 15 February 1973, p. 72; 22 February 1973, p. 62; 24 January 1974, p. 1; 22 July 1985, IV1; 7 March 1986, I1; 30 June, p. 3).

12.3.1 What about the future?

Despite the limited nature of past EC successes and the persistence of old issues, the members of the EC at the Maastricht summit made ambitious plans for a wider, deeper union. The creation of a common currency is to be the means for ensuring greater prosperity and closer political cooperation. How will this work, given the patterns of national politics discussed above?

The results may not be as beneficial as anticipated. The implementation of an EMU would be influenced by the factors discussed in this paper (Kaufman, 1982). Decision making in the EC is still heavily influenced by national governments that are committed to defending national interests. There are significant differences in the economic circumstances of the major countries. Finally, there are significant differences in the national political expectations that also drive national policy preferences.

Efforts to strengthen the EC through the creation of a common currency will probably spur a new round of contention and conflict. From a pan-European perspective, the benefits will undoubtedly outweigh the costs. However, the local losses may be significant. In essence, the member countries would be giving up their ability to protect domestic industries by devaluing against the national currencies of competing companies. The result would be the growth of more competitive companies and economies at the expense of the less competitive companies and economies. Given the continued commitment of all member states to the defence of their national industries, the result would probably be a search by the governments and industries in the weaker economies for new ways to protect local interests (Schukrecht, 1991; Goldstein, 1992).

Strengthening the roles of the Commission and Parliament in the EC could make the problem of local protection more severe rather than easier. There are two strategies for coordinating the selected industrial protection policies of the EC member states. One would be to prohibit the member states from unilaterally protecting local industries. The necessity for pushing forward the EC 1992 project 35 years after the Treaty of Rome suggests how difficult it has been for the EC to effectively achieve this goal.

The other strategy would be for the EC to protect all producers in the relevant economic categories throughout the EC. The EC policies governing subsidies for regional development, trade with Japan, the CAP, airbus, and HDTV all reflect Community wide protectionism and trade distortions. This strategy is likely to be politically attractive as long as EC policies are primarily determined by negotiations among the governments of the member states (Pierce, 1991).

12.4 CONCLUSIONS

The EC will endure. The major Western European states have all made membership in the EC an integral component of their strategies for economic prosperity. Trade among the member states trade has been growing at twice the rate of the trade with non-EC countries. Experience with membership seems to lead to rising support for the institutions (Inglehard and Rabier, 1978). However, stability will not necessarily reflect consensus. National differences on Community related issues will continue. Questions about the feasibility of the EC as a vehicle for political decision-making will undoubtedly persist (Kohn, 1978; Lavant, 1978).

The EC negotiations have succeeded primarily in areas that do not directly involve conflicts in the national positions of the major states. These positions generally reflect basic national expectations and established commitments in the areas of national security, prosperity and the roles of elites. Consequently, these positions are not likely to change easily in the short term.

Despite the inflexibility of national positions and the resulting endemic conflict in the negotiations, some progress has been made. All states have come to rely on the EC as a major component of their economic strategies. Proposals in areas that are likely to engender conflict have often been tabled. The result has been a *de facto* Community strategy of widening the alliance without deepening the levels of economic and political integration.

The effects of a persistent emphasis on national interest should be kept in mind when pressing for greater integration, especially in the development of a common monetary system. If devaluation was unavailable, then demands for economic protection would probably be met by internal market restrictions and by increasing the barriers against foreign trade. These patterns will persist as long as national interests are important in the politics of the EC.

REFERENCES

Alderman, G. (1986) *Modern Britain: A Domestic History*, Croom Helm, London.

Ardagh, J. (1990) *France Today*, Penguin Books, London.

Barker, J. (1916) *The Foundations of Germany*, Kenikat Press, Port Washington, N.Y.

Barnes, S. (1971) Public Opinion and political preferences in France and Italy. *Midwest Journal of Political Science*, **15**, 643–60.

Barzini, L. (1964) *The Italians*, Penguin, New York.

Behrens, C. B. A. (1985) *Society, Government and the Enlightenment: The Experiences of Eighteenth Century France and Prussia*, Harper and Row, New York.

Bitton, D. (1969) *The French Nobility in Crisis: 1560–1640*, Stanford University Press, Stanford.

Braudel, F. (trans. S. Reynolds) (1990) *The Identity of France: Volume Two: People and Production*, Harper and Collins, New York.

Brenner, M. (1978) Monetary policy: processes and trends. *Annals of the American Academy of Political and Science*, **440**, 110–20.

Burkitt, B. and Bambridge, M. (1990) The performance of British agriculture and the impact of the Common Agricultural Policy: an historical review. *Rural History*, **21**, 265–80.

Castronovo, D. (1980) *The English Gentleman: Ideals in Literature and Society*, Ugar, New York.

Caves, R. (1980) Productivity differences among industries, in *Britain's Economic Performance* (eds R. Caves and L. Krause), Brookings Institute, Washington, D.C., 135–98.
Clapham, R. (1961) *The Economic Development of France and Germany: 1815–1914*, Cambridge University Press, Cambridge.
Cunningham, H. (1986) The Conservative Party and Patriotism, in *Englishness: Politics and Culture, 1880–1920* (eds R. Colls and P. Dodd), Croom Helm, London, 283–306.
Dolan, M. and Caporaso, J. (1978) The external relations of the European Communities. *The Annals of* the *American Academy of Political and Social Science*, **440**, 135–55.
Edinger, L. (1968) *Politics in Germany*, Little Brown, Boston.
Fischer-Fabian, S. (trans. L. Segal and P. Stern) (1981) *Prussia's Glory: The Rise of a Military State*, Macmillan, New York.
Giddens, A. (1979) An anatomy of the British ruling class. *New Society*, **887**, 8–10.
Goldstein, W. (1992) Europe After Maastricht. *Foreign Affairs*, Winter, 117–32.
de Gramont, S. (1969) *The French: Portrait of a People*, G. P. Putnam, New York.
Habermas, J. (1992) Citizenship and national identity: some reflections on the future of Europe. *Praxis International*, **12**, 1–19.
Hamerow, T. (1969) *The Social Foundations of German Unification 1858–1871: Ideas and Institutions*, Princeton University Press, Princeton.
Holt, E. (1971) *The Making of Italy: 1815–1870*, Atheneum, New York.
Horne, A. (1984) *The French Army and Politics: 1890–1970*, Peter Bedrick, New York.
Inglehart, R. and Rabier, J. (1978) Economic uncertainty and European solidarity: public opinion trends. *Annals of the American Academy of Political and Social Science*, **440**, 66–97.
Kaufman, H. (1982) The European Monetary System and national policy constraints. *Comparative Social Research*, **5**, 107–28.
Kohn, W. (1978) Energy Policy in the Communities. *Annals of the American Academy of Political and Social Science*, **440**, 111–21.
Lavant, P. (1978) The decade of divergence and development. *Annals of the American Academy of Political and Social Science*, **440**, 13–28.
Lowell, A. (1914) *The Governments of France, Italy and Germany*, Harvard University Press, Cambridge, Mass.
Maehl, W. (1979) *Germany in Western Civilization*, University of Alabama Press, University, Alabama.
Melada, W. (1970) *The Captains of Industry*, University of New Mexico Press, Albuquerque, New Mexico.
Millot, B. (1981) Social differentiation and higher education: the French case. *Comparative Education Review*, **25**(3), 353–68.
Munro, W. (1938) *The Governments of Europe*, Macmillan, New York.
NYT. *New York Times*, various editions.
Namier, L. (1961) *The Structure of Politics at the Accession of George III*, Macmillan, London.
Pierce, W. (1991) Innovation and diffusion in the Single Europe: institutional structure and industrial prospects for the European Communities. *Technological Forecasting and Social Change*, **39**, 35–44.
Pinto-Deuschinsky, M. (1973) Stratification and policy in the British Conservative Party. *American Behavioral Scientist*, **17**(2) 285–92.
Price Waterhouse, (1989) *Doing Business in France*, Price Waterhouse, United States.
Putnam, R. (1993) *Making Democracy Work: Civil Traditions in Modern Italy*, Princeton University Press, Princeton.
Rubenstein, W. (1986) Education and the social origin of British elites: 1880–1979. *Past and Present*, **112**, 163–207.

Runge, F. and von Witzke, H. (1990) The European Communities: enlargement and institutional choice in the Common Agricultural Policy. *American Journal of Political Science*, **34**, 254–68.

Sampson, A. (1982) *The Changing Anatomy of Britain*, Random House, New York.

Santoro, K., Vissichio, L., Branchini, M., Sosa, A., and Rubenstein, A. (1987) Italian attitudes and responses to terrorism. *Terrorism*, **10**(4), 289–310.

Schukrecht, L. (1991) The political economy of EC protectionism based on Article 15, Treaty of Rome. *Public Choice*, **72**, 37–50.

Seward, D. (1978) *The Hundred Years War: The English in France 1337–1453*. Atheneum, New York.

Shinn, R. (1985) *Italy: A Country Study*, US Government Printing Office, Washington, D.C.

Shirer, W. (1969) *The Collapse of the Third Republic: An Inquiry into the Fall of France in 1940*, Atheneum, New York.

Smith, M. (1990) *British Politics, Society and the State Since the Late Nineteenth Century*, Macmillan, London.

Snyder, L. (1978) *Roots of German Nationalism*, The University of Indiana Press, Bloomington, Indiana.

Suleiman, E. (1978) *Elites in French Society*, Princeton University Press, Princeton.

Traugott, M. (1985) *Armies of the Poor: Determinants of Working Class Participation in the Parisian Insurrection of July 1848*, Princeton University Press, Princeton.

Trevelyan, G. (1987) *A Shortened History of England*, Penguin, London.

Washington Post, various editions.

Wall Street Journal, various editions.

Weiss, J. (1982) *The Making of Technological Man*, The MIT Press, Cambridge.

Winchester, S. (1982) *Their Noble Lordships: Class and Power in Modern Britain*, Random House, New York.

Zeldin, T. (1980) *France: 1848–1945: Intellect and Pride*, Oxford University Press, Oxford.

Index

Entries are arranged in letter-by-letter alphabetical order. Titles of documents are set in italic. References to figures are indicated by bold type, and those to tables are set in italic.

GPSR Compliance

The European Union's (EU) General Product Safety Regulation (GPSR) is a set of rules that requires consumer products to be safe and our obligations to ensure this.

If you have any concerns about our products, you can contact us on ProductSafety@springernature.com

In case Publisher is established outside the EU, the EU authorized representative is:

Springer Nature Customer Service Center GmbH
Europaplatz 3
69115 Heidelberg, Germany

The manufacturer's authorised representative in the EU is Springer Nature Customer Service Centre GmbH, Europaplatz 3, 69115 Heidelberg, Germany. If you have any concerns regarding our products, please contact ProductSafety@springernature.com

Printed and bound by CPI Group (UK) Ltd, Croydon, CR0 4YY

30/09/2026

02225494-0012